D0019466

From the Old Marketplace

From the
Old Marketplace

JOSEPH BULOFF

Translated by Joseph Singer

HARVARD UNIVERSITY PRESS
Cambridge, Massachusetts
London, England

This book is printed on acid-free paper, and its binding materials have
been chosen for strength and durability.

Library of Congress Cataloging in Publication Data
Buloff, Joseph.
[Fun altn markplats. English]
From the old marketplace / Joseph Buloff ; translated by Joseph
Singer.
p.   cm.
Translation of: Fun altn markplats.
ISBN 0-674-32503-6 (alk. paper)
1. Buloff, Joseph—Childhood and youth.   2. Jews—Lithuania—
Vilnius—Biography.   3. Vilnius (Lithuania)—Biography.   I. Title.
DS135.R95B85313   1991
947'.5—dc20   90-4649
[B]   CIP

*To my wife, Luba, and
my daughter, Barbara*

One lives only once
in his childhood and adolescence—
the rest is just a repetition.

—Barve's Son

Part One

I

⚭

AS BARVE'S SON told it, the old marketplace was once a deep, dark forest where the nomadic Slavonic tribes used to gather and in drunken orgies fling their firstborns into burning pyres to appease their terrible thunder god, Perun. They would prance around the flames in a savage chorus and swill a dark, bitter brew out of huge goatskins or bowls fashioned from the scooped-out skulls of the sacrificed children.

According to Barve's Son, sometime during the seventh century the forest was taken over by White Russian tribes, who were later supplanted by Ukrainian hordes who leveled the forest and transformed the White Russian settlement into a Ukrainian village. This Ukrainian village was subsequently burned to the ground by a gang of Lithuanian marauders who rooted out the Ukrainians and established a Lithuanian colony called Vilnius. In the twelfth century this townlet achieved the honor of becoming the capital of Lithuania under the benevolent rule of the grand duke Gedymin and was promptly seized by the Poles. In the eighteenth century, after the Russians, Prussians, and Austrians had clawed and chopped Poland into three chunks, Vilnius reverted to its former humble status and once more became a village—but a Russian one this time and marked as a mere flyspeck on the map encompassing the sprawling empire of her most Imperial Highness, Catherine the Great.

After many generations of methodical savagery, the beginning of the present century found the population of the former capital welded into a polyglot, multiracial mélange dedicated to the perpetuation of its ancestral feuds and inexorably linked to the heroic legends of its forebears. Left to the tender mercies of their conquerors, the townspeople were contemptuous of each other, secretly envious and resentful of the Russians; but they achieved a splendid unity in a deep and frank hatred of the Jews.

When and whence the Jews had come to the marketplace, Barve's

Son was uncertain. According to one of his conjectures, the bulk of them had been brought as captives along with the Khazars from far-off Asia when Perun had still been God. But although no trace remained of either the Khazars or their conquerors, the Jews of the marketplace were still very much in evidence and thought of as unwanted strangers who could neither be exterminated nor disposed of in any other fashion.

The fact that the Jews stemmed from a land not indicated on any local map—along with the theory proposed in the Holy Scriptures that held the Jews to be some sort of relatives of God, His Son, the Holy Mother, and the whole celestial family, which branded them renegade angels transformed by God's wrath into devils who were driven from heaven down to the marketplace—was not only accepted by the local population but consolidated the majority opinion that the quicker these same Jews were returned to their native habitat the better it would be for the marketplace and for the whole world. Well aware of the popular viewpoint, the Jews exhibited a remarkable indifference to this contention. What possible reason could there be to hurry back to heaven when any fool knew that within a hundred and twenty years the whole marketplace, as well as the entire city, would end up in heaven and the whole pattern of misery would begin all over again? No, it was infinitely more sensible to feign ignorance, to remain segregated, and to hang on in the marketplace until the Messiah made his appearance and redeemed all the people from all the ills of the earth and of heaven.

In this same marketplace, Barve's Son also asserted, the Uprising of 1863 had been squelched in a river of blood through the gentle ministrations of a certain General Count Mikhail Muraviev and his handpicked regiment of wiry, wild-bearded Kuban Cossack cavalrymen and flat-faced horsemen from the Ural Steppes.

The stone-hewn figure of the infamous general was now ensconced on a high pedestal facing the marketplace. Leaning against a naked sword, he looked down with an ironic smile that warned both Jew and non-Jew that the year 1863 could be resuscitated at any given time. And until this warning actually came about, for several-score years the Cossacks loitered about the marketplace without a stitch of honest toil to perform.

Wearing wide blue breeches with red stripes, silver earrings, and bushy mops of hair parted to the side, armed with swords, revolvers, and lead-tipped leather whips, the Cossacks wandered about aimlessly or sprawled beside the garbage bin, cracking sunflower seeds and yawning desperately.

The bin stood at the edge of the marketplace. From it stretched two long curving paths lined with stores and stands—gentile-owned to one side, Jewish to the other—and scattered among them, as if gone astray, were several Tatars, a few Greeks with great turned-up mustaches, a Turk or two in red fezzes, a ruddy-complexioned Georgian, and a Chinese with a queue—all carrying their businesses in their hands or upon their backs.

On the Jewish side was old Libbe's fruit stand. Next to her was Notte's kerosene shop and Artche's hat emporium. With the serenity of a dozing hen, unruffled by the buzzing of bees and flies attracted by the nearby vegetable and fruit stalls, Old Libbe managed between one customer and the next to darn a pair of stockings, while Notte—unhampered by demands of commerce—mumblingly recited the entire Book of Psalms. In the wintertime the marketplace women sat covered under a downy snow like white marble statues, with pots of glowing coals beneath their skirts. The men gathered about a communal fire pot to thaw out their ice-encrusted beards and philosophize about the fleeting events in the great wide world as well as about the enduring problems of their own world, the marketplace.

The communal fire pot was located to the right of the huge garbage bin. This fifteen-by-fifteen-foot bin was painted a bilious yellow-green, and from its circular opening on top—like a volcano's crater—issued a constant stream of vapor mixed with the odor of putrid vegetables and rancid fat that blanketed the entire marketplace with a cloying, nauseating effluvium. The bin also served as a popular meeting place for out-of-town merchants and for local customers who would agree beforehand to, "God willing, meet at the garbage bin . . ." Often, the bin provided a hiding place for a chicken loose from its coop or for an escaping thief. On still, moonlit nights, the bin's deep shadow helped the Cossacks lure the servant girls from the neighboring street.

Another reason for its popularity was the fact that behind it—that is, between the bin and the brown wall near which it stood—could be found the "little" marketplace, where the small fry set up their own shops and stalls and conducted a brisk and intensive commerce that could have at any time been envied by the impoverished merchants of the regular marketplace.

Here in the little marketplace, the barefoot, snot-nosed "merchants" tore worlds asunder, traded bones for buttons, buttons for chips of brick, grew wealthy in the morning, poverty-stricken in the afternoon. Here in the little marketplace, one could accumulate a fortune in an hour, go bankrupt in one minute, and be back in business again all within one short afternoon. Here there were warfare and truce, laughter and tears. Here everything bubbled with life. And odd as it may seem, here even the sun shone brighter than two steps farther on in the regular marketplace.

It was here by the bin that on one summer morning I opened my shop featuring silver bones, glass diamonds, and silk rags and by that very evening established the fact that my name was Yosik, that I came from the three-storied house with the red gates across the street, and that as a businessman I was a total failure. Perhaps this was because I behaved as if I had the exclusive patent to deal in silver and diamonds, or maybe it was because I lacked the patience to haggle with customers. Anyhow, after the initial flush of success, the customers began to avoid my establishment, and I was soon forced to close up shop.

What started me on my road to ruin was when I grabbed at a customer's sleeve and said, "You owe me four buttons from the day before yesterday and two from yesterday." The customer began to howl as if he had been attacked by one of the mangy marketplace curs. When his protests attracted a mob of youngsters, to my great astonishment instead of siding with me they began to scream: "There never *was* such a thing as the day before yesterday!"

Whether they meant it or were playing make-believe, the truth is that here, behind the garbage bin, the subject of yesterday's debts had never come up before. That which had happened in the morning, no one remembered an hour later. But I could not help myself. My memory haunted and tormented me, and with a peculiar obstinacy I recalled not only the debts from a day before but those from a whole week past.

And in addition to the curse of memory, I was saddled with the burden of tedium. Several times in the course of a day I would abandon my stall, don a set of reins, and let one of my customers drive me around the little marketplace. It was obvious that my ambition to be a horse outweighed my hopes for a mercantile career. But even in my role as a horse I was doomed to failure. Because it never transpired that I would complete a journey without dealing my driver a swift kick in the ass. And all because the driver refused to understand what the horse was trying to tell him.

"In all fairness," the horse would argue, "the driver must change places with the horse for a while and let the horse drive the driver." But here, behind the garbage bin, one lived only according to whim and will and adhered to no previously determined stipulations. How could a driver know beforehand whether he'd feel like being a horse later on? And anyhow, who had the head to remember in the afternoon what had been decided before breakfast? So all that was left for the deceived horse was to throw off his reins and plant a foot in the driver's rump. After a few such eventful journeys they began to regard the horse as the foulest creature ever to wander into the marketplace.

I myself was considerably disturbed by these incidents and decided once and for all to dispose of my business with its stock of worthless junk and to become a more respectable member of the community—as, for instance, a doctor.

The thought became the deed. I opened an office near the brown wall and got hold of a large spoon with which I began to examine the patients. But I failed again. The patients objected strenuously to the rusty instrument with which the doctor rammed down their throats some dark and suspicious home-brewed mixture.

One day in the midst of some spirited wrangling with one of my patients, I was interrupted by a certain Pevke, a lad celebrated behind the garbage bin for his rough-and-ready independence and proven reluctance to accept any man's guff. He had come to consult me about an operation. I changed patients on the table, but as soon as I began to push the infamous spoon down his gullet, he tore the instrument from my hand and threatened violence unless I promptly stretched out and let the patient operate on the doctor. It now became clear that this was no spontaneous act but a diabolical plan to repay the doctor with his own medicine for an earlier attempt to dun the "patient" for some "yesterday's" debts. A violent struggle erupted from which I emerged with a torn face and a bloody nose, a condition calculated to destroy the final vestiges of the doctor's prestige.

I was therefore obliged to take down my shingle and was reduced to going partners with one Berchik, a notorious simpleton and an orphan. Together we operated a bakery—not even near the bin, but in the very gutter of the marketplace.

With the lid of a shoe-polish can we stamped out round little tarts from sand. I knew that to draw customers to an unwholesome location required a definite attraction. And when a few of the curious finally wandered by, to whet their appetites I bolted one of the tarts and licked my lips as if it had been made of honey. Seeing that I still had not captured the confidence of my audience, I poked Berchik in the ribs, which clearly implied: "Well, stupid, now *you* swallow a tart and lick *your* fingers." But the idiot opened a pair of frightened eyes and refused even to sniff the filthy stuff. I measured my about-to-be-discarded partner with a deadly eye, kicked him heartily in the seat of his pants, stamped to powder the little "bakery," and ran away forever from behind the garbage bin.

The next day I returned—not to the little marketplace but to the big one, where from the very first moment I was warmly accepted and properly appreciated. There, it seemed, both the buyers and the sellers were in need of my zeal, energy, and enterprising abilities. On the very first day I became thoroughly acquainted with all the shops and stalls and began to serve the customers, to point out where one could pick up a cheap pair of boots, a pair of secondhand trousers, or where to find the chicken coops. And if someone needed to—I wasn't too lazy to direct him to the public outhouse, either.

I gave particular attention to Lazer, the old-clothes dealer who sold trousers that crackled like heavy cardboard. Once wrinkled, nothing could press them smooth again. And just because of this, Lazer particularly needed someone to hold the customer by the coattails until he had convinced him that these were "English goods" and that what was good enough for the English was certainly more than adequate for Jews.

Artche the hatter was also badly in need of help. He averaged one or two hat sales a week. But seldom did a customer not return the hat with the complaint that the hat was either too large or too small and that his wife "didn't like it in the first place." If I was present,

I would hold the mirror and allow Artche to manipulate the hat on the customer's head. And when the customer bent almost to the ground to look into the mirror and see (either because of the unnatural position or due to the poor quality of the glass) his face elongate until it resembled a horse's, he would be forced to agree that it was indeed not the hat that was at fault but the shape of his head. For these and similar reasons it was inevitable that within a short time I would become the most popular individual in the marketplace. Of course it occurred to no one that I performed all these tasks not so much for the sake of others as for my own gratification. Because I was running from earliest morning until late at night, covered with sweat and grime, risking life and limb to serve, I gradually convinced myself not only that the entire marketplace was my personal property but that all the storekeepers were merely my employees and that it was my job to supervise them.

I neglected no one. I kept a strict account of everybody and clearly remembered who had said which and who had thought what. The marketplace had no secrets from me. I even knew the location of the thieves' den—a cellar on Butcher Street to the right of the market, where I became a frequent and welcome visitor. I quickly became expert in the marked cards used there and thus was able to lend a helping hand by informing on the cardsharps who tried to cheat the pickpockets. For this I was often unjustly treated to a wallop across my skull, which I naturally repaid with a vigorous bite. One time I almost enjoyed an unexpected meal of a pickpocket's finger, which somehow had landed up between my teeth.

After each visit to this den I'd emerge with either a knot on my forehead or an ear with a sizable chunk missing. But this concerned me little. I didn't have the time to think of such trifles when the whole market was waiting for me: this one to help buy a hat, that one to help buy a pair of boots—even the chickens in the coops would have come to grief had I not crawled each morning into the garbage bin and retrieved a rotten potato for them to peck at through the bars.

Neither did I neglect the Cossacks. For them, I had a special weakness. For hours on end I'd trail along behind them and help them make their purchases: one a gingerbread cake, another a glass of apple kvass, a razor, or a whetstone for his sword. The Cossacks were appreciative and let me handle their leather whips and often even treated me to a handful of sunflower seeds. One of them, Arkashka, became a close friend.

One morning Arkashka was standing in a crowd of other sports watching as the Turk with the red fez placed a pea beneath one of three thimbles. Anyone who was willing to risk ten kopecks could try to guess under which thimble the pea lay and win a whole ruble the Turk was betting. As soon as I spied Arkashka in the crowd, I realized that my friend's ten kopecks were in danger. I was no less familiar with the Turk's tricks than he himself, and pushing through the crowd I pointed to his right hand where the pea usually lay between his fingers. The Turk leaped at me with his iron cane, but Arkashka wrenched it from his hands and, with a long, drawn-out curse that began with the Turk's father's father and ended with his mother's blood, demanded the silver ruble. But here I again interceded and prevented them from coming to blows because, outside of the Turk, I was the only one who knew that the ruble was only a hunk of lead and not worth fighting over. Following this incident, whenever I met Arkashka in the marketplace he would offer me a handful of sunflower seeds from the pocket of his wide breeches. I would then take hold of his sword and thus, cracking sunflower seeds, we would stroll through the marketplace.

From behind the garbage bin would pop up the astounded faces of the little merchants who looked agape at the bankrupt baker, humiliated doctor, and repudiated horse strolling with a towering Cossack, brandishing a whip, cracking sunflower seeds, and ejecting the shells with a burst as if he were a miniature Cossack himself. When I became aware of the envious eyes from behind the garbage bin, I adopted an even more spiteful demeanor to further annoy my former companions.

I was another thing altogether with my new partners in the big marketplace. They couldn't find sufficient praise for my spunk and valor. When, for instance, it once happened that two dogs suddenly became entangled and with shrill cries shattered the composure of the marketplace people, who milled helplessly not knowing what to do, it was I who came up and, catching their tails, separated the dogs. Or when a rat once raced through the marketplace, causing a frightful panic as the women scattered with skirts held high and the men leaped onto boxes or benches, again it was I who promptly grabbed a stick and with the agility of a cat cornered the rat, swatted him, then lifted him by the tail and carried him through the market-place to the garbage bin under the admiring eyes of all.

But my popularity was not destined to endure. It would seem that the market people grew quickly tired of me and wanted to rid them-selves as fast as possible of the "charlatan" (as Notte the kerosene dealer had dubbed me). Still, no one dared to show open impatience with me because, for all of my eagerness to please, they knew that I wouldn't hesitate to kick the rump of even Shlome the phylactery maker, who had a long, gray beard.

When my reputation as a charlatan reached my mother, she became very upset and tried to save her only son. She strove to convince me that it wasn't fitting for a boy from a respectable family to be a charlatan and for one my age to associate with thieves and, above all, with Cossacks who taught me oaths strong enough to peel the paint off the walls. But her words fell like snow on a burning griddle, because more than anything I mistrusted women.

I had, however, a special weakness for my father, who stood a full head taller than any one of the market people and could smash a half-dozen walnuts with a single blow of his fist or bend a silver ruble between his fingers. In addition, he had a long, turned-up mustache that lent him a startling resemblance to the Cossacks in the market-place.

But it wasn't only his strength and imposing appearance that drew me to my father. The close relationship between the father and his son, the charlatan, was largely due to the fact that the father had a good deal of the charlatan in him as well.

Prior to his marriage he had served for five full years in the army, somewhere deep in the interior of Russia. There he had learned to anoint his mustache with pomade, to play the accordion, and to sing risqué ditties. And this wasn't all. Long before his military service he had been regarded as something less than a saint by the market people. He smoked on the Sabbath, played billiards, seldom was seen in a house of worship. And when he returned from the army he had even forgotten the existence of God and allowed his son to eat food that wasn't kosher and permitted the roast to be carved with a knife intended for dairy food. The market people, therefore, were not disposed to lay all the blame on the son.

This was the father who used to urge the son to climb up onto the hanging lamp and to swing there until the fixture would tear loose from the ceiling and come crashing to the floor. And if this were not enough, he used to plant himself like a ladder so the son could climb up on him to the wall clock and take apart its "gizzards," attach the wheels to overturned chairs, and thus make a train with which to ride to the ends of the world.

The father drove the train with such a roar and a fury that it always jumped its track and turned over, and after each journey the son was left bruised and battered. All this, however, did nothing to deter my avowed determination to reach the ends of the world, once the idea had been planted in my mind.

My father then persuaded me to try my luck with a boat made from a sheet of newspaper to see if I could attain my goal that way. He slopped water on the floor to create an ocean. Once out on the open sea, however, as if out of spite, he created a terrible storm and doused me with a pail of water. But I maintained a remarkable resilience and bounced back from each fresh catastrophe with an even more intense zeal and iron-willed resolution to gain my objective.

One day my father led me to believe that the end of the world could be seen from a high mountain and indicated the armoire as a near substitute. Without hesitation I began to climb and, when I had finally nearly reached the summit, he pounded me over the head with a pillow with such force that it tore and a blizzard of down blinded me and I tumbled from the mountain, nearly breaking every limb.

It seems the father knew that no matter how often he cracked the son across the skull, either with a pillow or with a stick, he wouldn't be able to erase from his memory what he had once told him, and because of this he felt it his duty to prepare the son for any contingency or mishap that might crop up in his insane desire to reach the ends of the world.

The father thus actually strove with all of his powers to make his son a daring adventurer, a wild Cossack, an incorrigible charlatan, to convince his son that he would live forever and could therefore toy with death.

But presently an extraordinary event occurred in the marketplace. One cloudy morning, Barve's Son, in his long, ragged coat and green, patched cap, stood near Notte's kerosene shop surrounded by his usual circle of admirers.

Although each of them knew that Barve's Son was a pauper who lived somewhere in a dark attic room on Market Street, still no one ever called him directly by name, but always referred to him in the third person. "What does Barve's Son think?" or "What has Barve's Son to say?"—which could lead one to believe that it was the father who was being accorded the respect rather than the son. The truth was that the father was a plain, ignorant teamster who hung around at the edge of the old marketplace smoking his charred pipe or dozing in the wagon with his head pillowed on the rump of his horse, which constantly flicked its tail and at the same time chased the swarms of flies off its master's fleshy nose.

No, the title "Barve's Son" honored exclusively the son and not the father, for it was the son who, amidst the most abject poverty, managed to learn "all of the books in the world" and often came to the fire pot to share his knowledge with the common market folk.

With a small twig the erudite youth drew in the snow the map of the world; pointed out where Macedonia was located; explained how Alexander the Great rode the clouds astride an eagle holding a chunk of meat on the tip of his long sword before the anxious beak of the starving bird who, struggling desperately, bore Alexander into the sky. He also explained the reason for the recent eclipse and gave the causes for the miserable downfall of the mighty emperor, Napoleon. Yes, Barve's Son was a blessing, a symbol of the ideal child. Pregnant women used to wish each other "a boy, another Barve's Son."

And so that morning Barve's Son stood there and outlined in the sand the topography of the Far Eastern region around Port Arthur. The faces of his audience were deeply concerned, and for good reason. Barve's Son had just finished telling them that since the "runty, slant-eyed" Japanese had just handed the mighty Russian Cossacks a terrible drubbing, it should not surprise the market people if soon they were called on to take up guns and go out to defend the Cossacks.

As usual, illustrating his words in the sand, he indicated the strategic position of the Japanese army—and, above all, the Japanese fleet—and shortly speculated as to who would win the war and then in a quiet, conspiratorial voice concluded: "It isn't important who will win the war, the principal thing is 'the consequences.'" At this he snapped his fingers and clicked his tongue to imply that the consequences could be of such magnitude that it wasn't possible to describe them in words and quickly vanished from the marketplace.

This warning from Barve's Son, particularly the final, mysterious click of the tongue and snap of the finger, made a deep impression upon the market people. Scratching their beards and rubbing their brows, they quietly dispersed among their stalls and there attempted to interpret to each other the meaning of that odd word "consequences." Was this perhaps a hint that the Russians would lose the war and that the strange "runty, slant-eyed" Japanese were likely to invade the country and possibly even come to this very marketplace and make the Jews liable for the whole goddam mess as was usually the case—or was it a sly whisper that perhaps the tsar . . . and they put their fingers to their lips as if afraid to take another breath.

As with everything else that occurred in the market, I took this warning more to heart than anyone. I wasn't as frightened by the prospect of the Japanese navy steaming into the marketplace as vexed by the thought of the "runty, slant-eyed punks" beating the stuffing out of my beloved Cossacks. I could understand the market people's apprehension after listening to Barve's Son, but the idea that my giant, heroic Cossacks who rode so dashingly and brandished long lances and leather whips should be so helpless as to require the protection of the enfeebled little shopkeepers who were even afraid to start up with me—this was beyond my comprehension. I dashed home to my father, who would surely clear up all confusion. But my best friend confused me even further.

To begin with, he refused to be a horse and wouldn't give me the customary nighttime ride. And when I began to belabor him with questions about the Japanese, he pushed me aside impatiently and squatted in a corner with the same hang-dog expression as the others in the market. Filled with compassion for my father, I decided to leave him alone and to take the destiny of the market people, including my father's, into my own hands.

And thus a day or so later, armed to the teeth with two wooden swords and my pockets full of stones, I made my appearance behind the garbage bin and proclaimed that everyone must close up shop and place himself under my command so that I might lead them in an expedition against the Japanese. This firm and surprising demand created a panic throughout the little marketplace. One faction joined me immediately and proceeded to collect weapons. The majority, however, grouped itself around my old enemy, Pevke, whose memorable visit had cut short my brilliant medical career. This same Pevke now contemptuously refused to close down his business and participate in this reckless adventure. The bulk of the other merchants, particularly those whose business was flourishing, sided with him and, united in common indignation, began to hustle me from the marketplace. Enough had they suffered from me—enough had I plagued them with my damned memory, the device of total recall, and wearisome pretensions. And now I even had the gall to incite them to combat—enough! "Be gone, you snotty charlatan!"

But I stood firm, I pushed them all aside, and with the tip of my sword sketched out in the sand the contours of the world, and with silver-tongued oratory in the style of Barve's Son began to declaim about the Peril from the East. And when in conclusion I again made a tearful appeal for volunteers on behalf of the butchered Cossacks, the response was as expected—no one stepped forward. And for mighty good reason. What, in all fairness, did this ragged crew of timid youngsters of the ghetto have in common with those out-landish creatures, the Cossacks? They never had understood from where these strangers had come nor their status in the marketplace. But instinctively and correctly they read in the cold blue eyes the contempt the Cossacks felt toward them and knew that only a char-latan could befriend these bestial cavalrymen and chew sunflower seeds from their brutal hands. No, no one moved from his spot. Even those few who previously had flocked to my banner threw down their swords. Muttering darkly and agitating each other, they circled about me ready to heave me bodily from their midst. Still, not one of them dared to make the first hostile move. They knew me well as a chip off the old block, the heir of one who towered by a full head over the others, sported a magnificent mustache and a derby hat, and could snap a silver ruble with a twist of a finger.

But suddenly forward sprang Berchik, the orphan, my weaselly ex-partner in the gutter bakery. This weak-kneed imbecile, to the astonishment of everyone, summoned enough courage to step out of the crowd and threw two heaping handfuls of sand into my eyes. For a moment, I stood there blinded. The hypnotic power that had managed to hold back the frenzied mob now dissipated like air from a punctured balloon, and a moment later the protector of the Cos-sacks lay stretched out on the ground.

With gleeful shrieks of pent-up revenge they flung themselves at me—some at my legs, others at my midriff. Pevke tore the swords from my hands and broke them—then, seating himself upon my face, he began to empty my pockets of the stones. The howls of animal joy echoed so loudly that the big marketplace held its breath in fear that the Japanese fleet had landed, and presently the people came galloping behind the garbage bin to see who was being put to death first.

I wasn't sure what caused their reaction—pleasure or surprise—but rather than leap to their master's defense, they began to clap their hands and shake with laughter. Shlome the phylactery maker even stooped to look into my face to make sure his eyes weren't deceiving him.

Thrashing about desperately, I finally managed to sink my teeth into Pevke's behind and to throw him off me, and, seeing through one sand-filled eye Shlome's face close to mine, I snared both my hands in his long beard. As its owner yanked and tugged to free it, he was forced to also pull me out from under the tangle of kicking arms, legs, and torsos. And once on my feet, and without using my eyes, I managed virtually to walk up the side of the garbage bin and dive into its circular orifice.

Here in my aromatic sanctuary I slowly began to reconstruct the events leading to my downfall. It wasn't the aches and bruises that pained me now but the disgrace! Pevke's gall was as nothing compared to Berchik's sneak attack. That this cabbagehead—who wet his trousers when he saw a stray chicken escaping from Leibke the poultryman and hid himself all atremble between my legs—that this craven should turn out to be the architect of my calamity, this was more than I could forget or forgive.

But an even more distressing enigma was the behavior of the market people. Why did they respond with such rapture? Was it possible they didn't know that my motives were directed toward *their* salvation? Had they so quickly forgotten how frightened they had been after listening to Barve's Son? Rather than jeer, shouldn't they have leaped in unison to rescue him who alone stood between them and disaster?

Well, the die had been cast. The little ragamuffins who had attacked me would be reckoned with in good time. But the grown traitors would have to be taught a lesson. Because in that horrible moment when they mocked my humiliation they became a thousandfold more evil than the Japanese, whom I didn't even know! But these beggars who lived on my bounty and supported their miserable families from my stores, in my market, in my world—they would have to be wiped from the face of the earth! And this, naturally, would require the assistance of my brave father. Just as they were standing there patting their fat bellies and laughing at my predicament, I would run home and persuade my father to come at once and smash this ugly crew like rotten nuts between his mighty palms!

I crawled stealthily out of the hole, slithered down the side facing Market Street, and with an incredible burst of speed born of white-hot revenge flew home. But there an even greater surprise awaited me.

Father was not at home—and what was even worse, he was not expected to return, because that very same morning he had fled to some faraway land called America.

How was this possible? How could he have done such a thing? Had Barve's Son's warning frightened him so badly that he had fled to save his life and abandoned his only son to the mercy of the Japanese? The cursed memory that haunted my existence now recalled for me in disgusting detail how anxious my father had appeared that morning and how tenderly he had kissed me. This alone should have made me suspicious, because to the best of my recollections it was the first time he had exhibited such sentiment and delicacy toward me. But that had happened in the morning, when I was rushing to the garbage bin to organize my expedition and didn't take the time to evaluate my father's odd behavior. Only now I realized with bitterness that the kisses had been but another handful of sand thrown into my eyes, to keep me in the dark. Pure treachery.

If, as Barve's Son contended, the landing of the Japanese fleet in the marketplace was inevitable, and if my father's escape had been a plan to dodge the "consequences," wouldn't it have been just and fair and decent to include me in this scheme? What was left for me now? To erase from my memory Berchik's sneak attack? To give up the struggle against the Japanese? To remain hiding in the garbage bin defeated and humiliated? No! Defeated, maybe. Humiliated? Never! That Pevke had sat on my face and punched me meant not a fig! What was a punch more or less to one who had a piece of an ear missing and lacked a patch of hair from his scalp from previous encounters?

But the jeering of the market people who had laughed not at my defeat at the hands of the Japanese but at my father's deceit—

laughed knowing that he had deserted me, but keeping it from me—this I could not forgive, *would* not forgive. Even if my father's bravery turned out to be a mockery and he had truly fled at the first warning of impending danger, the market people were sadly mistaken about his son. They had probably forgotten that a certain Arkashka was still around and that a few choice words would suffice for him to mount up and gallop through the marketplace chastising with his lead-tipped whip the mockers and burning into their brains the proper behavior toward one to whom they owed their very existence and who had given so very, very much of himself in their behalf.

With this thought in mind, I stood by the window and watched the panes grow a deeper blue and the room darken. And when my mother approached with silent tread and laid her hand upon my head I shook her off because it had been she who with honeyed words had tried to estrange me from Arkashka. I'd be in a fine stew now had I listened to her and stopped being a Cossack, a cardsharp, a charlatan . . . To whom would I turn now that I had no one to pull me up the wall and swing me on the lamp? Who would stand up for me in my moment of darkest distress? Ah, how good that I had never paid any attention to that woman! And now when she again told me to drink my milk I refused. To hell with milk! The best thing was to leap into bed and get the night over with as quickly as possible. Because the faster time passed, the sooner I could meet Arkashka and plan my attack.

II

꧁ ཌ༇ད ꧂

THE GARBAGE BIN, as I've already mentioned, stood on the Jewish side of the marketplace. The soup kitchen on the gentile side was, all things considered, every bit its equal as a popular attraction. Here, in broad, greasy pots that hung on chains from the great iron tripods, *yushke,* the soup relished by the peasants who came to the market with wagonloads of vegetables from the neighboring villages, was boiling. They would sit around the long tables, licking the bowls and sucking their fingers with such gusto that the sounds carried as far as the fruit stalls. Around them milled the stray market curs wagging their mangy tails and waiting for the gluttons to tire of gnawing the bones and toss them to them for at least a sniff of the delicacy.

A special table was set aside for the gang of tailors, shoemakers, and journeymen who gathered at the soup kitchen more to talk than to eat. They were often joined by the market porters, butchers, and ordinary loafers and, wrapped in clouds of tobacco smoke blended with the dense, sour vapor from the soup kettles, argued passionately and attempted, each in his own fashion, to interpret Barve's Son's "consequences."

Some conjectured that they possibly, or probably, or certainly portended a revolution against the tsar. Others claimed it an obvious, clear, and positive indication of a possible street demonstration complete with banners and singing. Still others laughed at the ragamuffin who dared speak so familiarly about the almighty tsar, just as if he were a fellow swineherd.

It was at this very table that I hoped to meet up with Arkashka, but a good many days went by and, as if out of sheer perversity, neither he nor any of the Cossacks were to be seen in the marketplace.

I whiled away the long hours of waiting by fanning the fires under the tripods and dividing the bones fairly between the two mongrels, Zhuk and Lishk. The tastiest bones, however, I saved for Matzek, a ragged boy who came from Church Street even more starved than the dogs. Several times already he had asked me who had bitten the chunk from my ear and how I had lost a patch of hair—but now, more cautious than before, I was loath to supply any information that could be used to thwart my plans.

And so one day as I was in the soup kitchen busy feeding the dogs and Matzek, several women came running up from Church Street shouting in terror, "The Cossacks are coming!"

The debaters leaped from their seats and sprinted from the market-place into the adjoining houses. The terrified mongrels abandoned their bones and dashed after the fleeing mob. Matzek flung his bone aside and raced home.

Veiled in the vapor of the boiling soup, I stood rooted to the spot. All through my long wait I hadn't given up hope that my Cossacks would come to avenge their beloved little friend. And now they were here. But the frantic mob turning over tables, benches, and tripods snatched me up and like a scrap of paper in a wind storm carried me to the courtyard of the three-storied house with the red gate.

Once there, they quickly barricaded the gate with a huge iron bar and huddled in mute terror listening to the rhythmic pounding of the hoofs on the cobblestoned street. Cringing in fear, the women tiptoed along the wall and dispersed into the houses, but the men assembled in Pitche the tinsmith's cellar room and began to arm themselves with hammers, chisels, and brooms.

As evening approached, Pitche lit a tiny kerosene lamp, and the walls became alive with trembling shadows. In the dark and oppressive stillness it was hard to determine what was man and what shadow. For the life of me I could not understand their exaggerated fear, nor why they had brought me here. Several times I even tried to protest, but they quickly clapped my mouth shut. It was clear that I was a prisoner here and would so remain until the Cossacks came and set me free.

Presently someone came with bad news—there was a pogrom going on on Butcher Street; the Cossacks were burning houses, slitting bellies, cutting off women's breasts, and throwing people out of windows. At this horrible news, even the flame of the lamp appeared to shrink and cower. Even to me this carnage rang a mite too brutal. After all, not all of the market people were guilty and certainly not those from Butcher Street with whom I had had nothing at all to do. If these fools would now let me go, I would look up Arkashka and clear up the whole misunderstanding. I would convince him that the whole incident behind the garbage bin hadn't been all that serious and certainly didn't warrant cutting off breasts and throwing people out of windows. But a guard blocked the gate, and each time I came near he threatened me with a heavy club.

I was sorry I had begun the whole thing and was even prepared not only to forgive but to help them. But no, the fools still didn't show the slightest bit of trust in their one-time patron and treated me like a neglected orphan whose father had fled to America and left his son to shift for himself.

But soon a fortunate or, to put it more accurately, an unfortunate twist of fate arranged it so that my captors not only gave me my freedom but also restored me to my former status as their acknowledged savior and benefactor.

It happened that after several days of confinement in Pitche's cellar room the men began to suffer from an acute shortage of tobacco. They tried to substitute paper, dust, mud, until they finally decided that no matter what, one of them must run to Hannah's grocery on Church Street and bring back a pinch of tobacco to alleviate their tormented cravings. Although it was possible to reach Hannah's through a back street, still one had to pass Butcher Street, and because of this even the ones who were tearing their hair from desperation thought twice.

I immediately sensed a perfect opportunity to gain my freedom and promptly volunteered. At first they turned me down, but slowly they were forced to admit that despite my disreputable character, I was the swiftest of all the boys from behind the garbage bin; and the fact that the "charlatan" was "no bigger than a flea," and was the least likely to be noticed by the Cossacks, weighed heavily in my favor.

But the most advantageous asset the charlatan enjoyed was that due to his close association with the Cossacks, he had learned their intricately tangled curses with such fluency one might have thought he had been born somewhere in the Kuban steppes or on the banks of the Don rather than in the homely Market Street gutter.

And since no one could match my qualifications for the mission, it was finally decided to send the "snotty little charlatan."

They cautioned me to make myself even smaller, to approach

Butcher Street from the rear, and to cross it at the corner where Karadzalis's candy store was located. From there I was to sneak into Hannah's back room. Once there, I was to buy five five-kopeck packets of *machorka* tobacco and go back the way I had come. I was then to tap softly seven times on the red gate to let them know the charlatan was back.

"Suppose he is caught with the tobacco, you know how the Cossacks love *machorka?*" Pitche asked and compounded the question with another: "What would they think if they found such a small kid with so much money on him?"

At first these questions posed serious problems but, necessity being the mother of invention, solutions were found. The tobacco I would pour into my shoes, so that if I were caught, they would appear to be filled with mud. And in order that I should walk in comfort, Pitche, who had the biggest feet, suggested I wear his shoes.

To the second question, one of the frustrated smokers proposed that all the loose change collected be pooled and exchanged for a single silver piece which, understandably, would be easier to carry than the pile of kopecks and groschen. But this did not completely solve the problem until, burning with impatience, I interceded and promised to keep the coin under my tongue. This satisfied everybody and no one could dispute the "conniving ingenuity" of the charlatan.

They led me to the door of the gate. The crew standing guard peered through a crack to see if the coast was clear, and then, cautiously raising the bar a trifle, shoved me out into the street.

Free at last! Now I would show those stubborn imbeciles what I was made of! Get even with them? No! Just the opposite. In the few days I had been holed up in Pitche's cellar and seen how pitifully frightened and desperate they were, I had completely forgotten any grievances I might have had against them. Now I was more vexed by the brutality of the Cossacks who felt so free to slice open bellies and throw people out of windows. But Market Street was totally deserted. So was Butcher Street, with no sign of friend or foe.

"Where are they in their mothers', fathers', sisters' . . ." I slipped easily into the usual curse, going all the way to the ninth degree. It seemed that not only the market people but the Cossacks as well had dispersed from fear and left me alone—the only living person in a deserted city. An odd sensation of pride, amazement, and some sort of guilt came over me. I felt that I was part of this strange, confusing incident, and I pitied the Cossacks as much as the market people.

At that moment a frightened figure with a chalk-white face slipped out from Deaf and Dumb Alley. I recognized Barve's Son at once. It seemed as if he had been expecting me. He sprang forward and taking a bundle of papers from under his coat whispered to me, "Take these . . . run and warn everybody to get ready for tomorrow's demonstration. Tell them that the revolution blazes like a bonfire. The tsar is finished. This is a call to arms . . . Tell them to distribute these proclamations, to push them under doors and gates . . . Run quickly, no one must catch you with these."

If there was one person whom I still respected, it was Barve's Son, although when I had tried to repeat his famous speech about the "consequences" it had cost me dearly. I promptly ran to deliver his message.

I had taken perhaps a few dozen steps when I detected coming from behind me the familiar rhythmic beat of Cossack hoofbeats and, as I turned, I saw Barve's Son slinking along the hulking walls of the narrow street as if trying to impress himself into the very buildings in order to escape the two Cossacks who came riding down each side of the street and cornered him.

Under the whistling lash of the *nagaika* I watched my idol sink to the ground, leaving his blood-red shadow on the wall. The Cossacks vaulted from their saddles and tried to stand him upright, but his legs crumbled under him as if they were made of paper. They emptied his pockets, even took off his shoes but, finding nothing, they flung him aside in disgust and frustration.

They wiped their bloodied whips on their wide breeches and were preparing to remount when one of them caught sight of me and beckoned to me to come to him. When I didn't move, the Cossack passed the reins to his companion and started toward me with a grin on his face and his hand outstretched. But I left his hand hanging in midair and deliberately refused to acknowledge my old friend Arkashka. At once his smile vanished, and with the same outstretched hand he tore the bundle of proclamations from under my arm.

"Who gave you these?" he asked, furious. Receiving no answer, he pulled me to him and began to go through my pockets.

"What else have you got on you?" he kept asking. When I ignored his question he lost his temper and, holding me by the hair, began to shake me and shout, "Where did you get the papers? Where were you taking them?"

But my lips remained sealed.

It seemed strangely suspicious to him that I who was normally so locquacious should suddenly grow as dumb as if my tongue were paralyzed. This could mean only one thing—I was hiding something in my mouth. Whereupon Arkashka squeezed my cheeks together between his fingers as if they were tongs and began to snarl, "Answer when I tell you . . . Speak up when I say . . . At least let me hear a word from you!"

In the throes of a painful convulsion I began to gasp, straining every effort to bring forth from my compressed gullet the one word he wanted. I tore my lips apart and in full voice shrieked, "In your father's, father's, marrow, liver, guts, sour milk and putrid blood from over, under, and all sides!"

Arkashka shook as if drenched by icy water. My curse topped by three whole degrees the favorite one he so frequently employed, and he now looked at me with disillusionment as if thinking, "Is this your thanks for being your friend, sharing with you my sunflower seeds, teaching you to swear, and making a little Cossack out of you? And now you've taken up with the Jews who want to get rid of the tsar . . . So be it! From now on you're no longer a Cossack. Go along to your ragpickers!"

He picked me up by my behind and, balancing me in the air, threw me in the direction of Barve's Son. Then he leaped into the saddle and rode off with his companion.

"In your father's, father's . . . You stupid Cossacks, did you think you were dealing with Berchik the Fool? Even if you tore out my tongue I wouldn't have told you a damned thing because now I know you for what you are. I know you didn't slit bellies and throw people out of windows on my behalf. You whipped Barve's Son and took off his shoes because you were looking for *machorka* as well as the twenty-five-kopeck piece in my mouth, you lousy burglars and pickpockets. You don't even know that a stomach is a den without windows and anything that goes down there, even the governor himself won't find . . . And now the silver piece is in my stomach, and I spit through your mother's ears into your father's eyes—through your sister's ass."

This final tirade I had to cut short because suddenly something began to press under my chin and I knew that very, very soon now I was going to be another Berchik the Fool and bawl like a baby. My accursed memory, which always came back during a time of trouble to heap coal on the fires of my agony, now began to torment me unmercifully: "Well, now, you weak-minded charlatan, think back to all the things you did to serve those stinking Cossacks! The money you saved them buying shoe polish and watches and jackknives and rings. The troubles you went to to see they weren't cheated out of a single groschen. The servant girls you lured for them behind the garbage bin on Sundays. The war you declared on the Japanese when you heard they were beating the hell out of your beloved friends. Oh, ah . . . into their father's, sister's, brother's—mother's mouth!"

And what now? Go back and tell how you were grabbed by the ass like a mouse by its tail and thrown onto the ground? Admit how the Cossacks misused you and threw you out of their gang?" Add to your disgrace the open scorn of the market people? No! Never! I now had another mission to complete. I had to lead the people in a demonstration to get rid of the tsar . . . and his Cossacks.

When they heard the seven taps and opened the gate, throwing caution to the wind, they burst into a hurrah and carried me gleefully on their shoulders to the cellar room. But once they found out that I had neither tobacco nor money, they dropped me quickly to the floor.

From behind, one of them fetched me a hearty crack across the skull and cried out, "What did I tell you? Go send a cat after butter! Instead of buying tobacco he goes and stuffs himself on cookies and chocolate in Karadzalis's candy store. Give us back our money!"

"I got it! I got the money," I cried. "But first you've got to get ready, because tomorrow morning I'm going to lead you all in a demonstration."

The commotion stopped abruptly. I climbed up on the table and, unable to keep the yarn from unraveling, giving full vent to my imagination, I continued in the same breath: "I walked down Market Street and passed Butcher Street when suddenly Barve's Son jumped out at me from Deaf and Dumb Alley. But just then the Cossacks came riding up and picked Barve's Son up by his behind, slapped him, and threw him down and beat him with whips besides. They would have killed him sure if I hadn't stuck up for him. I got some rocks and threw them at the horses, and as they ran away the Cossacks had to chase after them. Then I picked up Barve's Son, carried him back to a safe corner, and sat him against the wall until he felt better. But while I was fighting with the Cossacks, the coin under my tongue slipped down into my stomach."

They began to scurry around as if ready to tear me to shreds. Because by this time it wasn't so much the loss of the twenty-five kopecks as the "unmitigated gall of the seventy-seven-times-damned charlatan who dared thrust a hot poker into the very hearts of the weary people." They were about to pull me down from the table when from under my shirt I pulled the crumpled piece of paper and waved it over their heads.

Eyes bugging, they began to read in chorus: *"Brothers and sisters, tomorrow—"*

As if a bitter frost had turned their bones to ice they were left standing there congealed. Could it be true? Was it a dream? Had Barve's Son's predicted "consequences" come about? Would they really come out from the cellar tomorrow and march through the streets? And if all this were indeed true, wouldn't they also have to believe the charlatan's incredible story: that he had actually swallowed the coin, routed the Cossacks, and rescued Barve's Son? That the sky had turned right side up and that the most fantastic miracles were happening and that they must indeed begin getting ready to be led by that son of a son of a son in a demonstration the following morning?

But how could one believe a creature that was barely weaned, whose tongue was already as crooked as the tail of a mangy cur, who spoke the language of the thieves, who cursed to shame a Cossack? Who would risk life and limb on the word of such a dedicated liar? No, this wrinkled piece of paper wasn't enough. He'd have to drop his pants at once and prove that the silver piece was really inside him.

They took me down from the table, seated me on the floor, and circled themselves around me with a far greater curiosity and amazement than they had exhibited at the famous "consequences" speech of Barve's Son.

I looked at them with pride restored, with the same self-confidence as on the first day when I came to the marketplace and took over their businesses, their worries and anxieties about making a living, and thus became respected and beloved, courted by the mighty Cossacks, sought out by the neglected mongrels and the starving chickens in the crates; the all-powerful benefactor in whose hands rested the destiny of Lazer the old-clothes dealer and Artche the hatter; one who singlehandedly dared to defy the Japanese, the tsar, and even the Cossacks.

III

ALTHOUGH AFTER SOME strenuous effort I managed to convince the market people that my tale of derring-do on Deaf and Dumb Alley was true, the result was a bitter disappointment. A demonstration did take place. People marched and sang, but they were promptly routed by a band of Cossacks. Some of the demonstrators were imprisoned, others given twenty-five lashes, and one was even hanged. Pitche the tinsmith was later heard to observe, "It would have been better already if the charlatan had squandered the twenty-five kopecks on cookies rather than bring them back in his bowels with such dazzling promises, which brought only disappointment and punishment."

The market people went back to their stalls, where the sun shone as always, and the Cossacks again sprawled around the garbage bin cracking sunflower seeds and yawning hugely as on the day after a wedding. Gradually, everything in the marketplace returned to normal. Even Barve's Son, save for the bruises under his eyes, showed nothing to recall the turbulent days. As usual he walked past the marketplace engrossed in his five-groschen booklets.

I too came back to the marketplace to begin anew. The first one to greet me was Artche the hatter, who lifted me in his large hands and said, "Ah, here is the little fellow who shits silver pieces." At this, Notte the kerosene dealer came running up and pinched my behind with rough fingers. Fat Doba picked me up and seated me on her huge, downy breasts like a suckling child. This coarse familiarity filled me with disgust.

What kind of idiotic antics were these, tickling me under the chin and rocking me on the bosom as if I were an infant? Had they already forgotten what I had done for them barely a week ago? Were they such nincompoops that of all the great events that took place they could only remember that I had defecated a silver coin? Fie!

I spat in disgust and left the marketplace never to see them again.

But only a few days later they all assembled at my house. I was already asleep when the sound of voices on the other side of the wall woke me. Mattes the baker had a squeaky little voice; Hershel the herring dealer spoke through his nose; and who couldn't recognize the hoarse voice of Notte the kerosene dealer who was now out-shouting everyone to the effect that, no matter what, when it came to affairs of war there was nothing anyone could tell *him*. But the others absolutely refused to concede this point.

"*Shmondaks* here or *shmondaks* there," Hershel snuffled, "still they gave the Russians a good hiding."

"The navy! The navy!" a shrill, piping voice cried out.

"What navy? Whose navy? The Russian admirals weren't worth a fig!" a fourth party interjected. Some agreed, others dissented, and presently they all grew weary of listening to one another and began to speak at the same time.

Soon a knock on the door could be heard and, from the warm reception accorded the newcomer, it could have been no one else than Barve's Son. As always, when in the presence of that revered fellow, everyone fell silent, and presently the velvet voice of Barve's Son could be heard. "Navies, admirals . . . it's all a lot of folderol, the main thing is—"

"The consequences," a sneering voice taunted him.

"Yes, the consequences," Barve's Son persisted, "because the war itself was nothing else but a consequence of consequences."

"I don't believe in any of your consequences. If you're against the tsar do the same as Benjamin, run away to America. If we all did this, we'd now be dancing a quadrille on roofs of buildings that reach to the clouds instead of bothering with some miserable conse-quences. Come on, Sarah, show us the letter."

"I was the first to see the postman," Notte boasted, but he was quickly drowned in a roar of objections, each one claiming, "I saw him first!"

The argument was terminated by the dulcet sound of Barve's Son's voice as he began to read the letter.

This was a letter from the father to his dearly adored wife, with kisses and fondest regards to his beloved son. It began with a descrip-tion of a land and streets paved with gold and with trains running over rooftops, with real black people, and with the strangest foods like cabanas and bananas. It went into a description of a sumptuous feast that Leibke the rag dealer from the old market arranged for his landsman, Benjamin, who after eight whole weeks of constant dizziness and vomiting into the stormy ocean finally arrived in the golden land. The banquet was held on the roof of a "skyscraper," where they danced a quadrille and raised their glasses to the very clouds in a salute to the old market!

It went on to describe how Leibke the rag dealer, the son of Kune Pessah the chicken plucker, had become a millionaire almost overnight in the golden land, how he wore silk socks and had teeth made of gold. This all was followed by a list of odd names like Morgen, Nechten, and Rockenflier, who were millionaires even richer than the rag dealer. One of those Jewish millionaires has given him, Benjamin, a job in a "shop." A shop is a cellar the size of half the marketplace. The only trouble is that it is a bit damp, and there are no windows, no air, and because of this, people get consumption. Consumption is a sickness where one spits blood and dies young. In the shop some hundred and thirty people work, but Benjamin had made friends with only four of them, with whom he is a boarder by a certain "missus." A "missus" is a widow who has two rooms and rents out one to boarders. This room has plenty of windows; the only trouble is that there are only three beds in the room so that they have to take turns sleeping on the floor. But all this is temporary until Benjamin works himself up and, like Leibke and the rest of them, becomes a millionaire. A millionaire is a person who has a million of the green papers, one of which "I'm enclosing so that you might know what I'm talking about." The letter ended with the salutation: "Long live Columbus! Your Benjamin."

In the deadly silence that followed I could hear from the other side of the wall the crinkling of the green paper, which was now being passed from hand to hand.

Everything was clear except the word "Columbus." Who the rag dealer was and what a "missus" and "consumption" were, my father had made quite clear. The only thing he had failed to explain was who in the world was Columbus and why he deserved a long life. But fortunately the same sort of curiosity had been expressed on the other side of the wall, and Barve's Son had to elucidate. I jumped out of bed and put my eye to the keyhole.

The erudite youth wet his gullet with a few sips of tea and with his finger substituted the breadth of the dining table for the stormy sea that lay between the old marketplace and the golden land. He placed a walnut shell in the midst of the ocean and added a matchstick for a mast. By this mast stood Columbus, and through his telescope he scanned the horizon seeking the shore of the golden land, America. For weeks on end the nutshell was tossed up and down in the mountains of water. The storm grew ever worse and the nights darker. Columbus lay exhausted and disappointed on the broken helm. Just when the winds congealed and the ship hung suspended on the crest of a petrified wave, someone pressed his behind to the keyhole and deprived me of seeing a miracle take place, on the table top—Columbus discovering America!

I could no longer contain myself and felt like dashing into the dining room, proclaiming myself Columbus, and leading them once again to that golden land. But who could tell? Why must I always drag along this miserable crew with me wherever I intend to run? Let them shift for themselves. Let them stew in their idiotic "consequences." As for me, I made up my mind there and then to run to America and join my father in his dance on the roof reaching up to the clouds.

Before daybreak I began to ready my ship and the necessary telescope. But before I was finished the sky became overcast and, as if the elements conspired to assist me, thunder ripped the sky and handfuls of sparkling crystals began to beat resoundingly against the rooftops. I quickly grabbed my ship and ran into the street. The gutters were already flooded with roaring waves that soon inundated the shoreline and the sidewalks beneath an angry sea. I began to steer the ship. The sea seemed more treacherous than the one that had confronted Columbus! Huge mountains of water blocked my course. Fiery snakes blinded me. Water whips lashed at me and tried to tear off my trousers. But clutching my pants in one hand, I took out the paper telescope from under my shirt with the other, and searched for a possible clue to the shoreline of the golden land. At that moment, a vicious gust of wind tore the telescope from my hand and cracked the ship in two. For another moment I struggled with the waves, hoping to float on the sodden piece of paper toward my goal, but a fresh torrent of rain struck me and swept a shoe from my foot. At the same time the capsized ship and crushed

telescope were caught in a whirlpool and soon sank in the abyss.

My courage did not falter, and I resolved to continue my journey, hopping along on one foot. The whipping rain lashed with stinging rods against my face and clawed the soggy rags from my body, but I skipped over the waves and scrambled through the nets of water, showing not the slightest trace of despair or exhaustion. I felt in every respect the equal of my illustrious predecessor. But soon an event took place that finally broke my courage, one that would have surely shattered the will of the famous Columbus himself.

The thunder and lightning abated, the driving rain slowly petered out, the water drained from the streets and gutters, and to my utmost disappointment I was left standing on the solid cobblestones of the littered street.

What indeed would the real Columbus have done if the ocean had suddenly dried out beneath his ship? How would he have felt when after all his efforts he discovered, under the dried-up ocean, not America but the old familiar marketplace, and the first to greet him was Notte the kerosene dealer?

"Where have you been? I got soaked looking for you. Come quickly. Everybody is waiting for you," he yelled.

Throwing me up onto his shoulders, he began to leap over the puddles that were now decorated with silvery spangles and colorful rainbows.

In the dining room was gathered the same group that had been present the night before. While their stalls were closed because of the rain, they were using their spare time to help my mother answer the letter from America. She was seated at the table, and they stood around her dictating their messages to my father. Artche the hatter had the floor:

"Whereas Benjamin writes in his letter that he will be a boarder only temporarily, and whereas according to all his calculations he must be, by now, if not a full millionaire at least a half millionaire, he must therefore help out his old friend Artche, who helped him arrange the match with the good and beautiful Sarah. Not that Artche was looking for a matchmaker's fee, but only because business was so bad that he couldn't remember the day when he had last sold a hat, and when he did sell one, it was as usual brought back the next day. And, besides all this, he had suffered a great misfortune

lately. A certain man had brought him a derby and had demanded his money back. How was this possible when in his whole life he, Artche, had dealt only in caps, occasionally perhaps a yarmulke? So how come a derby? But the man fetched the policeman, and how can a Jew stand up to the police? He, Artche, had to take his last few kopecks and exchange them for a derby that he had never sold and would never be able to sell."

Now Hershel came up to the table and asked that the letter tell how his customers had developed a habit of buying a piece of herring for a groschen, and demanding in the bargain a full glass of herring brine with it, and now they had all become so fond of the brine that they came with empty jars and he is left with the barrel of dried-out herring. "Save me, save me, Brother Benjamin!" he pleaded. And before he was finished, Leibke the poultryman pushed him aside and began to wail as he had the night before. He wasn't asking for millions, nothing like that, only to be brought to America, where he would be glad to sleep on the floor every night at the missus's and even get consumption, just to get away from the accursed tsar.

Suddenly Lazer the old-clothes dealer cried out, "Let the little fellow sign his name too. Sometimes when one becomes rich one's heart turns to stone. Maybe his son's signature will melt the stone, and the millionaire will take pity on us and send a whole ship to bring us to America!"

Notte pushed me up to the table. My mother gave up her place to me, put the pen between my fingers, and began to move my arm to show me how to write my name in the corner of the letter.

I looked up at the eager faces hovering over me and for a moment had a strong urge to disclose to them that all their hopes and expectations were for naught because that fairy tale that Barve's Son had spun for them was as worthless as his "consequences." It just wasn't possible to get to America . . . as I had just this morning found out. The only thing to do was to bring my father back to the marketplace to establish order on both sides of the garbage bin and to put things right, to drive away Arkashka and all the damned Cossacks and reinstate his son as the only master of the market . . . as he used to be.

But this required more than just my signature, and I began with several hesitant lines to draw a small figure with pipe-stem legs and

arms, then added fingers to each hand. Between the fingers I placed a sword and a spear on one side, and a torn flag on the other. Then I shook a fat drop of ink from the pen and dragged it across the sheet of paper in a series of strange zigzags to and fro, and ended it with a stripe. I signed my name with a dash and a period and walked away from the table.

IV

AFTER THE LETTER had been dispatched to America, I planted myself on the steps of Mattes's bakery to wait for the answer. There, I could sit in peace and contemplate how I might climb up to the roof some evening and poke a finger through one of the glittering holes in the sky.

One day as I sat there, my head cocked skyward, I didn't hear Matzek come up. Although his father was Jan the shoemaker on Butcher Street, he had hardly ever in his life worn shoes. The soles of his feet were like the bark of an old tree that wouldn't give even when he stepped on a piece of glass. His hair was rarely washed, and never combed; you could see the color of his flesh through his torn pants winter or summer. His small eyes beaming in a round face thickly sprinkled with freckles, he asked: "What do you see up there all the time?"

"A fiery balloon."

"That's no balloon, that's the sun."

"And what hangs in the sky at night?"

"The moon!"

"No, it's a mirror."

"That's no mirror, that's the moon."

"If it's a moon why is it cracked and sometimes whole pieces fall away?"

"I don't know. Come, let's ask my mother," he suggested.

Jan the shoemaker's only son lived in a cellar room on Butcher Street. A dozen or so worn brick steps led to a dark foyer with several doors. On one of these doors hung an angel with wings holding a boot in his hand. This was the entrance to the shoemaker's single room, which he shared with a blind beggar whose bed was partitioned off by a torn sheet suspended from a rope. From early morning till late into the night, Jan—a man with broad, drooping mustaches dangling beneath a blue-red bulbous nose—sat on a three-legged stool with a mouthful of nails that he spat out and hammered into something resembling a shoe that lay wedged between his knees.

Out in the foyer sat Felix, who had only one eye but many glittering rings on his fingers. His cap pushed way down nearly to the rim of his empty eye socket, he squatted on an empty beer barrel playing cards with fat Eunuch while the other inhabitants of the cellar stood around kibitzing. Among them was a Chinese with a pigtail called the Mandarin and a Tatar nicknamed Genghis Khan. The former peddled paper flowers and colored fans in the street while the latter went from door to door with a satchel, his principal customers being housemaids to whom he sold scented soap, wedding rings, and love potions. According to rumor, when the love potions and wedding rings failed to achieve their intended purpose, he also had a stock of candies filled with poison.

They both now stood around the card players and, as was the custom, helped them along. This led to bitter quarrels, convoluted curses, and frequent fistfights, following which at least one of the two had to be revived with a bucket of water. A third onlooker who stood out from the crowd was known by the imposing nickname of "Emperor." It wasn't completely clear if this was due to his tattered general's uniform with the dazzling cockade in the cap or his ability to down a whole bottle of ninety-proof vodka in a single gulp without a grimace. But whatever the case, he deserved this noble title if for nothing else than his tall figure and his splendid basso voice, which he often raised in sweet and touching song.

As we came down into the foyer we ran into Matzek's mother, a robust woman with ruddy cheeks and even ruddier arms and legs.

"Ma, what's up there in the sky, the sun or a fiery balloon?" Matzek blurted out without any preliminaries.

"The sun," she said and walked up the stairs to empty the slops into the street.

"Aha! I know better than you what's going on in the sky!" Matzek shouted triumphantly.

"Ask her about the moon," I prompted him. And the moment his mother came back with the empty basin he blocked her path and asked, "And what's up there in the sky at night, a moon or a mirror?"

"What kind of crap is that?" she asked pushing him aside impatiently. "Of course it's a moon!" And she passed through the door with the painted angel holding the boot.

"Ask her who shatters the moon?" I urged him.

From that day on, I ran to Matzek's place with questions, such as "Why does smoke rise from a chimney?" or "Why does a horse have four legs?" The real reason being that I wanted to hang around the crowd in the cellar. As Matzek strained to puzzle out the answers, the Emperor—in his cups, as usual—burst into song accompanied by the blind beggar on his accordion, and the Tatar sprang toward the ceiling and pirouetted like a top while the Mandarin giggled his approval in a shrill voice and kept time by clapping his hands.

I was deeply intrigued by this crew and made every effort to get closer to Matzek and his neighbors. I ran to the teahouse to fetch hot water for the Mandarin and helped the Tatar lift the satchel to his shoulders, but I made special efforts to assist Matzek's mother. I helped her empty the slops, sweep the floor, and wash drawers and soon managed to become an important member of the company, who looked at me not as a stranger but as Matzek's twin.

Along with the rest of the gang, my "brother" and I stood around the table watching the fierce contest between Fat Eunuch, who was a terrible player, and One-eyed Felix, who joked that he had pawned his other eye when he was once desperately in need of cash. Felix trimmed Fat Eunuch with regularity. He didn't collect his day's profits only, for the loser also had to treat the winner to a free ride around the marketplace in his ancient droshky with its canopy hanging in strips.

Felix would insist that the horse proceed slowly while he stretched his legs out to the driver's seat, draped himself with the canopy, and dozed off. Matzek and I hung onto the back of the droshky and finished off the day with our own free ride around the marketplace.

One evening Felix, who was the winner as usual, terminated the game and to everyone's surprise gave back to Fat Eunuch all the money he had lost. In return, he demanded a hundred free rides around the marketplace. Naturally, Matzek and I dashed right out and took our customary places on the rear axle.

It was quiet in the marketplace. You could hear the rustle of trees from as far away as Church Street. Fat Eunuch, swaying on the high seat of his carriage, dozed off and let the horse take over. Suddenly, Matzek tugged my sleeve—a strange, muffled sound was erupting from under the canopy. We knew for sure that Felix was under there, enjoying his due. Sometimes he snored, other times he wheezed, but we had never heard him giggle before. Besides, this wasn't his deep, whiskey growl but the thin, tinkling voice of a woman.

Holding our breaths, we strained to figure out the mystery. But the giggling promptly ceased, and all we could hear was the usual squeak of the wheels, the hoofbeats, and the snorting of the asthmatic horse. We looked at each other in amazement and waited impatiently for the ride to end.

When the droshky pulled up before the cellar, Matzek and I quickly sprang down and stationed ourselves by the side of the carriage.

Nothing could have surprised us more than what we saw next—from under the canopy jumped Matzek's mother, who silently slipped down into the cellar. Fat Eunuch whipped the horse and soon vanished, leaving the twin brothers standing completely flabbergasted in the middle of the deserted street.

I waited for Matzek to explain this to me, but he only stared without speaking.

"Maybe I'd better go home," I suggested, but he grabbed my sleeve. "I won't let you go till you swear that you'll never tell what we saw here tonight!"

"I swear that everything that happened tonight will remain secret forever!" I said with gravity.

"So will our friendship last forever. From now on, we're no longer make-believe twins but real, true-to-life brothers!" Matzek concluded.

To seal our brotherhood, Matzek took out the safety pin that held up his pants and pricked his middle finger, then insisted I do the same. He then pressed our fingers together so that the blood blended in a bond of eternal brotherhood.

From that day on, we both stood nearer to Felix and watched him closely. From my days in the thieves' den I clearly recalled that the trick of winning often lay in the way the cards were dealt. We were deeply concerned that Felix should lose, knowing that if he won, we would again have to perch on the droshky and listen to the strange goings-on between him and Matzek's mother.

One of us stationed himself behind Felix's shoulder and, looking at his cards, wigwagged to the other standing behind Fat Eunuch. But even this didn't help. Felix kept on winning and Matzek and

I were forced to accompany his mother almost nightly on her excursions.

One night as she was leaving the droshky she was met at the entrance to the cellar by her husband the shoemaker. Seizing his wife's hair and tucking her head between his knees, he began to pound it with the same hammer and the same force that he used on the old shoes. She tore loose, raced into the house, grabbed a pot of boiling water from the stove, and flung it in her husband's face.

The blind beggar woke up behind the sheet and began to shriek wildly. His screams quickly brought the other neighbors in their underdrawers. The Mandarin and the Emperor immediately joined the fray on the wife's side while the Tatar took up for the cuckolded husband. Matzek's mother's nocturnal adventures were no secret to them, and each of them had his own opinion concerning the matter. Now they finally had the opportunity to pound these opinions into the heads of the others with their fists and with anything else handy.

Soon the other neighbors joined the scrimmage, which didn't end until some of them lay in puddles of blood. The wounded husband and wife were carted away separately, putting a temporary halt to the fun.

The smoking lamp still dangled on the wall and its glass, like the rest of the things in the room, lay shattered on the floor. The beggar, with his flattened nose and huge flecks under the two chunks of dried cheese curds issuing from his blind eyes, stumbled about in one corner while the twin brothers huddled in the other.

The next evening when the inhabitants of the cellar again assembled in the foyer, they began to recall who had done what to whom, and it didn't take long for the fighting to resume with renewed enthusiasm. The rematch drew the participation of One-eyed Felix, and before it was over, Jan was missing some of his front teeth and the blind beggar, who for some reason had stood up for Jan, was nursing a cracked skull.

It was only natural that Matzek should side with his mother. After all, it was she who occasionally washed his face, hacked off his hair with a large rusty knife, and on long winter nights lulled him to sleep with terrifying tales about the accursed Jews. It was she who took him to church on Sundays and explained to him that the crucified figure with the pierced hands and bloody chest was the victim of these same Jews. At Passover time, it was she who hugged him close lest the Jews seize him and suck out his blood for their black holiday.

Although my sympathies were with the battered shoemaker, still I couldn't place myself against my twin brother with whom I had forged a blood bond of eternal devotion.

Crawling on all fours over the scene of the carnage, Matzek and I collected all the hammers, pliers, iron and wooden lasts, and brought them to the mother to use on her mate—until Jan in terrible indignation tore the burning kerosene lamp off the wall and hurled it at his wife, who leaped triumphantly out of the way with great agility and then tripped head over heels over me. She grew temporarily dazed from the terrible blow on the skull, but no sooner had she revived than she seized me by the hair and hurled me into the street with such wild rage that the angel holding the boot blew off the door.

The differences of opinion continued, with brief respites, for a long time. The combatants took a night or two off before resuming anew, and since I was by now persona non grata in the cellar, I went back to the bakery steps to speculate on how I could possibly drag down the cracked mirror of the moon, sell it in the marketplace, and thus help out my twin brother.

One night, Matzek came to the steps and began to sob: "I'm hungry . . . Since my parents have set out to cripple each other, I haven't tasted a bite of food."

I ran home and sneaked a big hunk of bread and a spoonful of butter out of our kitchen. Matzek wolfed it down in a gulp, then sighed, "The day before yesterday I made up my mind to drink some poison and die. And since you're my best friend and brother, you can't desert me and must take poison too, so we'll die together."

I looked at him in bewilderment. True, I had already seen several dead people, one of them being the janitor's daughter, Marinka. She lay in a white casket with silver fringes, all decked out in a white veil and flowers, and she looked very attractive.

Another time, I saw four horses with black hoods over their heads with holes cut for eyes drawing a black casket. A big crowd followed behind, while in front a children's chorus marched holding lighted candles and singing. It had been all very enchanting, but having now received a direct proposal to die, I felt somehow confused by it all. Matzek promptly came to my assistance. Taking out from under his shirt a small, greasy book with colorful pictures and gilded edges, he said, "After you take poison, you die and go to heaven." He pointed a finger upward, "That's where God is." He then placed the same finger on a picture in the book.

"Who is God?" I asked with an awkward smile.

"He's the King of Heaven. This is His house and there are His angels," Matzek said and leafed through the pages to a second picture in which plump naked toddlers with golden ringlets and silver winglets hovered among puffy clouds.

"I didn't know about these things—where did you get this book?"

"If you don't believe me, read it yourself," he suggested.

"I can't read."

"Neither can I," he confessed and promptly added, "But my mother can."

"Well then, read me what your mother reads," I pleaded.

"After you die you go up to heaven," Matzek "read," running his finger over the type and casting his eyes piously upward. "God sits there at a long table set with the fattest chickens, ducks, and grapes—"

"But what do you do there after you've eaten?" I asked with my whole being.

"You sing and you dance and you eat some more. Bells chime all day long and you play with the angels," he went on as fat tears trickled down his cheeks.

There wasn't any doubt in my mind as to the authenticity of his message. I had long since acknowledged Matzek as an authority on celestial matters, and now the remarkable book lay there before me, substantiating every word that he uttered with those spectacular pictures.

One thing, however, I couldn't understand: Why had Matzek kept all this a secret so long? Didn't he know about my gnawing urge to reach the end of the world, that enticing remoteness beyond the marketplace, the last street of the city at the very edge of heaven? How many times had I told him about my train rides and sea voyages—how I had climbed mountains and swum oceans and remained at the steps of the bakery just because my father had betrayed me and fled to America? But what was America compared to that golden house in heaven? Why hadn't Matzek shown me his magic book before? Why had he waited so long? If I could have spoken now, I would have asked him a million questions. My throat had grown constricted and I could barely mumble, "Yes, I will go with you, give me some poison!"

Unfortunately, he didn't happen to have any poison on him—he hadn't expected me to agree to the suicide pact so quickly and hadn't thought to prepare the poison beforehand.

Besides, even if he had anticipated my consent he wouldn't have been able to manage it, for since the brawling had commenced he couldn't find a piece of bread, much less poison, in his poverty-stricken home.

It would undoubtedly be far easier for me to prepare this celestial brew. After all, beside the two bedrooms and the room with the long trumeau mirror, we had a kitchen where you could put your hands on all the ingredients needed to cook up the poison just as Genghis Khan did when he concocted his deadly candies for the servant girls. It was nothing more than natural that I should agree not only to accompany my twin brother to heaven but also to prepare the means of getting there once he gave me the recipe. We kissed and parted with the understanding that we would meet the next day in the same place, from where we would embark to the end of the world and ascend to the Golden House of the Heavenly King.

When I came home, everyone was already sleep. I undressed quietly and slipped into bed, committing to memory the recipe Matzek had given me.

I pulled the blanket over my head so that no one could read from my face that this was to be my last night in this bed. Tomorrow, I would already be strolling on clouds. Let my father in America dance his quadrille with Leibke the ragpicker—I'd rather dance with the angels in heaven.

I had barely managed to close my eyes before an impatient dream flung me out of bed. Wearing only my nightshirt, I leaped out the window into the street below and whistled so loud that Matzek heard me in his sleep and joined me half-naked by the bakery steps. We climbed to the roof and, catching the tip of a cloud, were borne aloft by the wind to the very gates of the Golden House. We knocked on the mighty gate, it opened on its own, and we saw God sitting at a sumptuously set table surrounded by hovering cherubim. Matzek pitched right into the food, but my tongue had grown parched and my gums swollen from the excitement. In the corner hung the sun, which turned out to be just as I had always contended—a fiery balloon. On the opposite side hung the moon, which was again as I had imagined it—a round, silver mirror. But the thing that pleased me most was the great blue floor, which was pierced by thousands upon thousands of flickering holes. I stretched out facedown and put my eye to one, and oh—it was the marketplace below us! I recognized Pitche the tinsmith, Notte the kerosene dealer, and Cossack Arkashka. I yelled as loud as I could: "Hey, you guys—look where I am!"

God leaned down to me and asked with a kind smile, "What do you see there, my small friend?"

"My marketplace! Did you ever see my marketplace?"

"I never leave heaven. I don't know who you are, but I like you. Tell me what you want and I'll help you."

"Give me a stone so I can throw it down on Arkashka."

"That isn't nice—you're liable to hurt him. But if you insist, I'll do as you say—here is the stone, throw it. So there'll be one Cossack less on earth."

The stone fell with a terrible crash in the marketplace.

God laughed and patted my head. "Since you already made it thunder, I've got to pour down some water, because after thunder there must be rain."

"That's right, but forgive me, God, if I make one more suggestion. If I could throw some tobacco down on them they'd catch right on that it's me up here."

"You need only say, my son. Will a thousand packets do?"

In the meantime, Matzek had eaten his fill and begun to gambol with the angels.

"What's the time now?" God asked. "It's time you went home already, my children."

Matzek and I stamped our feet. "No, no, we won't go back! We want to stay here! Is this fair? We died and now you're shoving us back into life again."

"But you can't stay here in your present condition. First you must drink the poison, grow wings, and become angels."

"In that case, we'll be back here first thing tomorrow morning.

Come, let's not lose any time," I said, pulling Matzek's sleeve, and then turned back to God. "If I should oversleep, throw down a stone so that when I hear the thunder I'll know it's time to get up."

I didn't hear the thunder, but as soon as the first raindrops moistened my pillow I got up and sprang quickly out of bed. Wolfing down my last breakfast on earth, I began to concoct the poison.

V

FOLLOWING MATZEK'S INSTRUCTIONS to a tee, I filled a small bottle with salt and pepper, ground in a piece of horseradish, and added a slice of onion and a dash of vinegar. Then I went into the bedroom and watched Pelga make up my bed for the last time. I met my little sister in the dining room and stroked her hair tenderly. I was glad that my mother was no longer at home, since it would have been harder for me to say goodbye to her than to the others. Now that I was about to leave her forever, I appreciated how quiet and gentle she was, how superior to Matzek's mother, for instance. But I couldn't give myself over to sentiment for long. I had to hurry to the bakery steps where I was supposed to meet Matzek. But he wasn't there.

What could this mean? Was it possible that in his great despair he had borrowed a little poison from Genghis Khan and gone on without me? The bitter thought pierced me like a knife and I raced swiftly to the shoemaker's cellar.

Imagine my surprise to see Jan sitting calmly at a table stacked with empty whiskey bottles and playing cards with whom but his worst enemy—Felix! The usual crowd of drunken sots stood around— Matzek among them on top of a barrel—laughing in a strange, loud fashion and shouting "hurrah!" each time Jan slapped his cards on the table.

From his high perch, Matzek had no trouble spotting me and running up quickly. He asked in a sharp tone, "What are you holding there under your arm?"

"The poison."

"Where did you get it?"

"I made it the way you told me."

He took the bottle out of my hand, sniffed it gingerly, and grimaced. "It's no good. It doesn't even begin to smell like Genghis Khan's poison, and it shouldn't be in a bottle, it should first be cooked in a pot, then cooled, then cut into little bricks. Go home and make it over again and this time the right way. Or better still, leave it till tomorrow, and in the meantime come watch my father win all the money from Felix."

I grabbed him by his sleeve. "What's going on here?"

He gathered from my tone that it would be best if he told me right off.

"Last night my father made up with Felix. All the neighbors drank a lot of whiskey and ate up ten whole sausages . . . There was kissing and singing. They've been playing cards all night, and my father has already won ten rubles that he gave to my mother, and she has gone to the butcher's to buy meat for real meatballs, with cabbage borscht, groats, and—"

But he hadn't managed to list all the dishes before a fresh burst of laughter erupted from around the card table, which meant that Jan had won another hand. Matzek jumped back onto the barrel and left me there with the poison in hand.

I stood there for a moment in great confusion, then dashed from the cellar.

What had happened? How was it possible that Felix could lose his money to Jan, whom only a day before he had pounded so bloody? And how could it be that Jan, who was a far worse player than Fat Eunuch, should suddenly win ten rubles from such a cardsharp as Felix, then turn the money over to his despised wife to prepare a supper of real meatballs? No, Matzek had plainly deceived me. He had probably lost the urge to die during the night and had now come up with this pretext to get out of it. And what was I supposed to do after I had already said goodbye to my bed and my house? Give up the dream? Renounce the glories of heaven? Forget my friendship with God and turn back to the garbage bin in the market-place? No! Never! Whatever the reason that had changed Matzek's mind, for me there was no turning back! After all, the bottle of poison was still in my hand. I could drink it myself and go up to heaven alone . . .

Naturally, it would be better if Matzek, who was an authority on every last detail concerning heaven, would go with me at least as far as the entrance. And why shouldn't he? Hadn't we sworn eternal brotherhood with our own blood? Can twenty meatballs cancel out a few drops of blood? Never! I must run back to the cellar and demand that Matzek leave the card game along with his lousy sausages and meatballs and, whether the poison was good or not, accompany me to heaven this minute!

But by the time I solidified my decision and went back to the cellar, the game had already ended.

Jan wobbled on drunken legs and kept counting his winnings. Licking the remaining few drops from the emptied bottles, the cellar bunch wished luck, strength, and a long life to the winner.

Fat Eunuch, who this time had been merely an onlooker, had nevertheless parked his carriage by the front door to take the winner for a ride as usual. This time, of course, for pay.

The drunken crew soon spilled gaily out into the street, lifted Jan up into the driver's seat next to Fat Eunuch, and placed the reins in his hands. His wife and Felix were seated under the canopy while the Emperor and Genghis Khan stationed themselves on the running boards on either side of the droshky, singing and fifing along.

Matzek ran to secure his usual place on the rear axle where he found the Mandarin already curled up and grinning through his rotting teeth. Fat Eunuch began to lash wildly the emaciated nag that dragged the overloaded carriage over the crooked cobblestones, sending sparks flying over the merry crowd inside.

I ran behind shouting, "Matzek! Matzek!" But my twin brother made believe he didn't hear me.

I managed to catch up with him at Church Street, to seize Matzek by a leg and drag him down off the axle.

"What do you want from me?" he bristled. "Why don't you let me ride with my mother?"

"Why did you say the poison is no good?" I asked.

"Because it isn't."

"Let's test it and you'll see that it works."

"Not now, I can't now. Maybe tomorrow . . . Maybe the day after . . . Take it, hide it . . . We'll use it some other time," he mumbled, trying to get away from me. But I was adamant. I brought the bottle up to his nose to convince him that the poison was the best in the world, but he spat in disgust, "I tell you it's no good. It needs vinegar!"

"That's a lie!"

"Then it probably needs pepper."

"That's a lie, too. And you yourself are a lousy liar!"

And I smashed the bottle on the ground.

Matzek narrowed his eyes. "How dare you call me a liar?"

"Because you fooled me. You promised to take me up to heaven and meet God. Now I see that you've changed your mind and that everything you told me is a big lie."

"God is a lie?" Matzek shouted with his fists clenched. "Isn't it because you're a damned Jew that you don't believe in God? If that's the reason, then it's better that you smashed the bottle, because the poison wouldn't have helped anyway. You wouldn't have been allowed into heaven in any case because you're a Jew, and God hates the Yids because they killed Him and sold Him for thirty kopecks, and that's why He cursed them forever."

"You mean me, too?"

"You and your father and your mother and your whole family!" Matzek concluded with a shriek, then burst out in tears.

"I never heard of this. It can't be . . . My father is in America, and I can swear for my mother that she wouldn't hurt a fly. How is it possible that God was killed when I saw Him only yesterday alive and well?" I asked, choking back my tears and seizing upon my dream like a drowning man clutching a straw. "Last night I went straight up to heaven . . . and I tell you that He lives. He lives . . . I talked with Him!"

"You're crazy, you only dreamed it."

"No, I tell you He lives. You read to me yourself in that book that He lives."

Matzek wiped his eyes and lost some of his assurance.

"I don't know. Maybe He lives . . . And what's the difference if He does or doesn't? The Jews killed Him in any case. And if you don't believe me, come with me to church, and you'll see Him hanging there crucified on the wall."

For a while we both stood there with heads bowed as if the earth had suddenly parted beneath us and a deep chasm separated us. But soon he stretched out his hand. "It hurts me that I had to tell you this, but it's your own fault. If you weren't so stubborn it wouldn't have come to this. But you needn't worry. It doesn't bother me that you're a damned Jew. I love you and I promise you that this coming Sunday in church I'll stick up for you and explain that you're my best friend. I'm sure that God will forgive you."

Hope flashed momentarily before my eyes then quickly flickered out. I no longer had any faith in my twin brother.

"I'll go with you to church," I proposed.

"No!" he blurted out. He knew how seriously I took a vow and was apparently loath to get me riled up all over again. "It would be better if I went alone. It would be better if you weren't there. But don't worry, I assure you I'll fix everything."

Head bowed, I turned my way home.

On the corner of Church Street, I stopped to look back at the white building with the long, stained-glass windows where, the following Sunday, my fate would be decided. The building was surrounded by tall chestnut trees. Matzek and I had often squeezed through the iron bars of the fence to pick the fallen chestnuts, but now the yellow leaves had fallen and in the shine of the solitary gas lamps the naked branches appeared like long fingers stretched out to seize the Jew's head. I quickly raced past Market Street and home.

That night, I couldn't fall asleep. My memory took special pleasure in taunting and tormenting me with last night's dream and with Matzek's promise to go to church and beg forgiveness for me for a murder I had never committed. But it also reminded me of something that absolved me from the whole mess, and feeling suddenly unburdened and overjoyed, I shouted into the pillow, "No, he won't eat any meatballs!" With a curse on my lips, I fell asleep in satisfaction.

Early before dawn the next morning, I ran to the shoemaker's cellar and bent down to the window that looked out onto the sidewalk. The whole crowd was stretched out dead drunk on the floor. The Mandarin lay under the table, the Emperor squatted in the middle of the room with his head hanging and grunted one of his mournful songs, and the blind beggar wearily tugged at his ragged accordion, which emitted shrill, solitary chords. I pulled the rag from the broken pane and shouted, "Matzek! Matzek!" until he came out into the street.

"How does God know that I'm a Jew?" I challenged him. "He never comes from heaven. He told me Himself that He doesn't know me. If you go to church, you'll only be telling Him things He knows nothing about. And how do you know that I'm a Jew?" I seized him by his dirty shirtfront with suddenly renewed courage and firmness. In my moment of despair, I looked my ex-brother squarely in the eye and cried, "You and your mother and your whole family are low-down liars! I'm not a Jew!"

"My mother is not a liar!"

"Well then, let's talk to her right now."

"She is sleeping."

I offered a compromise, "Then let's ask your father."

"My mother said you can't ever come to the cellar again. Let go of me, you're tearing my last shirt!"

"Let's go ask your father," I insisted.

"No, I won't let you in our house anymore!" he said, blocking my path. With the same agility with which I had once vanquished Pevke in the marketplace and conquered the Japanese by the garbage bin, I now clamped my fingers around his lower lip and dragged him down the brick steps and into the cellar.

The drunken crew welcomed me with howls, but I ignored them and went straight to the corner where Jan sat on his three-legged stool guzzling his vodka.

"How do you know that I'm a Jew?" I asked him. He raised his wrinkled, grim face and, measuring me from head to foot with a pair of glazed eyes, broke into a laughter that flooded his eyes with tears and blasted a great blob of snot from his red and blue nose, leaving it dangling on his grimy mustache. Mixing his laughter with a cough, he still managed to cry out, "Of course I know. Everyone knows!" And he poked me rudely between the legs.

I clutched my groin not so much out of pain as out of astonishment, and before I even realized what Jan meant, the Emperor skillfully unbuttoned my fly and tickled me under my bare navel.

The Mandarin came crawling out on all fours from under the table. "Let me, let me take a peek, too! I've never seen such a thing in my life!" Genghis Khan grabbed the Chinese by his pigtail and dragged him back to the table. Then he took me aside and rebuttoned my pants and insisted that everyone beg my pardon. The Emperor promptly agreed. He stretched to his full height, laid his hand alongside his cap, and clicked his heels with military gallantry, "Pardon me, Sir!"

Receiving no answer, he hissed, "For the first time in my life I begged a Jew's pardon, but once a sheenie always a sheenie." And he left the cellar. The Mandarin with the flowers and the beggar with his accordion followed behind.

From behind the partition stepped Felix, accompanied by Matzek's mother. He pinched her cheek, adjusted the dirty patch over his hollow eye socket, and went outside too. Genghis Khan had already placed his satchel on his shoulders, but he lingered by the doorway, took out a paper cone of candy, and offered it to me.

I looked at the Tatar's outstretched hand holding the real poison that could have borne me to heaven as easily as a feather. But what good would it do me since I was a Jew, a sheenie, and heaven was closed to me forever? I turned away from the Tatar and buried my head between my knees.

VI

⚬✥⚬

ONE FROSTY WINTER day, a poor peasant woman wearing torn felt boots came to my mother, Sarah, to sell her milk. She said she had been seduced by a handsome scoundrel and her illegitimate child had died when it was barely two weeks old. She presented her breasts for inspection, and after Sarah had tapped the nipples and tasted the milk, she tore me away from her own meager breast—at which I had been clammering for several weeks with lips swollen from straining to draw out a bit of sustenance—and attached me to the fleshy mounds of the White Russian peasant woman.

In later years, Pelga would tell me that from the very first day at her breast, I behaved like a charlatan; that after the very first suck of her milk, I winked at her as if to say, "This is it!" and chucked her under her chin.

When Sarah, who was generally delicate, came out of a second pregnancy in a greatly weakened condition, Pelga took over the housekeeping chores. Along with this, my mother passed over to her the major part of my supervision, which turned me into a child with two mothers.

Between these two mothers stood the father who was proud of the fact that his son was "the world's biggest rascal, who could drive not two but six mothers to an early grave." But now, after the incident in Jan the shoemaker's cellar, I felt for the first time a need for a mother's comfort and decided to turn to Pelga.

I made this choice because once when Pelga was airing out the chest that she kept under her bed, I noticed there a colored picture of a woman with a naked infant in her lap and a silver ring around the baby's head. This had happened at a time when I was rushing off to engage the Japanese army and didn't have the time to pay attention, but now the similarity between Pelga's picture and those in Matzek's book came to me with particular clarity.

Next morning as Pelga squatted on all fours scrubbing the floor, I asked her, "Hey, what do you know about God?"

She trembled as if someone had struck her. "What business is that of yours?"

"Is it true that He was killed and betrayed by the Jews?"

"Bite your tongue!"

She angrily threw down the wet rag and, still kneeling, placed her thumb and two fingers to her lips, kissed them fervently, and crossed herself.

"What does it mean, what you just did?" I asked.

"It's none of your business. Go to the marketplace!" she cried. "Don't dare speak of it again. You have your own God!"

"Who is my God?" I asked, wondering why she was so angry.

"I don't know Him, I know nothing about Him! Why don't you ask your mother?"

"You're my mother too, aren't you?"

This was all that she needed to fill her blue eyes with tears. She pulled me close, pressed my head to her ample belly, and, dabbing her eyes, said in a milder tone, "Maybe it's because you have too many mothers and not even one father that you don't know who your God is. I believe that your father doesn't know who his God is, either. I never heard him mention God's name. In this damned house, I've nearly forgotten myself that there is a God in heaven. A big boy like you should know already who your Jewish God is."

"Who is the Jewish God?" I asked her.

"How should I know? My God is Jesus Christ."

I seized upon this at once, "In that case, you can tell me all about Him!"

"I told you already that this is none of your business. You've got no right to know, to talk, or even to think about my God."

"Why?"

"Because you're a Jew, and you must think about your own God!" she raged with fists clenched.

That I was a Jew was no longer news to me. All that I wanted to learn from her was whether it was somehow possible for a Jew to go up to heaven and play with the naked angels too. But from her rage I gathered that this was an almost hopeless goal, and I asked with resignation, "If that's the case, maybe you can tell me where the Jewish God hangs out."

"Let me be. I already told you that I can't talk about your God. Tomorrow I'll get your grandfather to explain it all to you. Now go to the marketplace!" And, glaring at me, she added, "Don't you dare mention a word to your grandfather about what was said here, or the old fool might blame me for everything. Not a word, you hear!" And she pushed me out of the house.

I was left standing behind the door with a feeling of disappointment. Maybe it was stupid of me to drag my family into my personal dealings with God. But it was already a lost cause, for Pelga left the floor half washed and ran to find my other mother. They locked themselves in the bedroom to decide which of the grandfathers to call on for help.

The first grandfather (my father's father) was a squarely built fellow with Mongolian features. All he lacked was a long pigtail down his nape to resemble the Mandarin in the cellar. People in the marketplace often wondered how such a Chinaman had cropped up in a Jewish family. Barve's Son tried in his unique fashion to show that in the past, the Mongols who rode on wild goats and held swords between their teeth had conquered Europe, including the old marketplace, and it was quite possible that Reb Mordecai was one of their descendants. The further fact that he was too partial to the grape was additional proof that although he may have been a Jew, there was great doubt as to whether he actually stemmed from the People of the Book—Abraham, Isaac, and Jacob.

For Pelga, all this was enough to choose the other grandfather, who was no more than a simple tailor but who was named Moshe and whose appearance was a true facsimile of one of her colored pictures of the ancient Hebrews—tall, lean, with a pair of kind, myopic eyes under dense brows and a drawn, parchmentlike face framed by a long, sparse beard.

And early the next day, Grandfather Moshe burst into my bedroom and in a cracked voice demanded, "What's this? What's this? What does it mean you don't know that you're a Jew? You know to play with dogs and with cards? Get dressed this instant and we'll go to cheder. You'll know at least that a Jew must go to cheder. I talked to the rabbi yesterday and he's expecting you." And before I even managed to ask what all this meant, Pelga dragged me out of bed, threw me into a tub of water, and proceeded to wash and scrub me with such vigor that she seemed anxious to skin me alive, Sarah feverishly prepared fresh underwear for me, and all three helped me wolf down my breakfast.

Dragging me by the hand, Grandfather Moshe turned from one street into another. The women trotted behind as if someone were chasing us with a knife.

Finally Grandfather stopped before a gate. He put on two pairs of glasses, peered at the number, and said, "Yes, this is it!"

We passed through a narrow, filthy courtyard and entered a dark antechamber where freshly washed underwear hung on ropes, stretching from wall to wall.

From behind a wet shirt peered a face whose gender it was difficult to determine at first glance. It was wearing a dress that was sharply tucked up to one side, disclosing heavy men's underdrawers, and you could spot a sparse mustache beneath its nostrils. But apparently the face was familiar to Grandfather, for he greeted it with a pleasant, "Good morning, Rebbetzin!" Adjusting her dress hurriedly, the rebbetzin responded in a hoarse, masculine voice, "Good morning, good year!" And she led the visitors inside the cheder.

On a pair of old, scarred benches sat a few children chanting and swaying to and fro. Facing the children was a small individual with a round, smiling face framed in a yellow-red beard. He sat half sunk in a chair with torn straw stuffing, and only a pair of cushions kept him from falling completely through the seat.

When the group came in, the rabbi stopped the chant, crawled out of his chair, and bowed to the guests. He pinched the new pupil's cheek and seated him on the rear bench.

"When I'm through with them, I'll deal with you," he said. He bowed to the guests again, indicating that they could go, snuggled back into his chair, and nodded to the children who promptly resumed swaying and chanting.

There wasn't one familiar face on the bench. Looking at their backs, I wondered who they were and where I had been dragged off to. But sitting there and listening to their chant, it soon became clear to me that I was in the right place. Because as far as I could make out, they were singing about that which interested me more now than anything else in the world—God.

Finally, the singing stopped and the children quickly scattered with shouts of joy.

The rabbi enjoyed a good yawn and a hearty scratch under the armpit, then, beckoning with a finger, summoned the new pupil, who was already waiting on pins and needles, to a seat on the front bench. From his waistcoat pocket he drew an old, folded sheet of paper and spreading it out on the bench said, "You see this small duckling with one leg drawn up into the belly and the other on its back—that's an *aleph*—oh,oh,oh,oh!"

I looked at the rabbi with a good deal of disappointment. Still, I managed to get hold of myself and repeated after him, "Little duckling, belly, leg, *aleph*, oh,oh,oh,oh!"

The rabbi gave another long yawn and, pointing to a second letter, continued, "This box which has a dot instead of a wall in front is called *beth*—bo,bo,bo!"

I read impatiently, "Box, dot, wall, bo,bo,bo!"

"This . . ." The rabbi placed his finger on the third letter and again opened his mouth to yawn, but this time I stopped him.

"Can't you tell me which of the Gods the children were singing about before?"

Caught with the unfinished yawn still in his mouth, the rabbi jerked as if someone had doused him with ice water. "What do you mean, which God—there is only one God!"

I moved in closer. "Who is He?"

"What kind of question is that? Don't talk nonsense, and repeat after me. This with the crooked leg is a *gimel*—go,go,go!"

"I don't want no duck, box, or crooked leg!" I said, pushing the grease-stained alphabet aside. "Why don't you chant with me the same as you did with the others?"

"How can you compare yourself to them?" he asked, "You're just a beginner."

"In that case, I'd rather go home." I got up from the bench.

The rabbi jumped up and cried, "Belle-Pesel! Belle-Pesel!" The face with the mustache appeared in the doorway.

"How do you like that—the boy is going home!" the rabbi appealed to her in a whining tone.

The rebbetzin wrung her hands. "What do you mean? We barely get a new pupil and we should lose him so fast already?"

"I tell him to repeat 'duckling,' 'belly,' '*aleph*,' and he asks me who is God."

"Well, are you too dumb or sick to answer him?" she grunted hoarsely.

The rabbi began to defend himself. "Who doesn't know that God created heaven and earth, all the oceans and mountains?"

"Where can this God be found?" I persisted, thinking about the God in my dream and wondering if they were one and the same.

"What do you mean, where? Everywhere and all over, in heaven and on earth!"

"On earth? On what street?"

"On all the streets, in all the cities, in every country, over the whole world!"

"Yes, but doesn't He have one definite place, a house?"

"Certainly. The whole world is His house," the rebbetzin interjected.

"But doesn't He sit somewhere in one place by a table?" I asked, ignoring the rabbi and turning to the rebbetzin, who seemed much sharper.

She looked at me for a moment with a helpless smile, then began to rail at the rabbi, "Why don't you answer him? These things are for you to know!"

But he only sat there dumbfounded, tearing at his yellow-red beard with a trembling hand.

"I'd better go home!" I threatened again.

The rebbetzin ran up to the rabbi in despair and, pulling him out of his chair, she cried, "A plague on all my enemies! He asks you a question, why don't you answer him?"

She grabbed me by the arm and sat down next to me on the bench. "The boy is right. I want to know who God is, too. Speak!" she ordered, her face grim.

Under her demanding stare, the hapless rabbi began to pace through the room wringing his hands and mumbling, "Strike me, God, if I know what to tell him."

"How does He look? Does He have long hair?" I persisted.

"God doesn't look like anything since He can't be seen, heard, or touched," the rebbetzin said, making an effort to help her distressed husband.

"Have you by any chance a picture of Him?" I asked bluntly.

The rebbetzin sprang out from behind the bench and stamped her feet on the floor as if she no longer cared whether she lost the pupil or not. "The Jewish God takes no pictures!"

Now that the rabbi felt his wife on his side, he regained courage and, following her example, slammed the table. "The boy is crazy! One dares not talk this way about God."

"Why?" I asked and again began to edge toward the door.

"Because God is holy and His name is holy. God is mighty and omnipotent, and His name mustn't be spoken. What did you think, that for a couple of lousy rubles' tuition you could come here to profane God's name! To hell with the money . . . Don't you dare speak that way about the Almighty!"

"I want to know God's name," I mumbled through clenched lips.

"Where do you come off to know God's name? And what business is it of yours?"

"With God's name, you can build worlds and destroy worlds!" the rebbetzin cried, outshouting her husband in a bellowing chant. "You can part oceans and raise mountains. You can even make a man, a living man out of stone and clay—a Golem!"

For me, all this was still not enough. True, it was already clear to me that my God was the Jewish God, but from the way these two poor people strained to explain it to me, He was a God who had no name or recognizable face. And although He appeared to be everywhere and over all, He had no definite address where He could be reached. I had already placed my hand on the doorknob, but the very last word the rebbetzin uttered stopped me. I turned around and asked, "What did you say—a Golem? What's that?"

"Ah, if you ask about Golems—that's something we can talk about. Sit down on the bench again and we'll talk." And she wiped the bench with the edge of her dress, then, taking the rabbi's arm, pushed him out the door. "You, go! . . . You'll find a dish of groats in the kitchen. Go eat and leave the boy to me." And before he had even closed the door behind him, she went on chanting with the same fervor, "The Golem is a man made of clay . . . Believe me, this is worthwhile hearing. Come, let's both sit here."

"Of clay, you say?"

"Yes, of clay . . . a living man!"

"How can that be? Who made him?"

"A big rabbi. A Gaon . . . the Gaon of the Great Synagogue."

"I don't know what you mean."

"You never heard of the Vilna Gaon? He was . . . he was a shining beacon for us Jews. He made the Golem so that he would provide the Jews with fish for the Sabbath. He would send the Golem down to the bottom of the river and use his knowledge of the fish language to lure them into a large net, then distribute them among the Jews . . . Come, sit down on the bench."

I didn't move, but I did let go of the doorknob. The rebbetzin probably noticed this, and she began to chant with more feeling, "He fashioned him out of clay and sand and water. And since the Gaon, may he enjoy bliss in paradise, knew the alphabet and the Pentateuch and the Gemara by heart, as well as all the secrets of the cabala, he also knew the name of God, and he wrote this name on a piece of paper and put it inside the Golem's head, and the piece of clay was transformed into a living man."

The extraordinary story, and particularly the lamenting and heart-rending tone in which she tried to chant it in her hoarse voice, enraptured me. Still, I shook my head in pure contrariness. "No, no, it can't be! If he was a man, how could he go underwater and not drown?"

"Of course he could!" she said, her voice rising to a higher pitch, which left her big eyeballs all bloodshot from the strain. "He could also leap like a bird from roof to roof. He could conceal himself so that no one could see him and fly through the air like a wind on a cold day. There was nothing he couldn't do. Oh, take pity and sit here with me on the bench!"

"But you yourself say that he was a man. How then could he be a wind?"

"He was a man and still not a man. The Gaon sent him to the synagogue to put out the candles on the Sabbath because, even though the Golem had the appearance of a man, he wasn't a true man and wasn't obliged to obey all the rules and customs of the Torah, and could therefore violate the Sabbath. His chief duty, however, consisted of protecting the Jews during a Christian holiday or on a market day, when the drunken peasants began to carry on and beat them. The Gaon sent out the Golem . . . oh, my . . ." She seized her throat abruptly as if something had burst in there, and the falsetto voice suddenly plummeted to a bass. "The Golem used to crack their skulls and break their arms and legs. They couldn't do a thing to him because he would jump up onto the roof or dive underwater and stick out his big stone tongue at them. When the governor general found out about him . . . oh, God, God . . . The Golem, I mean the Gaon, sent the Golem the—how is he called? The gover—gover—governor . . ."

She strained to bring out the words that had grown entangled in her stretched vocal chords. I came up closer to her. "Why should you strain yourself to sing? Why must we talk so much? Let us better go to the Golem. Where is he now?"

"In the attic of the Great Synagogue."

"Is it far from here?"

"I've never been there."

"Well, call in the rabbi and ask him."

"My God! Why do you torment us? Why are you driving two poor people to an early grave? I have to heat the stove. I have to knead the bread. I have to scrub the floor. Why did you come to drain our blood? I should leave everything in the middle of the day and go crawling up to the attic after a Golem? Anyway, the Golem is no longer a Golem because the Gaon took the paper with the holy name out of him and turned him back into a hunk of clay."

"Why did he do that?" I cried angrily.

"Because there's no shortage of fish in the marketplace now. Even paupers like us can afford a piece of carp for the Sabbath. Any time he is needed again, he'll be brought back to life."

"How?"

"A new Gaon will come and again put the scrap of paper with the name of God into his ear. But let God save and protect us. Better we shouldn't need him!"

"We do need him!"

"Who needs him?"

"I need him!"

Whether it was because my last demand frightened her or because she finally realized that all her efforts had been in vain, that her strength was drained, and that she was losing a pupil in any case, she suddenly clasped her face in her tanned, masculine hands and burst into tears.

I let her cry for a while, then proceeded. "What was written on the paper?"

"I told you. God's holy name," she said, wiping her nose on her sleeve.

"But you said that God has no name."

"He has, He has! God has a thousand names, as for instance, God of Abraham, Isaac, and Jacob. God in heaven. He whose name I mustn't mention because I haven't washed my hands yet. The Lord of the Universe—and so on and so on, but one of the names is the holiest of all the names, and this particular name is only known to the greatest sages, great rabbis, great Gaonim. Where do I come off, a poor weak woman, to know about such things? When you grow up and become a great Gaon, God willing . . . and you will, too, I can see as sure as today is Thursday that—you're not like other children . . . You will be a Gaon, and you will make a Golem. Why not? It would be good for the Jews. But in order to be a Gaon, you must come to cheder every day and study your a-b-c's," she said, holding the greasy alphabet before my face as the tears flooded her red eyes.

For a while, I stood there with my head hanging and said nothing, then I blurted out mechanically, "Duck foot, belly—oh,oh,oh,*beth*—bo,bo,bo . . ."

The overjoyed rebbetzin turned her eyes heavenward with hands clasped. "Blessed be He whose name can't be mentioned."

From that day on, I raced to the cheder with the same impetus with which I had once raced to the marketplace. To be a Gaon, not in heaven but here on earth . . . not to drink poison and die but to live . . . to learn the Torah, the Gemara, to arrive at the holy name, then to come to the marketplace in the company of a stone Golem . . .

From the very thought, I saw the letters of the alphabet begin to tremble. The "ducks" flipped upside down, and the whole alphabet stretched and turned into the old marketplace, which was full of confused and astounded market people.

The pickpockets raced from the thieves' dens to look at their old associate; the ragamuffins, from behind the garbage bin, piled one on top of another to gaze at their former partner; the Cossacks halted their horses to glance at the little rabbi standing in the center of the marketplace next to a huge stone giant.

With one leap, the little rabbi sprang up on the Golem's back, cried the holy name, and all that could be seen now was a mighty wind racing through the streets and down into Jan the shoemaker's cellar.

The storm shattered the door with a crash, blew away the cards, and scattered the drunken band, stripping their trousers and flinging them into the street. Running bare-assed along Butcher Street, they screamed in frightful terror, "Help! Help!" But no one could help them, for who could stop a wind? All they could hear was the clatter of stony feet upon the cobblestones and a thunderous laughter issuing as if from heaven.

Soaring on the wings of my inflamed imagination, I quickly jumped from the alphabet to the Pentateuch, from Abraham the Patriarch to Moses, and from the edge of the sea to the desert, where I caught up with the other pupils in the Land of Israel. And long before we got to the Destruction of the Temple, I already sat on the front bench, chanting louder than all the rest.

VII

⟨⟩

WALKING HOME FROM cheder one afternoon, I noticed a crowd in the marketplace. It was obvious that this had nothing to do with Barve's Son since the crowd was broken up into several groups, which wouldn't have been the case had the learned youth been giving one of his discourses. What then could it be, I wondered, and before I even realized what I was doing, I was in the marketplace.

As I crossed Market Street, I wondered how I would be received by the market people after having stayed away so long. But the coldness and indifference that I encountered were worse than I had imagined—they didn't even turn around to look at me. This wasn't the way I had visualized my return to the marketplace, but since I had already made the mistake of showing myself, it would be foolish to leave without at least finding out what had aroused the people so.

I moved from group to group and finally discovered that they were all discussing the same remarkable event that had occurred during the time I had been away. Although every group, and each person in every group, managed to voice his own version of the occurrence, it was clear that this had to do with some musician whose name was Paganini.

According to one witness (which a second verified and a third corrected slightly) the story had happened this way: On a very hot day some time ago, a stranger with a violin under his arm stopped at a marketplace stall to drink a glass of apple kvass. He was lean, tall, with extraordinarily long legs, and dressed in a black cape and a shiny top hat. He seemed to be very thirsty. He put the violin case on a nearby bench and, mopping his brow with a silk handkerchief, refreshed himself with a glass of kvass. In the meantime a barefoot boy came up from behind him, opened the case, took out the violin, and commenced to play. The stranger looked about and was momentarily dumbfounded. When he recovered he cried out, "God in heaven, I could swear that this boy would grow up to be a second

Paganini!" He stooped to kiss the boy's head and said, "I make you a present of the violin. When you have bedazzled the world with your artistry, you can pay me back." He then thrust the violin case into the boy's hands and vanished from the marketplace.

According to a second version (that someone had heard from someone else, who had heard it from a third party), it had all happened altogether differently.

The real Paganini, the master himself, had come to play a concert in the great town hall. Naturally, only the rich people could get inside, while the poor gathered outside hoping that at least a few of the violin chords might escape to them through the walls. In all the excitement, no one noticed a small, barefoot boy wandering about backstage. After the first number, called "Perpetuo Mobile," Paganini was forced by a call of nature to put down his violin on a nearby table behind the curtain and visit the men's room. Without asking anyone's permission, the boy picked up the violin, went out on stage, and began to play the very same number.

Well, the ensuing stir couldn't be described by the market people since none of them had been able to scrape together the price of admission, but they did know that the audience rose as one and demanded that the concert be finished not by Paganini but by the barefoot boy. And that wasn't all. Whether it had actually been Paganini (who according to one loudmouth expert had died a hundred years earlier) or some other musician who presented the violin to the boy wasn't as important as the fact that some wealthy patron promptly outfitted him in a velvet suit and hired a music teacher to prepare him for the conservatory in St. Petersburg.

And before I could even finish running from group to group to form a clear picture in my mind of this remarkable event, the people all drifted over to the kvass stand, which stood at the edge of the marketplace at Church Street. Dazed by what I had heard, I tagged along.

The incredible story about Paganini that had stunned me to such a degree was still as nothing in comparison to the sight that met my eyes next. Walking from Church Street in a velvet suit and carrying a violin case under his arm was no one else but Berchik the Fool, my erstwhile partner from behind the garbage bin.

My senses reeling, I leaped aside and peered out from behind a nearby stall at my former partner who, despite his fancy attire, had changed little. His pale, drawn face with round eyebrows over gray eyes retained the same dull, piteous expression.

When Berchik (to whom the market people now referred as Boris) came up to his mother, Beille the kvass vendor, he was instantly mobbed by the market people, who flocked around him like so many gabbling geese.

"Boris, is it really true that you're going to a conservatory in St. Petersburg?"

"When are you leaving? This summer or next winter?"

"You have your train ticket already?"

"Leave him alone, he didn't come to talk to you but to his mother."

"Oy, if his father were only living—what pleasure this would give him!"

"What happened at the concert in town hall?"

"Who was the stranger who drank the kvass?"

"Did he really call you Paganini the Second?"

"Is this really Paganini's fiddle you're holding?"

"Is it true Paganini got the cramps after he heard you play?"

"Why should you only play for the rich—let the poor people hear you too!"

"Don't push, take it easy, he'll play. He'll play!"

And that's how it turned out. A moment or so later, Paganini the Second thrilled the marketplace with his enchanting, magical tones.

Silently I poked my head through the wall of backs surrounding my former partner, who stood with eyes closed, ear resting on the violin, and trembling fingers racing over the strings.

If with my own two eyes I had seen Moses parting the Red Sea or Elijah rising up to heaven, I wouldn't have been more flabbergasted than I was by what I was witnessing now. It seemed to me that not only did Paganini the Second soar up to heaven but he carried the whole marketplace along with him. I literally felt the ground move and powerful winds lift me, and I clamped my eyes on Paganini as if to hold on so that the winds wouldn't dislodge me.

How could this be? How could it have happened? And how insignificant everything I had ever done in the marketplace seemed in comparison with what this small fool had accomplished now . . . How could I have allowed myself to be sidetracked to some forsaken cheder, and squander so much time on fables from the Pentateuch and Scriptures, and be convinced by that foolish little rabbi that if I was a good boy I would grow up to be a Gaon and bring life to the Golem, which lay covered in cobwebs in the attic of the Great Synagogue? Who the hell had plucked me from the marketplace at the very time that Paganini the First stopped to have a glass of kvass? There could be no doubt at all that if I had been there at the time, it would have been I who was given the violin. I would be Paganini the Second, now playing to the enraptured market people.

But the worst rub of all was St. Petersburg. If I hadn't abandoned the marketplace so casually, *I* would be wearing the velvet suit with the laced shoes. *I* would be going to the conservatory. I would be playing in the town hall, the same hall with the gilded figures in front balancing great baskets of flowers on their heads . . . More than once, I had passed this building with the white marble stairs illuminated by the golden yellow glow of the great chandeliers. More than once, I had wondered if I would ever have the chance to go in there and see what went on inside. And, finally, when the opportunity presented itself, where was I? In some stinking stuffy cheder getting my brains addled with Moses and Elijah the Prophet.

Moses and Elijah the Prophet may have been great men once, but what were they to me? After all, had I known them personally? Could I be partners with them in a bakery? But I had played horsey with Paganini the Second. I had sold mud pies with him. He had been an equal partner in all my enterprises. And just as if we were still partners, I followed every flicker of his fingers with a happy smile and vibrated along with him as if I were helping him play, as if I were holding the violin, as if I were pushing the bow. True, he had been a lousy partner and had once even thrown sand in my eyes, but this didn't bother me now—I would have gladly let my eyes be plucked out for the chance to be a partner to such a miracle of miracles.

When Paganini finished, I wanted to leap forward and help him put the violin back in the case, but the crowd blocked my way and, thrusting me aside, surrounded the little artist to rain kisses on his head and hands. Some kissed the violin, and some even the case. And after his mother had treated him to a glass of apple kvass, the jubilant crowd escorted him from the marketplace to Seminary Street, and there finally dispersed to let him go home.

My heart pounding, my brain reeling, I trailed behind. "To hell with cheder," I vowed silently. "I'll propose a new partnership to him. Starting tomorrow, we'll give concerts in the marketplace. I'll put him up on a crate. He'll play and I'll hold the violin case . . . Then we'll both face up to that rich patron and demand that he either send both partners to the St. Petersburg conservatory or neither of us will go."

Such thoughts leapfrogged over one another faster than I can now describe them . . . because by the gate of the seminary courtyard I had already caught up with Berchik, given him a good-natured slap on the back, and exclaimed, "Hey, how are you doing?"

Paganini the Second jerked away from the unexpected slap and measured me from head to toe. "Who are you? What do you want?"

I would have taken it as a joke if not for the serious expression on his face. I was temporarily taken aback as if I had really stopped a stranger by mistake. But I soon got hold of myself and in an apologetic tone asked, "Isn't your name Berchik?"

"No, it's Boris."

"Remember when we ran a bakery together?" I said, trying to prod his memory.

"What bakery? What do you want from me?"

"Behind the garbage bin, by the gutter in the little marketplace," I prompted him.

"I don't know you," he replied with a kind of fatuous solemnity, then spun about sharply and left me standing there completely perplexed.

The entire encounter lasted perhaps a half-minute, yet it was a half-minute destined to become one of the most important turning points in my life.

As soon as I saw Paganini the Second turn the corner into Glass Street, I dashed wildly into the seminary courtyard. I knew that there was a private passageway that led out into Glass Street. With the speed of the wind I spun through the complicated corridors, and when I reached the middle of Glass Street, he came up short in astonishment. The same boy who had stopped him a few minutes earlier in the marketplace now stood facing him in the middle of Glass Street with his head cocked upward and staring up at the seminary tower.

He obviously had no knowledge of the passageways in the seminary courtyard and couldn't figure out how I had gotten there ahead of him. But he was even more intrigued by what I was gazing at so intently up there on the roof.

At first, he passed me with affected indifference, but he soon looked around and, seeing my eyes still fixed on the roof, he could no longer contain himself and came up to me. "What do you see there on the roof?"

I had been anticipating the question and was ready. "There is a . . . man standing there."

He looked around. "Where?"

"There, there!" I said, pointing my finger in an indefinite direction.

"I don't see anything," he said with irritation and a foolish smile on his face.

"Stand here next to me," I said. And when he came over, I put my hand on his shoulder and, looking him straight in the eye, said, "See the chimney from which the smoke is blowing?"

"Yes."

"See that drainpipe on the side of the seminary tower?"

"Yes."

"That's where he's standing, under the drainpipe."

He stretched his neck and peered upward. He did see something there, but he couldn't be altogether sure if it was a man or the shadow of the chimney. I suddenly yanked my hand away from his shoulder and said in a conspiratorial tone, "Go away, get away from here fast!"

"Why?" he asked in confusion.

"Because the man will soon jump off the tower, and I must talk things over with him."

"Jump off a four-story high tower? How is that possible?" he asked in complete seriousness.

"He's not an ordinary man you might see walking the streets, and if you can keep a secret, I'll confide in you . . . That man up there on the roof is made of clay and stone."

"I don't understand."

"Did you ever hear about the Golem?"

"It seems I have . . . but I don't know . . . I don't remember," he said, shrugging his shoulders.

"You don't remember nothing and you don't know nothing! Don't you even know that Gaon made a man out of clay who could become invisible whenever he wanted to. He can walk the streets, he can stand on roofs, he can go in your house without you seeing him."

"Come in my house without me seeing him?"

"Yes! But the one who knows the holy name can summon the Golem out of his own invisibility."

"What does it mean, the holy name?" he asked, blinking his eyes as if his brain were spinning.

"Go away, go away from here! Because if I should utter the holy name right now, he's liable to jump down from the tower and trample you and your violin to pieces under his stone feet!" And I began to shove him away, as if actually ready to carry out my threat.

"Yes, I'd best go home," he agreed, pressing the violin case to him.

"Where do you live?" I asked.

"On Green Street, first floor." And he made a move as if to leave.

"Get going!" I hurried him along. "I'll tell the Golem all about you."

These last words worked their intended purpose. He wanted to leave, but his feet wouldn't move, as if I had poured sticky tar under him.

"Who is this Golem and how do you come to know him?" he asked in a trembling voice.

"I can't talk now. I'll come by your house later and explain everything. But for now, leave me alone." And I began to wave to the rooftop.

His head hunched down between his shoulders, his feet dragging, Boris soon turned the corner into Green Street. I followed him at a distance, then quietly tiptoed up to the first-floor window of the small house.

I watched as he put the violin case on the chest beneath the round mirror and, with a disturbed look, stationed himself to await my arrival. He didn't have to wait long.

"The Golem saw you and he likes you," I whispered in his ear after he had let me in. "I'll let you meet him tonight."

"Why tonight? I'm afraid of the dark."

"With me around, you don't have to be afraid. The Golem only wants to look at you for a few minutes. He can't stay long because he has to go back to the attic in the Great Synagogue. I told the Golem how marvelously you play the violin and he wants you to play something for him."

Until now, Boris had seemed to be the same simpleton as ever, full of incredible naiveté, but the moment I mentioned the violin a change came over him. His round eyebrows stretched into two half-moons, his lower lip climbed over the upper, and his voice grew even shriller. "Who are you?" he cried. "I don't understand you! I never heard about this Golem before. The whole story must be a lie. There was no one on the roof, or I would have seen him. I don't believe that a person can make himself invisible. Why did you attach yourself to me, and why are you making me crazy? If you think you can scare me with that Golem you're wrong, because I don't believe that you have any connection with him. I know you! You're that charlatan, the horse thief who used to hang around with the Cossacks in the marketplace. And you can't tell me any more fairy tales!"

I let him conclude his diatribe and, after a short pause, replied. "Now you remember me because you're afraid of the Golem. But if you don't believe in him, why are you so afraid?"

"I'm not afraid."

"If you're not afraid, why don't you come with me to the marketplace tonight, where I'll introduce you to him and you can see him with your own two eyes?"

"I don't want to see him, I don't want anything to do with such horrible things. Yes, I'm a coward, and I beg you to leave me alone."

"When you're with me, you've got nothing to fear from the Golem."

"But I don't want to be with you! My mother warned me a long time ago to keep away from you because you're a charlatan, a cardsharp, and a bastard. Your place is with the drunks on Butcher Street, and it's beneath me to associate with your kind."

I licked my suddenly parched lips. "I don't care what your mother says about me. If you dare whisper even one word about the Golem to your mother or to any of the other market people, your life won't be worth a groschen. If you don't believe in the Golem, forget about him."

"Yes, I promise that I won't say anything about your Golem," he said in a tone that seemed to apologize for his brutal frankness.

"That's fine. If you don't believe in the Golem, forget about him. This must remain a secret. I offered to let you meet the Golem because I trusted you, and for this reason you should trust me too. I share something with you, you must share with me as well. We must be friends always, everywhere . . . and when I tell you to bring your violin, you must bring it, and when you tell me to bring the Golem, I'll bring him."

He blinked as if straining to understand what I was saying, then grew hysterical. "It's a lie, the whole thing is a lie!"

I waited until he had calmed down somewhat, then resumed. "If you can't understand it, I'll show you how I too can make myself invisible. Come here and look in the mirror. Do you see me in there or not?"

He came over and took a look. "Yes, I do."

"You see there a living person before you," I said. "I move my hands, I talk to you and now in one second, I'm gone!" and I stepped aside. "Where did I go? If you tell me that anything that's seen once is seen always how come you don't see me anymore? You can't deny the fact that I'm still in the same room with you."

"Oh, that's a mirror," he whispered like a whipped dog.

"The Golem is like a mirror too."

"You told me he's made of clay and stone," he said, trying to nitpick his way out of the situation.

"When you see him, he is made of clay. But when you don't, he is a mirror," I said, hammering my point home.

Such gobbledygook might have confused an even greater intellect than Paganini the Second. By now almost completely crushed and demoralized, he still tried to cling to something to save himself from the net into which I had drawn him. Suddenly his dull eyes flickered as if struck by a happy notion and he cried out, "You're a liar, because if what you tell me about a mirror is true, then I'm a Golem too!" And attempting to mimic my agile movements, he went on. "Here I am in the mirror . . . and there I'm not!" And he jumped aside with a triumphant smile that seemed to say, "And what do you say to that?"

I came up to the glass, looked in, and with complete insouciance remarked, "What nonsense! You certainly are there."

"It's not true!" he shrieked in a frantic falsetto.

"I say that you're in the mirror, and if you don't believe me, come here and look for yourself!"

Paganini wiped the cold sweat off his pale forehead with the silk kerchief. For a moment we faced each other waging a silent, bitter duel with our eyes. Finally he bowed his head and said in a broken voice, "Maybe you're right . . . maybe I don't understand. Maybe you know these things better. Maybe you actually can make yourself disappear—who knows? I'm beginning to believe everything about you. I'll tell you the truth—I'm timid and I'm afraid of such things. I never like to think or talk about evil spirits."

"The Golem is no spirit," I corrected him sharply.

"Not a man and not a spirit is even more horrible! Aren't you at all scared to meet him at night in the dark marketplace? And how did you come to him in the first place?"

"I didn't come to him, he came to me."

Boris twitched for the last time like a fish out of water, and said in a barely audible tone, "Why to you? Who in the world are you?"

I drew myself up to my fullest height. "Guess!"

It was apparent that he was completely crushed, left without a shred of resistance, and utterly convinced that he was facing an awesome, irresponsible, dangerous boy who was involved with an even more frightful and terrible Golem.

"If that's the case . . . then I'll come. Where shall we meet?" he asked in a daze.

"At the little marketplace behind the garbage bin. And don't forget to bring this," I said, laying my hand commandingly on the violin case.

"You mean the violin?"

"Yes, we'll play for the Golem. Both of us will play. We were always partners, remember?"

He wanted to respond but his mouth wouldn't function. All he could do in his dumb, helpless fear was stare at me with glazed eyes as I opened the case and took out the violin.

During all this time, he hadn't grasped what it actually was I wanted of him, and he apparently thought it would be better to offer no resistance and thus perhaps be rid of me. But he saw now that not only he himself but also his violin faced great danger. I might take the violin with me as hostage so that he'd be forced to keep his promise and play for the Golem.

Any moment now, he was liable to hurl himself at the door, stretch out across the threshold and, with his waning strength, cry, "No! No! Over my dead body! Help! Help!" But he saw that instead of heading toward the door, I walked farther into the room, carefully tucked the violin under my chin, and began to run the bow over the strings.

The violin squealed like a rusty hinge, and I recoiled at the horrid, unexpected sound. Dazed, I looked at the bow. Had I made a mistake in my urgency and picked up the poker instead? No, the bow was a bow all right. With fresh resolution I began once more to slide the bow forth across the strings, but once again I was forced to stop—for such an unbearable rusty screech could have only been produced by a poker drawn over some other hunk of metal.

"Why doesn't it play?" I asked, turning to my trembling partner with a furious, puzzled glance.

Boris shrugged. "I don't know, I don't know. Maybe you need the notes?" And, pulling open a drawer, he quickly took out a stack of old, wrinkled pages that he spread feverishly across the table.

I leaned over the table and stared fixedly at the obscure, senseless circles, loops, and lines, then remarked, "Why is it that when you played you didn't need notes?"

"Because I know them by heart," he said, nervously twining his fingers.

"All these notes by heart?"

"Even more," he admitted in a humble and embarrassed tone.

"Give me the violin and I'll show you." And he reached out a pale hand.

I wiped away the drops of sweat that had formed on the tip of my nose and, with a look of bitter disappointment directed at the hunk of creaking wood, laid it on the table.

Boris seized the violin as a mother would seize her frightened child, tucked it deeply under his chin, and soon the child that had found its mother emitted a joyful, heart-rending cry.

The sun peered into the windows.

Flocks of pigeons took wing.

Trees swayed.

Lions roared.

The violin grew ten times larger, and the room became too small for the racing instrument. I huddled in a corner as if to make more room for the suddenly converging birds, trees, streams, and forests, but the more I scrunched down the narrower the room grew, and I emitted a frightened cry: "Enough! Enough! I'm not the guilty party. The rabbi . . . the rabbi fooled me! Stop! Stop!"

But my incomprehensible pleas grew muffled and lost in the tempo of the now wildly throbbing violin. Boris no longer heard or saw me. Eyes closed, he swayed—climbing mountains, uprooting trees, taunting savage beasts.

"Enough! Enough!" I pleaded, and soon dashed from the room.

I ran with fists clenched in the direction of the cheder. I hurried to face the red-bearded rabbi and his gravel-voiced wife and shouted into their faces, "You fooled me, you took away my marketplace and my people and handed them over to an imbecile. You deceived me with that foolish talk about a clay Golem and with your promise that I would grow up a big Gaon, learn the holy name, and make miracles! And in the meantime, Paganini the First came to the marketplace and, like the blind Isaac, chose Berchik to be Paganini the Second. He gave him his violin for keeps and taught him to play, and now Berchik is Paganini the Second and what am I?"

But what kind of answer could the little rabbi give me? Wouldn't it be better to go to Paganini himself and explain the error, the misunderstanding, the swindle? But where could he be found, this Paganini? He had long since left the city and, according to some of the market people, he was already dead a hundred years. In despair I stopped in the middle of the street and turned to a lamppost for advice. And when no answer came, I burst out crying. Within an instant, the street flooded and, in the strange vortex of watery hoops, the houses began to split, topple, and melt like sugar in the pool of my tears. The sodden lamppost crumbled under my hands, and its light scattered in a glowing mist all around me.

Through my gushing eyes, I spotted a man with unusually long legs and a high top hat. I recognized him at once—it was Paganini the First, the real, the live, the same who had stopped at the marketplace for a glass of kvass! I rushed toward him.

He seemed to be in a great hurry and strode along faster than I could keep up with him. To my delighted surprise, I soon saw the great master turn into Market Street and walk straight into the courtyard with the red gates. It was obvious that he was coming to see me.

I flew through the kitchen into the dining room like the shadow of a racing pigeon. And when I came into the bedroom, Paganini already stood inside the long trumeau mirror waiting for me.

"Why? Why?" I gasped in a tearful voice. "Why did you give the violin to a stranger and not to me? The marketplace belongs to *me*— I should be the one to play for the market people. Why did you pick a stranger to be Paganini the Second? What was your hurry? Or was it that you didn't trust me? Show me how, and you'll see that I can play too. Give me a violin." And as I stretched out my hands, he gave it to me. "Now show me how to hold it." And as I moved my hand he corrected me.

I pantomimed his movements and reminded him of the melody of the "Perpetuo Mobile," which he seemed not to remember, and there was music inside and outside the mirror. My fingers raced so skillfully across the strings, and the bow swayed with such grace, that Paganini grew enchanted on the other side of the mirror and began to accompany me in a remarkable duet.

A cold shiver ran through me, as if I had grown frightened by my own miracle. I no longer knew who followed whom—I Paganini on the other side of the mirror, or he me on this side of the mirror.

It appeared as if we were competing in skill and grace, and the sweeter one played, the more tenderly did the other accompany— until I reached the very highest note.

"What are you crying for, little fool?" he chanted from inside the mirror. "I didn't mean you any harm. I looked for you, but I couldn't find you so I gave the violin to your partner."

"No, no, he got it from you by deceit, the way Jacob got the blessing from his blind father," I sobbed.

"Foolish boy, the blessing is not in the violin but in the one who plays it, and since you play the way you do, you don't need a violin, you can play without it."

Inspired by his flattery, I began to sweep the bow up and down as if flapping a wing and, with the fingers of my other hand, gripped the neck of the invisible violin, which now began to rattle and gasp as if choking from an excess of rapture. Eyes closed in deep concentration, I saw Paganini move his hand out of the silvered glass and place it tenderly upon my flushed brow. "From now on," he said, "your name is Paganini the Third, and I proclaim to the whole marketplace and to the whole city that neither the First nor the Second but the Third is the real Paganini, the truest and greatest of them all."

VIII

A FEW DAYS later when I learned from Barve's Son that Paganini had actually died some hundred years before, I knew that no one would help me and that if I wanted my own violin I'd have to manage it myself. I undertook the task.

I carved a board in the shape of a figure eight and stretched cotton strings across it. For the bow, I used a thin stick to which I attached strands of hair that I plucked from Fat Eunuch's nag's tail. For the next few days, I paced around my room with the board under my jaw, humming the "Perpetuo Mobile."

Through the window I saw the neighbors looking up to see where the wonderful music was coming from. Could this be Paganini the First, the Second, or maybe someone who was even better than the two of them? Because this music sounded as if it issued not from a wooden violin but from some instrument that sighed, wept real tears, and seemed to possess a human soul.

The wonder and curiosity reflected on the upturned faces below strengthened my faith in my musical skills, and particularly in my violin, and after a few weeks of ardent rehearsal I felt ready to make my debut in the marketplace as Paganini.

For a while, I considered holding a tryout behind the garbage bin; I was afraid of again being jeered at in the big marketplace. If it happened to me once more, the marketplace would be lost to me forever.

Still, I had the premonition that this time it would be different, that this time they would like my strange music even though they had already heard "Perpetuo Mobile" twice before played on an ordinary violin. But which Paganini could play the same number on the strings of his own throat? My music would be something novel, something they had never heard in their lives. Maybe just because I would be playing on two sticks, they would more readily realize their mistake in idolizing Boris. Maybe they would understand that it was actually for *their* benefit that I had gone to the cheder to learn how to animate the Golem in the Great Synagogue. And just because I would be demonstrating my musical prowess on two pieces of wood, perhaps they would be touched, perhaps their memories would be jogged and they would remember and accord me the respect I deserved.

With these hopes in mind, I came to the marketplace, mounted a box, took out my violin from the kerchief in which it was wrapped, and began to "play."

The crowd that gathered broke into laughter after the first few notes. This time, though, it wasn't mocking laughter but an outburst of delight. Some began to accompany me, others clapped along in time with the music. They joined hands and formed a circle. The marketplace shook under their pounding boots, the stores and stalls began to jiggle, even the garbage bin didn't remain still for long.

Hens and roosters began to hop over each other, wildly clucking inside their crates. A circle of marketplace pigeons swooped overhead. This was wondrous—far, far beyond the wildest reaches of my imagination.

What was a Gaon who made a stone man come to life next to a Paganini like me, who could make a whole marketplace dance? When Boris had played his violin not long ago, there had been great enthusiasm, but also impertinent questions.

"Was it actually Paganini the First who gave you the fiddle or was it Mechel the wedding fiddler?"

"Who gave you that velvet suit? Did your mother make it from an old blanket?"

"Are you really going to a conservatory in St. Petersburg, or to Slobodka to play at a wedding?"

But when they danced to my music, there were no questions. It was as if they had been waiting for my strange concert before I had even thought of it.

Possibly this was due to the strange rumors that had been floating lately over the marketplace, or maybe it was on account of the ugly slanders spread by Red Itzik, the pockmarked bookkeeper with the horsey ears.

This detestable creature with the sharp tongue (it should only shrivel) surely had had something to do with the reception the marketplace now gave me; it was this very same Itzik who had an uncle in America who wrote him stories of how my father, Benjamin, had married a millionairess in America, had stolen her millions, abandoned her, and would soon be showing up at the marketplace.

Although Barve's Son had already branded these rumors as silly, he did have to concede that whether Benjamin had indeed married or robbed anyone, two things were sure—he had a lot of money now, and he was on his way home. This started a lively discussion among the market people.

"He's coming. The only question is—will he bring the millions with him?"

"Just one million wouldn't be enough for you?"

"For me it would be enough if he'd pay me the few rubles he owes me for arranging a match with Sarah."

"Sarah grew up in *my* house . . . I held his son at his circumcision."

"His son was once the big boss in my store."

"My store he squandered by giving presents to his Cossacks."

"Remember how he dropped his pants in my house once? In the middle of the room, right on the floor . . ."

"Would you ever believe that such a little stinker . . . ? Did you ever hear such playing?"

"Next to him, Paganini is a mutt."

Hershel the Snorter went so far as to grunt, "When you have a father who's a millionaire, you can even play on a broom."

Everyone found it necessary to congratulate me several times a day on my success, to take the occasion to ask about my father, and to propose that I stage the next concert at *his* stall.

The enthusiasm over my concert and the feverish anticipation of my father's arrival lasted for weeks, until one day there was a commotion in the marketplace over the rumor that my father had already boarded the ship . . . the train . . . the droshky . . . And the crowd raced toward the railway station.

In the distance, we saw Fat Eunuch's carriage coming. My father sat inside, dressed in a checked suit and a gray derby, carrying a cane with a silver head, and shifting a long fat cigar from one side of his mouth to the other.

The crowd parted to make a path for the American millionaire, who took a roll of green bank notes from his bosom pocket and stuffed them into the hands of those who pressed in around the carriage.

Sitting next to the millionaire were my two mothers, Sarah and Pelga. I climbed up onto the folded canopy in back of the droshky, lay down happily, and hummed the "Perpetuo Mobile."

Events then began to race. A week later, the millionaire and his household abandoned Market Street and moved to the aristocratic Boulevard of St. George. I was pushed and pulled into a suit of real velvet, patent leather shoes, and a silk handkerchief and put out on the wide, handsome avenue to commence a new life as an heir to millions.

IX

IN MY NEW, privileged circumstances, it might have been expected that I'd get a real violin with which to go to a conservatory in St. Petersburg and become if not a Paganini then at least a good musician. But it happened differently. A short time after I had exchanged my ragged pants for the long, elegantly pressed, brand-new trousers, I lost all my ambition to provide music for the poor market people and became involved instead in a new adventure that more befitted a millionaire—namely, an adventure with a woman.

I must, however, admit that I didn't come to this completely by chance nor without the proper preliminaries.

Every Thursday after we moved to the Boulevard of St. George, there assembled in the foyer of our rich new house the poorer members of the family and some of the indigent acquaintances from Market Street, and they waited for the American millionaire to dispense some largesse for the forthcoming Sabbath. At first blessings were heard for the philanthropist, but soon a new voice began to express itself in tones of envy and rancor. "If that's all that's coming to us, then the millionaire might just as well have stayed in America with his missus."

"What missus? Which missus?" people asked each other. And the "missus" soon became an important subject of discussion in the foyer.

The story of my father's connection with this missus was simple. When he arrived in America, he became a boarder at a certain missus's house. All that was known about her was that she had bleached blonde hair, heavy legs, and a broad behind, and since this missus had other boarders in her small apartment too, my father slept on the floor. This information came from the letters that he had written to my mother. Then he stopped writing and didn't even answer the extraordinary letter that I sent him. The reason for this was that the missus took pity on her poor handsome boarder and moved him from the floor into her bed. This in itself wouldn't have been so terrible. The trouble was that she would no longer let him out of her bed.

How he managed to free himself from the bed, and how the poor boarder turned into a millionaire, was discussed in the foyer in dozens of whispered versions.

The one most believable was that lying in bed one day the missus whispered a secret in his ear about an invention of her late husband's, a furrier who had discovered a way to dye a cat's tail so that it looked like silver fox. My father promptly began to exploit this invention, and since all this took place in America where everything is quick and easy, it naturally didn't take him long to become rich.

What actually had brought him home? There were various explanations for this as well.

The most interesting was that after becoming a millionaire he decided one bed wasn't big enough for two people and soon went off to another house with an even larger bed.

This displeased the missus. When she went to his new house and found him in bed with another missus, she took a bottle of carbolic acid from her purse and flung it at the bed. The lucky thing was that my father was lying face down; otherwise he would have gotten up blind and scarred. But this frightened him enough so that he caught the next ship home.

Whether all this was true or not, after I overheard the story in the foyer, the "missus" stuck in my mind.

I couldn't gather any more details, since it wouldn't have been proper for me to question the paupers, and I didn't dare go directly to my father.

Besides, something else occurred to occupy my interest, this time not in the foyer but inside the apartment. Pelga became pregnant. The most startling thing about it was that the one responsible was the Cossack Arkashka.

Father summoned the Cossack to our house. Arkashka came and respectfully stationed himself with cap in hand, leaning on his sword in the doorway. After some brief preliminaries, Father issued an ultimatum. Either the Cossack married Pelga right away or he'd report him to General Renenkampf. It was no secret that my father was close to the commander of the city garrison. Soon after his arrival, his reputation as a silver fox expert had spread through the city, and he was promptly summoned to a certain lady who turned out to be a general's wife. She introduced the American to Madam Renenkampf, who made him the creator and guardian of her extensive fur collection.

When it came to payments, my father dealt with the general himself, who was known as a heavy drinker and gambler who had trouble paying his debts. This, naturally, allowed my father to establish the friendliest contact with the most powerful military figure in the region.

Despite all this, Arkashka kept his nerve and vigorously denied any responsibility for the forthcoming baby. My sympathies lay on the side of my family. But at this moment, something occurred to change my prejudice against the Cossack.

This happened after Arkashka hinted that possibly he wasn't the child's only father, whereupon Pelga leaped up from the table and dealt him four lusty blows, two on each cheek. Arkashka bowed his head to block the blows with his elbow, which gave Pelga an opportunity to seize him by his hair and shake him so hard that his silver earring was torn loose and rolled somewhere under the table.

What this offense actually consisted of was not clear to me, but the punishment that he had now received seemed too harsh whatever his guilt might have been.

Arkashka had been the legendary hero of my childhood, and seeing this same hero now—with a sword strapped to one side and a revolver to the other, standing with his hair disheveled and his cheeks flaming while a trickle of blood ran from his mouth—I was seized with such a feeling of anguish that I was about to hurl one of my convoluted tenth-degree oaths (that this same Cossack had taught me) on the head of my second mother, who at that moment became to me a kind of second American "missus." But the fact that I was now a millionaire's son had already begun to affect my manners. I bit my lip in silence.

Presently, my father stood up, embraced the beaten Cossack, made him sit down, and lectured him for a long time, mixing his Russian with the three American words with which he ended every second or third phrase—"yes," "all right," "good-bye."

What these three words meant neither Arkashka nor any of us knew, but it was obvious that the ignorant Cossack was no less impressed by them than the high military authorities had been. Arkashka wiped his bloodied lips with his sleeve and smiled foolishly.

When Father detected signs of weakening in the Cossack, he took a thick roll of bank notes from his breast pocket and, spreading them out on the table, slapped him amiably on the shoulder. Calling him by the familiar "thou," he said something like this: "*All right* . . . say *yes,* the match is arranged, and *good-bye.* If you weren't the father of Pelga's child, I'd be damned if I'd let you have her for a wife. *Yes* . . . if I wasn't married to Sarah, I wouldn't mind marrying Pelga myself . . . *all right* . . . but even so, Pelga still was the boss of the household and she raised all my children.

"And what harm would it do you if she raised you such a boy as Yosik? Because, talking among ourselves, who are you and what are you? A lousy Cossack who eats and sleeps with his horse, and all you know is to beat up Jews in the old marketplace. Is this a life? You should know that you're taking a wife from a rich man's house and that you are getting a dowry of a thousand rubles. *Yes* . . . If you could add two and two, you'd know that on your salary you'd have to work two hundred years to save up this amount. *All right* . . . Don't be a fool, be a man, take your wife, take your money and say, *yes* . . . *all right* . . . *good-bye* . . . Go home to the Kuban Steppes, buy a house and a cow, and live a good life. Believe me, with such a wife and dowry people will envy you!"

Arkashka hesitated a moment, then went over to Pelga and kissed her on the head and hand, which made her burst into tears and run from the room.

A few days later, Pelga took off the key ring that she had worn for so many years and turned it over to my mother, who presently opened all the drawers and took out sheets, pillowcases, nightgowns, dresses, a whole bunch of spoons, forks, and various other utensils. Arkashka packed this all in large sacks and carried the loot to the wagon waiting outside.

My two mothers embraced and kissed each other for a long time on their hands and faces. Then Pelga turned to me, pressed me tightly to herself as if trying to squeeze me into her swollen belly, and sobbed, "I'll name my child after you!"

Arkashka dragged her away, sat her down in the loaded wagon, and followed behind on foot.

Until the wagon was far down the street, I accompanied it with my tearful eyes. I was deeply touched by the parting with my second mother, but I was perhaps even more affected by a feeling of compassion for Arkashka, who trailed after the wagon like a dog on a string.

I didn't have the slightest inkling of what and where the Kuban Steppes were, but I was positive that there wasn't as gay and bright a place on earth as that which lay between Butcher and Market streets.

Since we had moved to the aristocratic boulevard it had occurred to me more than once that if I could, I would give up all my wealth to go back to the marketplace, because for all its beauty and affluence, I had learned something here that I had never heard of or experienced in my whole life—boredom.

A wide boulevard with handsome houses and fine trees, but where were the people? And if a couple of people did finally show up, they barely walked or talked. No one fought, no one kissed, the children lay hidden inside the houses and only used the boulevard to go from house to house. Whether it was a Monday or a Tuesday, it was always the Sabbath on the boulevard—quiet, peaceful, and boring. And now, with Pelga and Arkashka gone, the deserted boulevard was twice as long and empty.

It's no wonder, then, that when I saw for the first time (actually not on the boulevard but on the nearby Pilna Street) two boys in the uniforms of gymnasium students standing talking to a girl leaning down from a second-story window, I grew flabbergasted and rooted to the spot. If this had been Market Street, now, it would have been simple to strike up a friendship, but here in this fancy neighborhood, dressed in my fancy clothes, I knew that the manners from the old marketplace wouldn't do. It had been hinted to me in the house a few times already that here you didn't simply go up to a person and start talking; here, you had to doff your cap and excuse yourself for troubling them first. In all my imagination I couldn't fathom what I might possibly say to somebody to make me beg their pardon first. And what was there to talk about in general on this desolate boulevard? What happened here worth discussing? But be that as it may, I had finally seen that people *did* speak here, and ignoring the advice from home I tried in my own fashion to strike up a conversation with the students.

As I walked past them, I intentionally dropped a coin, and as I made believe that I was searching for it, I waited for one of them to offer his assistance or even make an actual move to help. But they both ignored me in a rather strange fashion.

A few days later when I saw them again talking to the girl in the upstairs window, I took courage, smiled broadly, and asked: had they by any chance found a lost coin? Both of them put out their tongues and spat at me. At the same time, one stuck out his foot so that when I tried to avoid the spittle, I tripped and sprawled out on the sidewalk.

Back on Market Street I wouldn't have stood for this and would have hurled myself at them with feet flying, but here in this aristocratic setting my patent leather shoes with the white pearl buttons kept my feet in rein.

This in itself would not have been enough to stop me. Actually, it wasn't so much my patent leather shoes as the boys' stiff, blue, fitted uniforms with the thin rows of gleaming buttons running the whole length of the chests, the thin white stripes along their trousers, and especially the large cockades on their caps that petrified me into inaction.

Shortly after I had become a millionaire, my father had led me to the same government gymnasium that these two students attended, judging from their uniforms. But there, my father had been most politely informed that Jewish applicants were only permitted to take the entrance examination from a quota of ten percent, and out of this ten percent all but those who got the very highest grade of "five" in every subject were further eliminated, so that eventually only a third of them would be finally enrolled at the gymnasium.

All those necessary "fives" that moved me from the first category into the second were purchased by my father with heavy bribes for each separately. But then, I was still one of four or five Jewish candidates who faced further elimination. Dividing us by thirds left one and one-third Jew eligible for enrollment. We still had to draw lots for the final privilege: the possibility of going through the whole procedure again a year later. But since I was the one who drew the blank number for which a bribe wouldn't help, my chances of wearing this uniform even a year from then looked very slim indeed.

The uniform that my father had already ordered from Uri the tailor was canceled just as the tailor was cutting the trousers.

At the time, these complications hadn't disturbed me unduly, since I had little liking for school anyway, but as I gazed now at the two boys in their dazzling uniforms it struck me that their arrogance stemmed primarily from the fact that they weren't dependent upon these mathematical intricacies in getting their uniforms— they weren't Jewish. I therefore rose silently from the sidewalk and quietly slunk away.

But this humiliation wouldn't let me rest. And if I lacked the nerve and courage to send them flying, nothing could keep me from toying with the notion that if I couldn't take the street away from the students, perhaps I could take the window with the girl away from the street.

Not that I had any interest in the girl; on the contrary, after the incidents with Pelga and the American "missus," the female sex held little attraction for me. Besides, I didn't know who and what this girl was. I only knew a half of her, the upper half that leaned out the window. I had never seen her in one piece. But even half of her would now be enough for me to avenge the insult. And just as fortune had so perversely frustrated me during the drawing of the lots, it now favored me here under the window in a most remarkable fashion.

One day I noticed from afar the half-body dangling from the window again. This time, the two students weren't around. It seemed to me this was the perfect opportunity to walk by and beg her pardon.

"Why do you beg my pardon? I don't know you," she said with a friendly smile.

"I've been told that around here you must excuse yourself before you meet somebody."

"Who told you that?"

"Isn't it so?"

"Do you live here?"

"No."

"I saw you pass by a few times."

"That means that you *do* know me."

"Now you must excuse me, but I don't know you."

"Strange, where I come from there are no people who don't know each other."

"I don't understand. What school do you go to?"

"I don't go to any school. I'm a stranger."

"Well then, who are you and where do you come from?"

Her question was a quite natural one under the circumstances, and I should have expected it. Still, my heart fluttered and I suddenly felt my knees buckle. She would never have asked me this if I had stood before her in a uniform. Without it, I suddenly felt naked and so flustered that I let slip a word that I instantly regretted, but it was already too late.

"From America," I mumbled, and, to make matters worse, added, "I come from far-off America."

She stared at me as if I had dropped down from heaven. The magic of the word "America," with which my father had managed to spellbind generals, now seemed to make an even greater impact on the girl.

"You are an American? Oh, how interesting! Oh, how exciting!" She clapped her hands as if they were wings ready to fly out the window and exclaimed in English, "Do you speak English? How wonderful! Please talk to me in English!"

My face flushed, my heart pounded, I was hopelessly trapped. The asphalt seemed to have melted around me, and I couldn't move. In my deep confusion, I barely uttered my father's three famous words: "*yes . . . all right . . . good-bye . . .*"

She leaned down even lower, as if about to spring down on me, and went on in English: "What's your hurry? Are you busy? Wouldn't you like to talk to me? Oh, America, America!"

What now? I thought. Where do I run to now? Where can I catch a ship? How do I save myself from America?

"I can't hear what you're saying?" I said aloud, cupping my hand to my ear.

"Ah! Why then are you standing in the street?" she said in Russian. "Why don't you come upstairs? . . . the first time that I'm meeting an American . . . I'm thrilled. Please come up!"

"What a bloody mess I've gotten myself into!" I raged to myself. At the same time, I couldn't tear my eyes away from the sleekly combed hair and the shining eyes that gazed down at me with such tenderness.

Who is she? I wondered. How does she come to know English? Maybe it wasn't English at all? Maybe I should make her repeat it? Maybe I should have again answered: *yes, all right,* and *good-bye?*

After all, such a sweet face wouldn't want to harm me, to splash me with carbolic acid and drag me off to the Kuban Steppes. Why in the world was I so terrified? Why *shouldn't* I go up to see her? Hadn't I come here to take her away from those arrogant students? And now that I had the opportunity to teach them a lesson—should I back out?

"How do I come up to you?" I asked in a voice that wasn't my own.

"Turn at the corner of Pilna and St. George," she said with an impatient wave of the hand.

I started to walk and felt my heart would burst under the heavy American stone that I had hung around my neck.

I halted several times to see if maybe—but no, she still kept pointing her hand, which from a distance and in the glow of the afternoon sun seemed to be made of gold. "Right, right . . . on the corner . . ."

I dragged myself up the few marble steps that led to a round foyer with a red plush-carpeted floor and a great trumeau mirror set in a gold-flowered frame that filled the whole right side.

I plastered myself to the mirror with such joy.

There within the mirror stood my good old friend Paganini the First, who smiled at me. "Fool, why are you so scared? You don't speak English, neither do I . . . Did you know how to read music? Still, you play the 'Perpetuo Mobile' better than all the Paganinis in the world. So don't worry, I'm still with you. Just as I draw the bow over those strings while you hum the melody, you'll now move your lips and I'll do the talking."

I took the steps leading up from the foyer in one jump and gave the bell pull a vigorous tug.

X

〰️

NIURA OPENED the door. And as incredible as it may sound, it
was I who spoke first—and in English.

She tilted her sleek head sideways as if straining to better understand my strange dialect. This encouraged me enormously, and I
rattled on with the same glibness with which I had opened the
conversation.

The only thing I couldn't do was look her straight in the eye. But
to my relief, just then a small, white poodle with a pink ribbon
around its neck came trotting in from a side door. The dog leaped at
me with a shrill barking that drowned out all my bold gibberish.
I stopped and directed my "English" at the dog, who turned out to
be the only one to understand it, for he quickly calmed down and
began to lick my hands.

I straightened up and said to Niura, this time in Russian, "How
do you come to know English?"

"I take lessons twice a week from a tutor . . . but now that I've
heard you speak, I realize how little I really know."

"Well, in order for us to understand each other better, let's speak
Russian, which is a much better and nicer language than English. I
must tell you that I personally don't like English. As a matter of fact
I hate it, I despise it!"

She chased the poodle away, then turned back to me. "It's odd
that an American should dislike his own language."

I spun on my heels in feigned embarrassment. "Not only the language . . . I don't like America in general."

"That's interesting, but—why are we standing here? Let's go to
my room."

All this had transpired in the windowless foyer with the only light
coming from a flickering flame under a red shade beneath a holy
triptych set in a silver frame in the corner of the room.

As Niura walked past the triptych she crossed herself swiftly and led me into another room. The walls were hung with many paintings and photographs. To avoid her gaze I busied myself studying them, but I quickly turned away as if something sharp had pricked my eye. In a flowered frame decorated with butterfly wings stood my two enemies with arms around each other.

"Who is this?" I cried, louder than I had intended.

"That's my brother Sasha, and the other is my brother's best friend, Romek Zavatski. His father is Polish . . . a general in the Russian army," she added with a sweet smile. I felt my knees buckle and, trying to reach for support, I nearly knocked over with my elbow a miniature set in a round frame. Trying to cover up my clumsiness, I pointed to the picture and asked again, "Who is this?"

"That's my great-grandfather, Voktuzen . . . from Dorpat. A Latvian baron," she said, and with visible pride straightened the picture. Then she pointed to another door. "And that's my room."

I began to edge toward the door as if walking a tightrope over a snake pit. Not until she had closed the door behind us did I draw a free breath again. There the walls were decorated with large yellow chrysanthemums, and the soft rug was stitched with leaves and flowers. I went to the window, looked out at the deserted boulevard, then turned back to her with a forced smile. "Oh, how nice it is up here!"

"Sit down." She pointed to a chaise longue. She herself sat down on the floor and tucked her legs beneath her.

"Why do you hate America?" she asked.

"Oh, it's very complicated," I said with a deep sigh. "My experiences there weren't too pleasant. Actually, it isn't America I hate so much as the people there, especially the women, and particularly a certain missus."

Her sweet little face became one big question mark. I bowed my head under the heavy burden of my experiences with the "missus," then smilingly murmured, "yes, all right, good-bye . . ."

"What, you're leaving already? Please don't go yet, I beg you. Tell me about it."

"Your brother and his friend are liable to find me here. They might chase me away again."

She took my hand and led me away from the door. "That's silly. Why should they?"

"I don't know. You saw what they did to me the other day."

"That was very rude of them."

"They why didn't you stick up for me and call them off?"

"I didn't know you then . . . This is my room. My brother has his own room. He doesn't know that you're from America. If he did, I'm sure he'd be very happy to know you."

"Well . . . you see, I have nothing more to do with America. I ran away from America."

"Where are your parents?"

"I ran away alone . . . on a ship."

"I don't understand."

"I was a boarder at a certain missus's. A horrible woman with fat legs who wanted to splash me with carbolic acid . . . I saved myself by running away. That's why I don't want to talk anymore about America."

She looked up in amazement. "I've never heard of such things. If it makes you uncomfortable, let's not . . . Let's talk about something else. I like the way you talk. Come sit here on the floor with me."

Her words and particularly her tone displayed sincere compassion for my woes, and I realized that with a few words I had managed to make her lose her enchantment with the land and the language that had urged her to ask me up to her room in the first place.

The question was, if not America, what else was there for us to talk about? It surely wasn't right to sit in total silence.

Should I tell her the truth: I didn't come from America but from the old marketplace? Should I tell her that I sold hats there, fed chickens, raced pigeons, played cards, made a Golem, and became a Paganini? As for America, the only thing I knew was about some missus with fat legs and dyed curls and three English words. How much more explicit I could have been about Pevke from behind the garbage bin, about barefoot Matzek from the shoemaker's cellar, or about Boris my partner . . .

But no, no! I would then also have to tell her why I wasn't wearing a uniform. And if she had swallowed all my lies until now, she surely would never forgive me this last single truth. She'd surely chase me out and spit at me just like the others, despite all her assurances that she would stick up for me. The graceful way she had crossed herself before the icon was still fresh in my mind. And could a woman generally be trusted, even one with such pretty legs and long pigtails? These questions demanded an immediate answer. I could not stretch my escape out longer and just wander alone at sea without sails or rudder, with no particular destination. For a while we faced each other silently, she begging, "Don't go," and I replying, "Damn it, I don't have anything more to say." But talk I must, at least to try to disentangle myself from the heedless prattle that had put me in the position of a miserable boy with a most unpleasant problem. My decision came quick and final.

"Tell me, do you know Paganini? You don't? You don't know Paganini the First?"

Her mouth fell open, but no words issued.

"Did you ever hear about Paganini the Second? No? Never? Well—I'm Paganini the Third."

The tip of her tongue lay paralyzed on her lower lip.

"Did you ever hear the 'Perpetuo Mobile?' That's a musical composition of Paganini the First's. A shame I don't have my violin with me or I'd play it for you. But if you'll allow me to come again sometime I'll bring my violin with me."

"Why don't you run home and get it now?" She clapped her hands as if she would suddenly turn into a mechanical doll.

"No. I can't now. It's too far and too late. Another time . . . maybe tomorrow."

"But what's your hurry? It's still early. Come, sit down next to me here on the rug and tell me all about it," she said, moving closer to me and nearly touching my feet. "Are you a musician? How wonderful . . . please tell me all about you."

"Would you have a couple of sticks here?" I asked, my eyes searching the room. "If you do, I'll play the 'Perpetuo Mobile' for you."

"Of course I have." She jumped up and soon came back with a bundle of kindling. I selected two pieces. She settled back on the floor and with blazing eyes put her hands between her knees ready to listen to the concert.

Her tilted face lay before me like a page of music on a stand. It was just as Paganini had promised. The violin did not follow the notes, but the other way around—the notes reflected what the violin played.

"Play, play . . ." the "notes" on her face seemed to urge me. "What are you—a musician or a liar? A chance passer-by at my window or some suspicious nut who wormed his way into my room? Do you come from America or from the basement on Butcher Street? What's the difference? Who cares . . . Just don't go away. You're so different from anyone I've ever met before. I know Romek, Petya, Grisha . . . I've known them all for years, still you've grown closer to me in the short time I've known you than all of them put together. Is it possible that I've met you? Sometime . . . somewhere . . . long ago? Well, then, why didn't I invite you up the first time I noticed you from the window? Why did I let them spit at you and kick you? Never again! Now I'll be your best friend because maybe it's really true that some missus was after your life in America and you escaped by ship. Nobody likes to talk about unpleasant experiences. It was very tactless of me to bombard you with unnecessary questions. But never again! Please forgive me and please, please don't stop playing."

I stood with one eye closed and with the other read the pleading on her face. I "played" my old humming melody until she suddenly leaped at me and draped herself around my neck. I grew frightened and the sticks dropped from my hands. A strange, sweet ache, one I had never known before, coursed through my body as if someone had stabbed me with a blade made of sugar. My trembling legs buckled and, with Niura still hanging around my neck, I fell onto the soft flowers of the rug.

XI

❦

WALKING HOME THAT evening, I saw that the two long rows of gas lamps along the boulevard glowed with a rare splendor. The cobblestones ground the light beams into diamonds and strewed the street with billions of stars, brighter than those up in heaven. Hopping from foot to foot, I tore off my jacket and flung my cap into the gutter. No longer was I the lonesome millionaire in the accursed desert of the boulevard, but once again the happy charlatan from the old marketplace.

This was on a Thursday. I couldn't be mistaken, because it was the night when the people assembled in my father's foyer to collect their handouts for the coming Sabbath.

It was enough for me to glance at the familiar faces to guess that they were somehow perturbed. I quickly gathered from the quiet, mournful whispers that a pogrom was brewing in the old marketplace.

"How come? . . . Who? Why?" I pleaded, but they had only one little story to offer that was too much for even my wild fantasy to fathom.

It seemed that a small gentile girl, the daughter of a janitor on Butcher Street, had gone to a barber's a week ago in the marketplace. He had promptly honed his razor, slit her throat, then drawn out her blood with which to make a few bottles of wine.

In the furthest stretches of my imagination, I couldn't conceive of a bearded girl going to a barber's for a shave. Second, what was a barber doing in the marketplace? As far as I could recall, there were only shoemakers, capmakers, bakers, herring vendors, but no barbers. And third, who knew the market people better than I did? I knew that outside of my grandfather Mordecai, who liked the grape a bit too much and was therefore known as the Jewish drunk, there wasn't a single one among them who would kill for a bottle of wine. This foolish prattle seemed too childish for even children to accept.

Unfortunately, the market people were right. A few days later, a pogrom was in full force in the marketplace.

The streets were blocked off by the police, and I couldn't get there until it was all over.

Small groups of men and women stood bunched around the market street. I stationed myself behind a couple shocked and shaken by the terrible disaster.

Notte's store was a pile of boards, Artche the hatmaker's place lay in shambles, Hershel was rolling a greasy barrel and gathering up scattered pieces of herring from the ground. Lazer the old-clothes dealer, his head bandaged, rummaged around for his "English" goods. Fat Doba, harnessed to a cart, picked up pieces of her rusted metalware that were scattered as far as the chicken crates. The crates were nearly all empty; only a few abandoned hens staggered around clucking mournfully. The famous garbage bin lay overturned as if it itself had been tossed into an even larger bin along with torn baskets, broken crates, and cracked barrels. The policeman known as the Karaite ran around tripping over his sword and angrily chasing the beggars and thieves who gathered like crows around a pile of manure. The few frightened, loyal cats lay hidden and left the mice to scamper freely all over the place. Lishk and Zhuk barked hoarsely with tails curled under their legs, howling into the sky.

Who had done this and why? What hoodlums, what hooligans had dared wreck my marketplace, my most precious possession? Well . . . My secret dream someday to sail my conjured-up boat with my captured treasure, Niura, to the market now lay shattered forever among the ruins. A wild rage came over me and, shedding all my manners of the boulevard, I screamed aloud the good, old, reliable curse, "From your father's father up to your mother's mother, from under, from over, from every side into your guts, through the lungs into your bitchy blood!"

The couple in front of me turned around with sheer terror in their faces, as if expecting one of the hooligans to hit them from behind. I recognized them at once. "How are you, Rabbi and Rebbetzin?"

"God bless us if it isn't our own Yosik!" she exclaimed, clapping her hands.

"Yosik, Yosik . . ." the little rabbi scratched his neck. "Oy, oy, you're still the same old rascal. How can a Jewish boy use such language? Maybe God punished the marketplace for these ugly words?"

"It was me who used such filthy language," I said through clenched teeth, "so why did God punish the market people? I thought the pogrom was made by drunken hooligans, not by your God."

"*Your* God? Oy, oy, oy . . . the same rascal!" the rabbi said with a grim face. "There is not such thing as *our* God and *your* God. There's only one God, and not a thing gets done in this world without His will. Did you already forget everything that you learned in cheder?"

"I remember well all the stories that you told me about God, but I ask you why He would want such a thing to happen?" I was waging a dispute with him as in the past.

"Who knows God's ways and purposes?" The rebbetzin took over in her customary chant and casting her large cow eyes heavenward. "One thing is certain—He doesn't punish without reason. The marketplace richly deserved it. Jews were so involved with business that they forgot to pray. They ate without making the benediction. They didn't even wash their hands at the soup kitchen. They didn't bother to kosher their meat. And what about all the card gamblers and swindlers? And what about studying the Torah? . . . They've even stopped sending their children to cheder . . ."

"Who is this barber?" I asked impatiently to cut off the tedious diatribe.

"What barber? Which barber? That was only an excuse for the hooligans. God needs no pretext. He exercises His justice as He sees fit. And if you hadn't run away from cheder, you'd understand everything."

"Of course," his wife interjected. "When you didn't have tuition money you came to us in cheder, but as soon as God put you in the lap of luxury, you ran away from us."

"Why do you bother me with your cheder?" I screamed.

"Don't shout! Have some respect for your elders!" The rabbi stamped the pavement with a tattered boot. "A Jew must go to cheder. You would do the right thing if you came back now."

"I don't need any cheder. I'm no longer a Jew!"

"Mercy upon us!" the couple cried in unison.

"If God made the pogrom He's no longer my God either!"

"Woe is me!" the rebbetzin seized her husband under his arms as if afraid that he would collapse right then and there. But he twisted out of her grip and, fixing the blasphemer with a contemptuous glare, cried out, "Know that the pogrom is nothing compared to what God can wreak in His rage and righteousness! I've taught you enough about how great and almighty He is, and no one is safe from His wrath! If you think you can hide in your fancy boulevard among the goyim you're mistaken, for He will seek you out, punish you, and crush you like a worm!"

The rebbetzin tugged at his sleeve, but he wouldn't budge. He hadn't yet said the most important thing, and he went on in the same outraged tone: "Because of the guilty, the innocent must suffer. And if you want to know who the real hooligan is, it's you! Because of one Jew like you, all Israel is punished. For one lout like you, God may destroy all Jews."

"If God will destroy all Jews—" but the rabbi wouldn't let me repeat my famous curse. He spat at me and, tugging at one another, the couple fled from their former pupil as if from a devil.

I wiped the flecks of spittle from my handsome suit, glanced for the last time at my devastated marketplace, and quickly turned back to the Boulevard of St. George.

But how could I face Niura now? To come again as an American violinist was too much of a risk. To show up with my true face, as a simple boy from the marketplace, which had suffered such a dreadful humiliation and awesome punishment, was more than I could manage.

In the meantime, Niura dangled from the window as usual and waited for me to come by. And after time passed and I still didn't show up, she went down to the street to look for me. I watched her from a corner of the window. She wandered around for a few days, then was joined by her brother Sasha and his friend Romek. They both held thick sticks and I could almost see their scowling faces.

What had she told them about me? She couldn't have been too careful with her words, and I couldn't much blame her. What could I seem to her now but some American swindler who had wormed his way into her room posing as a violinist, who had thrown her to the floor, and who had fled without so much as a good-bye, not even leaving a name or an address? When it turned out that the "American" was the same boy in whose face they had spat a day before, it was only natural that the two boys should be caught in the grip of a furious desire to kill or to cripple the nervy imposter. Watching the sunset from the side of the window, I saw myself caught and chained behind the bars of a fantastically beautiful prison. The prismatic shadows of the last sun rays on my suit turned it into a handsome prisoner's garb and even reflected colorful chains on my knees.

I was abandoned by the Golem, cheated by Paganini, and, what's more, betrayed by Niura, another English-speaking missus, who would, without hesitation, have thrown carbolic acid in my face had I only given her the chance.

But these fleeting moments of self-pity were soon washed away by a wave of self-justification and replaced by a sweet feeling of revenge for the pogrom at the market, for the unattainable uniform, for the damned boring Boulevard of St. George.

I had settled accounts with the arrogant students and taken Niura away from them, at least for one afternoon. Now, as I looked out from the window of my hiding place, I could see them squirming in the net of my imagination in which I had so skillfully trapped them.

XII

~~~

MOSHE REITBARD was a tailor about whom the market people often jokingly said that if he could sew a button as well as he could study a page of the Gemara, he might have to enjoy a smaller piece of the Leviathan in the other world but he'd surely have more to eat in this world. To this Moshe would reply, "A fish swims better than man, and a deer runs faster. There are animals with a sense of smell that extends for miles, a lion is stronger, an elephant lives longer—but one thing they cannot do, and that is pray and study the Torah."

Long before sunrise he already sat by a small kerosene lamp, covered by a shade cut out of an old newspaper, and was deeply absorbed in the faded yellow pages of the Torah with the tiny little letters of the commentaries, which would have ruined the finest eyesight in a short time. And Moshe was actually extremely nearsighted.

His two pairs of glasses with the cracked lenses apparently didn't help much. He would tuck his long beard to one side, which would allow him to put his whole face close to the book and run his thin nose across the page as if anxious to sniff the holy words before exposing his eyes to them.

When the last stars would fade in the sky, he would blow out the lamp, close the book, wrap himself in a prayer shawl and phylacteries, and station himself in the eastern corner to pray and praise the Almighty for the great honor he had bestowed upon man, a tailor who could do that which all the other creatures in the world could not—pray and study the Torah. True, after sixty years of studying he conceded that he didn't know or understand much, but was it possible in sixty short years to absorb the Torah, which was deeper than the sea and bigger than the whole world?

And thus Moshe stood in the corner and prayed silently until he heard the first muffled groans of his wife, Liba. Slowly and deliberately he folded his prayer shawl, boiled some water in the teapot, sliced bread and brought it to his wife in bed, and, sitting down facing her, mumbled a chapter of the Psalms.

Dunking the bread in hot tea and chewing it slowly with her toothless gums, Liba looked at her husband with a pleading glance to forgive her that her legs had become paralyzed, forcing her to give up her fruit stall in the marketplace so that her Moshele had to leave his holy books and slice bread, brew tea, and even sweep the house for her.

Her anguish grew even deeper when she saw poor Moshe sit down to patch an old jacket or to turn a pair of worn pants. And when he cast a loving glance at her above the two pairs of glasses, it was scant comfort, for she knew that even if *he* forgave her, God would not. What had she done to her Moshele after he had spent better than three quarters of his life studying the Torah, praying day and night, making countless benedictions, performing good deeds—all that so that when his time came he would rise up to paradise?

Suddenly he had to tear himself from the holy books, cut short his prayers, risk his hard-earned place in paradise, and, all on account of a measly piece of bread, become a tailor. And all this because of her, all because her legs had failed her, and after fifty years of running she had suddenly taken to bed and had to be served breakfast in bed like some princess—woe unto her! If she had a thousand pairs of legs and if they all became paralyzed, it wouldn't pain her so much as it did to see her Moshele struggle to thread a needle, his hands too long for the thread and his legs so slight that the jacket slipped off his knees every minute. She bowed her head in shame. Her eyelids drooped like a sick hen's, plagued by the thought that she would never run again, never move again, spend the rest of her life like a duchess, never doing a thing or leaving the very bed in which fifty years earlier Moshele had taken her as his wife.

Fifty years both winter and summer, even before God drew the sun from the sheath, she used to run to the market to wrangle and haggle with a sleepy or frozen peasant over his cartful of raw apples or little pears and rush back home again to her children—suckle one, bathe a second, patch the pants of a third, then run right back to the market, open her fruit stand, then rush home again and clean, wash the floor, rinse out the drawers, prepare breakfast, and run back to the market again . . . And soon home again, comb the children's hair, give them the cheder tuition, take out an interest-free loan, beg an extension of the rent, polish the candlesticks, and prepare for the Sabbath.

For nearly fifty years she did this. What else could a person do in fifty short years when fifteen of them had to be spent nursing a sickly son who every Monday and Thursday lay down with another sickness and for whom you had to find a *feldsher,* leeches, cupping glasses—and when this didn't help you had to run to measure graves, jump over a broom, and lay pebbles on the grave of the famous *Graf* Potozki, who converted to Judaism. And then when all this effort came to naught and in his fifteenth year the son had died, what more could she do than cry a bit, mourn a bit, recite a few prayers, then promptly run to see about little Elke, who had gone to have a tooth extracted and the dentist, cursed be his memory, pulled a piece of the tongue out with the tooth, which promptly caused poisoning of the blood? What more could she do but run to the rabbi to cast away the evil eye, give to charity, shove garlic up the girl's nose, pour salt in her ears, even bring in a gentile quack? But as if out of spite, the girl got bluer and bluer and soon joined her brother in the other world.

The only sliver of satisfaction she derived came from her eldest son, Sheike, a locksmith, a brawny youth handsome and sturdy as an oak. But he began to pal around with the rebels, and no more or less than slapped a policeman, and while she was still observing the mourning period for Elke, they brought her the news that the apple of her eye was being dragged through the Lukish suburb, shackled, barefoot, and with a shorn skull.

She promptly took off on the run. Moshele even complained to her that she was violating the period of mourning, but she took the sin upon herself, grabbed a pair of old shoes, a shirt, a hat, made up a bundle of them, and raced to the outskirts of the city to bid farewell to her precious.

But it didn't end with this, because only now did she begin to race around, knock on doors, ask, seek, inquire to which prison her darling had been sent. But where do you run to shout your protest when there are more prisons than blades of grass in a field?

If she had lain in bed like a princess and hadn't raced here and there, wouldn't Feigel who was already along in years have remained a spinster? If she didn't run from matchmaker to matchmaker and didn't pound her breast and didn't swear and didn't promise that she would pay out the dowry, would Abramele have stood with Feigel under the wedding canopy? Like hell he would!

True, for all her running she still couldn't keep her promise in time and Abramele begged, dunned, and demanded his due. With each new child that Feigel bore him his demands grew more insistent. He slammed the table and cried, "Go, run, seek, bring!" And she ran, ran here, and there, and slowly paid it off. And when the bandit had collected the whole dowry, he left the house one fine day without a fare-thee-well and never came back. Feigel tore her hair and wanted to drown herself, but Liba promptly ran and got a new interest-free loan and set up a grocery store for her daughter, the deserted wife who couldn't make it on her own.

When she was done with this and came back to the market, a new challenge awaited her already. This time it was her younger daughter, Sarah.

True, with Sarah she no longer had to worry about a dowry, since her youngest was as pretty as a picture with lots of prospective grooms after her, but as if out of spite Sarah fell in love with a boy named Benjamin.

On appearance alone, this youth was something out of this world—tall, slim, with a head of curly black hair, a mouthful of teeth like pearls, and a trim mustache that had turned more than one girl's head already. The trouble was, however, that he was conscripted into the army and sent away for a whole five years to faraway Russia.

Sarah waited patiently and faithfully. Liba guarded her like the apple of her eye, didn't let her dip a finger into cold water, so that when her destined one came back from the service, God willing, he would find her with the same peaches and cream complexion with which he had left her.

Finally, he returned, even healthier and handsomer than before, and Sarah brought him home for the first time.

Liba ran and prepared a meal that would have made the tsar himself lick his fingers.

When they sat down at the table and Moshe was in the middle of the benediction, he suddenly began to mumble and gesture in mute language, "Mmm . . . mmm."

"What's the matter?" The ex-soldier had started to eat before he said the blessing. It soon turned out that in the five years Benjamin had been a soldier, he had completely forgotten all the blessings. Moshe left the table angry, and Liba ran after him and was forced to come out with the truth—that the bride was no longer a virgin and that he must come to the wedding so that they wouldn't be disgraced before people.

Moshe let himself be persuaded. He came, but sulked in a corner. But when he first saw the groom's father, he went into shock.

In came a square-cornered figure with a great, round face and a pair of small, slanting eyes and the sparse beard of a Chinese, his top hat askew, his legs wobbling, obviously filled with vodka. Moshele almost fainted.

After the wedding Liba would take a brief rest, but not like a countess, God forbid, not for long, only for a while because soon a war broke out. Benjamin after five year's service in the army had had enough of it and vanished overnight and left Sarah pregnant in the care of Liba, so that for Liba the running started all over again. Who else would be able to help Sarah, who after her first pregnancy lost the peaches and cream in her cheeks and after the second became as weak as a fly altogether?

And so she dashed about until one day she felt that her left leg had grown strangely heavy. At first, she ignored it and joked about how she could manage to run more on the right leg than the left, but soon the second leg started getting heavy too and instead of the legs carrying *her*, she had to drag them instead.

But even if she had had to drag a thousand legs, she wouldn't have stopped running. She swore with a thousand mute tongues—no, no, no! She would have never stopped running if she hadn't fallen flat on her face one day. The good market people carried Liba back to her home and put her to bed. She flung her head back on the pillow, guilty and ashamed.

But Moshele, who never ran anywhere, sat calmly patching an old, tattered jacket and didn't stop mumbling one chapter of psalms after another.

From time to time he cast a quiet smile at his foolish wife who, he observed with his knowing eye, was still racing to and fro in her mind. "For whom? For what?" He smiled. "Why run when a deer can run faster and doesn't get anywhere anyhow? An insect had twenty legs, what good did it do him? Where did it get him? Why run, bustle, worry about things which, like everything else in the world, were totally and completely in God's hands?"

He was right. For who could have thought that one fine day God would send an angel not from heaven but from America of all places, an angel who could not remember a single word of the tens and hundreds of prayers or blessings.

This angel plucked Liba from her iron bed on Market Street and carried her over to the Boulevard of St. George, where he placed her in a carved, wooden bed with downy pillows and sat Moshe down with a whole pile of new holy books under a large, bright lamp with a lampshade that reflected all the colors of the rainbow.

True, some fifty-odd years ago Liba had dreamed a dream that a hundred and twenty years hence an angel would come down from heaven and, placing Moshele up on his wings, fly him to the sky and there seat him among all the holy saints for the great banquet. As for her, she knew that there was no room for women in paradise. That paradise was for men only. That a decent Jewish woman was given one life, a short one at that—on earth.

But now, as she focused her misty eyes, observing Moshele at the carved table in a padded chair with his head buried in a large volume, his beard spread across one page of the holy book, so calm, so serene, she knew that all this was out of this world.

In place of her wasted legs, wings suddenly sprouted that lifted her from the bed and made her soar around Moshele's illuminated head like a butterfly in paradise. She began to sing a praise to the Almighty, to the Everlasting, and the other ten names of God she knew. But the paralysis that had started in a single toe and spread to the hips had by now reached her tongue, and her praise to God was left congealed in her throat unheard by anybody.

She gathered the remnants of her waning powers and beat her wings . . . but she bumped into the ceiling and like a caged pigeon fell back to earth with a smile. She didn't know that Moshele had found his final rest lying on the page of the holy book just half a night ahead of her.

This is the short history of Grandmother Liba, who exerted an indirect but nevertheless distinct influence on subsequent events. Somebody will remember her and will make a remark—that to die beautifully is perhaps the greatest achievement in life. Yes, these two simple humble people died beautifully.

But since every person is destined to have at least two grand-mothers, it is necessary to devote several pages to the second grand-mother, who through ironic chance also bore the name Liba.

XIII

⁕

THE WAY BARVE'S Son told it, the Lithuanians settled in the ancient forests between the Niemen and Danube rivers because that area offered a better hiding place in which to defend themselves against their worst and most powerful enemies, the Slavs, who came from the west and south and plundered them without mercy. It's no wonder the Lithuanians held the ancient, mighty trees to be their good and benevolent gods. But a few centuries after they had driven off their enemies and adopted Christianity, they sawed down these mighty gods, tied them into large rafts, and floated them down the Viliya River, where the Jewish merchants bought them for resale.

These merchants were husky, big-boned men with red, thick napes and heavy beards.

Legends were told in the marketplace of the strength of one of these merchants. It was said that after he bought a tract of forest, in order to prevent having other trees substituted for those he had selected, he would either place his thick neck against the trees and break them, or tear them out by the roots. This legendary hero was the father of Grandmother Liba the Second.

She was a living witness that the stories told about her father's strength weren't completely fabricated. A tall, healthy woman with a powerful voice and an even more powerful laugh, she might not have been able to tear a tree out of the ground, but she did once slap her youngest son for playing hooky from cheder and promptly knocked out two of his teeth.

Just like her counterpart, Grandmother Liba the First, she knew that the other world was reserved for men only, and she therefore decided to get all she could down here on earth. With the same enthusiasm with which the market people recalled her father's strength, they also lauded her wonderful cooking and baking and her lusty appetite not only for food but also for ninety-proof vodka, which she could toss down without so much as a grimace—a sight certainly worth seeing.

Whether her husband, Mordecai, would enter paradise concerned her little so long as he brought her all his earnings while still in this world. And such earnings as a mediator and broker for various businesses were quite respectable. Besides, it must be told that Mordecai was no slouch himself when it came to food. As for the juice of the grape, he could more than hold his own with his burly wife.

He carried a head on a pair of broad shoulders without the help of a neck, while from two slits in his Mongolian face peered out two amiable, yellow, leering eyes. And although like my other grandfather he was a pious Jew who wouldn't swallow a drink or a bite of food without first uttering a benediction, he had his own version of paradise and believed that when the Messiah came the water in the river would turn into vodka and his goblet would be the great bell from the church.

This couple had three sons. The eldest, Elchik, was a journeyman for Uri the tailor, whom he drove to an early death by his rebellious socialistic antics and especially by his flirtation with Uri's wife. Elchik promptly married the young widow and became an even bigger exploiter than had been his employer.

Grandmother Liba was proud of him. She had less satisfaction from her second son, Benjamin, whom she described as "the handsomest youth ever spawned on God's earth." Such a fine figure of a man, she felt, deserved a dowry of at least a million rubles. But all he managed to acquire was a job at a fur-cap maker's at four and a half rubles a week, and the girl with whom he fell in love, Sarah, had neither millions nor so much as a broken needle for a dowry. This was enough to cause Grandmother Liba untold aggravation.

If someone had told her then that one day her beloved son would go to America and come back a millionaire in his own right, she would have collapsed from excitement.

But the son who caused her the most grief was her youngest son, Abraham, known to one and all as Abrashka.

He was the one whose teeth she had knocked out because he wouldn't go to cheder, but this hadn't helped much and he had grown up, as the market people put it, "a tragedy upon the Jews." This phrase wasn't taken lightly around the marketplace, since what was bad for Jews was considered bad for the whole world.

In contrast to his two towering older brothers, Abrashka was small and slight, with a pair of squinty eyes that he had inherited from his father. Wearing tight, skimpy trousers and a crushed hat cocked sideways, holding a twig in his hand and a burnt match between his lips, he hung around the edges of the old marketplace where he neither bought nor sold, was neither merchant nor coachman, neither rabbi nor thief, a man without a trade or a profession, unwilling or unable to work or earn a kopeck—in a word, "a tragedy upon the Jews."

Many times Grandmother Liba drove him out of the house, but he always came back and threatened that if he wasn't fed and given a ruble or two for spending money, he would slit his throat. And to prove it, he drew a flashing knife from his pocket and waved it in the air. Grandmother Liba, who was almost twice as big as her good-for-nothing son, would beat him up as usual.

Still, she took his warnings seriously and after she had reddened his cheeks properly, she fed him, gave him the demanded sum, and again threw him out of the house. A week or two later, he'd be back with the same threats.

Once, when he began to wave the knife in the air in customary fashion, she grabbed him and threw him down the stairs even before she had fed him. A few minutes later she heard a soft moaning outside the door, and when she went out to look she found her youngest son sprawled across the front steps with his throat slashed. She worked desperately to save him. She comforted him with her mighty hands until the suicide refocused his upturned eyes. Then she carried him into the house and began to stuff him with everything in sight. And when he was sated and had accepted his usual fee, the suicide wiped the red paint off his gullet, stuck a match between his lips, and, twirling his twig between his fingers, again vanished for a few weeks. From then on, he never came back into the house but each time was found dying anew on the steps.

One can well understand Grandmother's irritation over all this, but what tormented her even more was her curiosity to know where her ne'er-do-well son vanished to between one suicide and the next.

She did everything she could to find out. She followed him, spied on him, questioned him—first she alone, then together with her husband and her other sons. They all kept trying to sniff out his hiding place but to no avail.

It just so happened that I was fated to finally uncover the great secret.

Since I hadn't been allowed to enter the gymnasium, my father had no choice but to enroll me in the Russian-Jewish junior high school. There was no quota here—both the pupils and the teachers were exclusively Jewish—and out of respect for my father, the American millionaire, I was put a grade ahead of the other children of my age group and degree of knowledge.

At first, the school held little appeal for me. They didn't have handsome uniforms here. The pupils wore dark satin tunics with flat, dark buttons and dreary black caps on their shaven heads. Nor did I display any outstanding scholastic talents. The three times that I was called on during an examination I received almost the worst possible marks. Still, I gradually became accustomed to the new conditions and began to get closer to my new schoolmates.

The only thing that bothered me was that the gymnasium that Sasha and Romeks attended was located on the very next street, so that to avoid them I constantly had to sneak to and from school along back streets. I also made sure to stay away from Niura's window on Pilna Street. This constant skulking down side streets was unpleasant and always filled my heart with worry and dread. At the same time, I was sure that the longer I hid from her the greater would be her effort to find me. And the more she sought me, the less would I be able to forget her.

Quite a few months passed by, and I began to lose all hope of ever seeing her again because in order for that to happen, it would have to be triggered by something that even my boundless imagination couldn't conjure up. But young as I was, I was fated to learn that life is sometimes stranger than the wildest stretches of imagination, for I did meet up with Niura again, and not only with her but with my two archfoes as well.

But prior to the meeting with Niura, walking home one day, I suddenly encountered my little uncle, the ne'er-do-well, vagabond Abrashka.

A man can be a devil to the whole world yet at the same time be an angel to somebody. So even as Abrashka brought shame and heartache to the whole family, he brought me something that made me conscious of certain powers within me and roused in me longings toward which I later directed my entire existence—the longing to perform, the lust to hold an audience in the palm of my hand.

XIV

~~~

MORE THAN ONCE in later years I had occasion to remember this meeting with my uncle. And more than any other event in my youth, it would emerge in my memory with the capricious unexpectedness and incredible reality of a dream.

Looking back through the perspective of time, this fateful meeting reflected in my memory like a distant, fluttering image with oddly sharp outlines and capriciously shimmering colors, like a view of something that's a thousand miles away and still close enough and clear enough to touch.

I recall with particular clarity approaching my house on my way home from school and seeing my little uncle's figure in the distance.

"What's he doing here?" I wondered. "Where is he going? Can he be on his way to kill himself in front of Grandma, or has he already gone through his act and is he heading for his usual hiding place?"

Both notions proved false, for the mysterious little man stood with legs crossed and leaned against the corner building without stirring.

His quaint appearance, his total self-absorption, his indifference to the world around him, and particularly his tragic-comic behavior at his mother's had roused my curiosity, and I had tried more than once to ingratiate myself with this odd member of the family. Unfortunately, Abrashka never showed the slightest interest in me . . . so that when I saw him now I didn't know whether to go up to him or not. But before I could make up my mind he beckoned to me, and I ran over to him.

With a fervor I hadn't expected from this skinny, cold-blooded runt, he exclaimed, "I've been waiting for you here a long time already. I knew that you get out of school around this time. Now, come with me!"

"Where to?"

"Don't ask!" he said, dragging me by my sleeve. "I know that you're one of the boys and that you'll help me out. It's a matter of life and death. You must save me!"

The sudden compliments, and particularly the desperate appeal for help, threw me momentarily. Still, I didn't resist and let him drag me along because even in my confusion I knew that this was a rare opportunity to get involved in one of his fascinating suicides, about which I had heard so much but which I had never had a chance to observe. But the moment I realized that we were heading away from Grandmother's house, I stopped to point it out.

"Grandmother lives the other way."

"What grandmother—which grandmother?" he said, seizing my hand again. "It's one of the greatest things . . . You won't believe your own eyes and ears. But I'll show you everything, explain everything to you." And catching sight of a passing droshky he added with the same impatience, "Let's get in. It's late. We must hurry, we must run, we must fly . . ." And once in the droshky, he cried to the driver. "To the Lukish horse market, my man, and don't spare the horses. Do us a favor—hurry, hurry!"

"What is it, a fire?" the old coachman asked with a smile.

"Worse, much worse than a fire. Drive, old man! Drive, my dear fellow!" my uncle pleaded.

Bounced around by the pounding of the metal springs over the crooked, pointy cobblestones, Abrashka nearly climbed on top of me and shouted in my ear, "You're going to be a midget! You don't have to be afraid. I know that you're not the timid type and that I can depend on you. You'll save me, otherwise it will all come down on my head as if it was my fault the midget died!"

I recalled what had been said several times in the family, that Abrashka wasn't in his right mind and would one day go crazy altogether, and I looked at him now with fear and suspicion.

"Yes, Yes, you'll be a midget!" the lunatic cried, his eyes flashing. "You'll be disguised. You'll be made up. You'll look like Vaska Sibiriak, the devil take him! Of all the days, he had to pick today to croak. Ate like a pig last night and, in the morning, stretched out dead on the floor . . . Gorodenko will go crazy!"

"Who will go crazy? Who ate like a pig? Who is Gorodenko? And where are we going?" I wanted to ask these questions but I didn't get the chance because Abrashka licked his cracked lips and went on with even more fervor.

"You'll put on a mustache and beard to make you look older. I know that you'll do it for us, or else it'll go badly with me and the whole carnival. I promised Gorodenko that I'd come up with a midget. All you need to remember is that you're forty-five years old and come from Siberia and have a giant mother and an even bigger father. Gorodenko will introduce you to the public. You'll be led out on stage riding a lion. Then I'll get into a box and you'll stick a few swords into me. Then a girl, Sonka, will get into another box and you'll saw her in half. And at the very end, I'll hand you two frying pans and one egg. You'll break the egg into one pan and cover it with the other, and from between them will fly out a live chicken. The band will strike up a march, the crowd will cheer, 'Bravo, hurrah for Vaska Sibiriak . . .'"

Abrashka jumped up, lost his balance, and fell back in the seat with a crash. "The main thing is you musn't tell anybody, especially Grandma. I'll take you home tonight. You only have to help us out this one night. The other nights aren't so important because the people only come on market day, and they happen to want a midget. When this Vaska was healthy, you could make a good groschen with him . . . So he goes and dies on me!" he concluded with a face as if about to burst into tears.

By this time the droshky had entered the Green Bridge, where it had to slow down, but Abrashka poked the driver in his behind and pleaded, "Drive on, my good man, drive on! The bridge is made of metal, it won't collapse." And seizing the whip from the coachman's hand, he whacked the horse across his hind legs. The horse leaped with such a sudden jerk that all three of us grabbed one another to keep from tumbling out. Tossing as if in an epileptic fit, the droshky now snaked its way through the crooked streets of the Lukish suburb until, finally, in the distance we saw the horse market.

On market day, there was a terrible commotion. The congestion and noise of people and animals filled the neighboring streets. Horse dealers—some with blue, bulbous noses, others slim youths in patent leather boots and with black, darting eyes in tanned faces—drove glossy frenzied stallions that had been fed potions to make them whinny thunderously and spray foamy spittle through flaring nostrils. Cows, calves, bulls, and goats all tried to outsnort each other but were no match for the unearthly squealing of the desperate hogs that lay packed five or six to a huge sack. The sack heaved with heart-rending screams like some accursed, fantastic creature.

Business was conducted here in the same frantic fashion with cursing, arguing, and bitter fights—following which the combatants made up, kissed, got drunk together, then started to fight all over again.

The streets around the marketplace were jammed with all kinds of bars, wine cellars, and dens where, over a bottle of vodka and a hard-boiled egg, it was remembered who had been the first to insult whom, thus igniting the fighting and the making up. This strange ritual went on until nightfall, and before the crowd dispersed to their homes, they stopped at the sideshow and, after throwing a coin into Gorodenko's hat, caught a glimpse of the famous magician—the midget Vaska Sibiriak.

The sideshow booth was an old wooden shack painted yellow, with a red cloth over the entrance and several colorful paper lanterns at the sides. The windows were boarded up and decorated with posters showing various poses of a square midget wearing a top hat and tails. Two tattered Russian flags fluttered proudly on the crooked roof.

When the droshky stopped, Abrashka leaped out first. His face was covered with drops of sweat the size of chickpeas, just as if it had been he and not the horse that had been pulling the wagon.

"How much?" he asked the driver, and before he even heard the answer he turned to me. "You got any money? Pay the man, I'll pay you back later."

I felt around in my pocket. "I don't have enough."

"It'll be enough," he said. He scooped the change from my hand, gave it to the driver, and headed quickly for the carnival booth. The driver glanced at the coins, then sprang down from the box and ran after us, shouting, "Wait, hold it!"

Abrashka shoved me quickly behind the red cloth but remained outside himself. I heard my uncle outshout the enraged cabby. "What do you want? What are you hollering about? You think you're in one of your filthy dens? This is a circus! This is a temple of art! You see those flags there? . . . We have a permit from the governor himself! You think you're dealing with horse thieves or hog drivers here? Do you know who you drove in your droshky? It's an honor for you and your old nag! . . . Did you ever hear of the famous midget, Vaska Sibiriak?"

That's all I heard, for suddenly it grew quiet out there.

For a while I stood there in the dark, but soon my gaze was drawn to a half-open door through which a subdued light penetrated. I edged toward the door and looked inside. Several mangy apes were jumping around in one cage, while a lion lay in a larger cage next to it. An elderly man in a dirty shirt, torn pants, and a drooping mustache that nearly hid the bottom half of his face stood leaning against the bars of the lion's cage calmly smoking a pipe, trying to blow the smoke into its eyes, and tickling the sole of its paw with a twig. The lion didn't resist and merely twitched his great, bristly brows in a lazy helpless fashion.

The old man tugged my sleeve and murmured, "Come." He led me into a small backyard strewn with all kinds of crates, boards, rags, and piles of dirt on which several chicks were feeding. In the center of the yard stood a lean, brown horse. A man dipped a wide brush in a bucket of lime and painted him white. From somewhere came a cracked voice that intermittently screamed and emitted lengthy curses.

Abrashka came and pushed me toward a low, crooked door. "Don't be afraid, go on in."

Inside sat several people wolfing down long chunks of sausage. A man stood with his back to the door and cursed the others in the same voice that I had heard out in the yard.

"I got him!" Abrashka cried and shoved me forward.

The man with the hoarse voice turned toward me.

If someone were to poke two fingers into a round chunk of dough and attach two black springs from a wall clock as a mustache, he'd have a perfect picture of Gorodenko. This piece of dough was adorned with a big black tie under its chin and a small derby on the back of the head. The most remarkable feature, however, was not the face but the belly, which began right under the chin and curved in a great arc almost to the knees.

Gorodenko glanced at me and then resumed screaming, this time in a piercing voice like a saw hitting a knot in a board. "Too big, too big, too big!"

Instead of answering, Abrashka leaped toward the door and was soon out of sight.

"Come back here, you damned plague. Come back here, you scurfy dog!" Gorodenko shouted after my vanished uncle, and, turning to me, snarled, "Get out of here before I slap your face and knock your teeth out!"

I didn't stir. Why was he driving me away? Why did he want to knock out my teeth? Hadn't I come here of my own accord and paid my own fare to help out a midget who was dead? Why did I deserve to be driven away and slapped besides? I wondered.

Gorodenko kept on "Why are you still here? Don't you understand what I'm telling you? You're no good to me . . . too big and you look like a boy. I need an old midget who is smaller and looks his age. That scum, Abrashka, fooled me into thinking he'd bring me someone who looked like a midget. Who'd believe he's a midget!" he said, turning to the others who calmly chewed the sausage with no intention of answering him.

"The cabby believed it," I muttered darkly.

The others looked at me, and Gorodenko, who had turned away, turned back to face me. "What did you say? What cabby?"

"The one that drove me here."

"What did he believe?"

"That I'm the midget."

Gorodenko shook his mighty head as if shooing a pesky fly off his nose. "What kind of nuisance is this—take him out of my sight! Why are you sitting there? Why don't you speak? Enough stuffing your faces already, goddam you and the midget both! What now? It's late already . . . It's time to start the show. Where is Abrashka? I'll tear his arms and legs off this very day yet or my name ain't Gorodenko . . . Enough eating, I say! Get dressed . . . Where's my bell?" And he started to push his way through the doorway.

I followed him and said through clenched lips. "What about me?"

"Go home!" he snarled waspishly.

"It's too far to walk there. Somebody will have to take me. Abrashka took all my money. You'll have to give me the carfare home."

"How do you like this punk? Who needs you, up your mother's father's mother!"

"Give me money! From your father's father up your mother's mother from under, from over, through your lungs and liver, in your son-of-a-bitching blood!" I fired back at him with assurance and expertise.

My unexpected reply hurled the eaters off the bench and sent them to the floor rolling with wild laughter.

Nothing in the world could have helped me more than this spontaneous outburst from these boorish gluttons. It was as if with their raw laughter they had pierced the inflated delusions of their brutal employer. Within seconds, the awesome, ominous Gorodenko became a piece of limp rubber. It was a few minutes before he could be heard or seen again. He took a red kerchief from his pocket and wiped the steaming lump of dough resting on his shoulders, sucked a breath of fresh air into his great belly, then turned back to the group still rolling around convulsed with laughter.

"How do you like this little bastard? Pure gold! My dear boy, where have you been?" he said and patted my head with a syrupy smile. "Come over here, let's hear it again." And after I had repeated the oath with clarity, force, and some additional variations, he began to ring the bell and with restored authority ordered, "Bring in Vaska's clothes. Let's see how the lad looks in a top hat and tails."

My fate was sealed.

From then on, events begin to race with the haste of a dream's final phases—in a turmoil of cursing and lengthy oaths, I am carried, shoved, made up, and dressed. Soon, I stand in a dark corner togged out in a small top hat and tails. A beard is glued to my chin and a pointed mustache bristles under my nose.

On the side is the painted horse with a silver fringe on its head. Sonka sits astride him, wearing a pink leotard with glittering sequins around the hips. On the other side lies the old, weary lion, dozing. Next to him stands the old man with the drooping mustache. He pokes his foot into the lion's side to keep it from falling asleep. On the platform, under a piercing gaslight, the sausage eaters dressed in clown costumes, festooned with bells, walk on their hands, stand on their heads. Gorodenko strolls among them wearing white gloves and a black frockcoat with three rows of gleaming medals on his breast. He conducts with a black baton and shouts, "Hop, hop . . ." A monkey rides a dog horseback. The white horse dances a waltz, and when the music stops Gorodenko announces the main attraction of the program, the greatest wonder of the world—Vaska de Sibiriak!

Abrashka flies like a demented bat from corner to corner. He tugs a box, he pulls a rope. Someone kicks him in the rear end, and when he straightens up to respond he gets a crack on the skull. He then drapes himself over me and whispers quickly in my ear, "Remember everything you've been told? Go sit on the lion . . . You're on!"

I get a good grip on the lion's tangled mane. Abrashka and the man with the droopy mustache scramble around at the lion's rear and shove him out of the dark corner and onto the lighted stage.

A foul cloud of cheap tobacco . . . the nauseating stink of sweaty feet . . . lumpy heads with swollen, bulbous noses . . . swarthy, cunning faces with flashing eyes . . . The wild blare of trumpets and loud, frantic drumming . . . Gorodenko's cracked voice: "How old are you, Vaska?"

"Forty-five!"

"Why are you so small?"

"Because my father didn't make me bigger."

"Why didn't your father make you any bigger?"

"Because he didn't have the time."

"Why didn't he have the time?"

"Because he had to make twelve more children!"

Thunderous laughter . . . a shower of falling coins.

My uncle lies all scrunched up inside a small box. I stick six swords into it and he comes out all sweaty but alive.

On the table in mortal fear lies my wife, Sonka. I saw her in two even pieces with a saw and she springs up from the table happy and in one piece.

I crack an egg and a live chicken comes out of it. Holding the fluttering bird by its legs over my head, I begin my greatest, most terrible, most destructive, twenty-fourth-degree oath assembled by Gorodenko. "In your father's mother's guts . . . "

The walls shake from the wildly aroused public. They stomp their feet, fling their hats, kiss, embrace, and begin to fight . . .

The light goes out . . .

In the dark, heads bob, hands wave, big gasping mouths shout, "Hurrah! Hurrah!"

XV

⟋⟍⟋⟍

THE KNOWLEDGE THAT I was in junior high school only because I hadn't been accepted in the gymnasium, and particularly the fact that my father had had me placed in a higher grade than that in which I belonged, put me in a very uncomfortable position.

I tried to justify my inability to keep up with my classmates scholastically by claiming that I hadn't come to school as they had, but only as a casual, temporary visitor, a kind of passing stranger—actually a violinist by profession on his way to St. Petersburg to enroll at a conservatory.

At first, my assertion evoked astonishment and some respect, but after a few months had gone by and I still scratched my neck and looked up to the ceiling or feverishly searched my pockets as if seeking the answer there each time I was called on by the teacher, and after I never got more than a one or a two (the lowest possible marks), the astonishment turned into frequent, spontaneous laughter mixed with open scorn. I was, therefore, forced to "come out with the truth" and inform them that I wasn't a violinist in the pure sense of the word but actually a magician who prior to entering school had worked in a circus. And in order to prove this contention, I demonstrated a few tricks to them right then and there.

One day, I even brought in an egg from home, and when the boys gathered in the bathroom during recess I pulled a living chicken out of the egg. The trick completely mystified them and although some still tried to mock me with the fact that on the way to school the front of my tunic had been mysteriously bulging and making cackling sounds, still the smoothness of my presentation and the authenticity of the magic phrases I employed in the process evoked the opinion that even if I wasn't a true magician I surely wasn't a simple student, either. Therefore I didn't need to study or know anything, and a one or a two was good enough for me since I was there accidentally and temporarily and merely to amuse and entertain them.

The most remarkable thing was that the students' opinion soon became that of the teachers, too, who began to look at me as at some strange little "ignoramus" who had stumbled into their school out of the blue, one who didn't even begin to know where he was or what was going on, one whose clumsiness frequently threw the whole class into hysterical laughter.

My indifference to my colleagues' reaction, my frank admission that I knew nothing and understood nothing, and particularly my desperate struggle to guess the answers, provided my teachers with more amusement and satisfaction then was the case when I occasionally did come up with the correct answer.

This correct answer came like a disappointment to one and all, a kind of deception on my part, and I therefore strove not to provide the proper answers but to give them what they expected of me.

Some of the teachers appreciated this and sometimes even gave me a higher mark than I deserved, especially Gerasim Isakovitch Dalski, who once gave me a whole five.

He called me up in front of the class and asked, "How many continents are there?" I thought it over and went through my usual routine of looking up at the ceiling, scratching my brow, and biting my lips, and finally came out with "four," adding in the same breath, "possibly there is one more or less, but on the basis of more or less it must be four."

As usual, the teacher and the pupils had a good laugh. I bowed with the dignity of a mandarin and said, "I see that I haven't guessed right. But I am more than sure that I wasn't far wrong, and even if I was, what's the difference? No matter what I gave you—six or ten—I still wouldn't get more than a one or two for it. That's my luck."

After a full minute during which the teacher tried to outlaugh the pupils, he wiped away tears of joy and said, "That's not true. This has nothing to do with luck. The bad marks you get are for not giving the correct answers. If you had said five continents, you'd surely have gotten a five."

I smiled with the same fatuous imperturbability. "If that's so, then give me a four for my answer of four."

The class commenced to applaud.

Gerasim Isakovitch raised his pen. "You have a bad opinion both of yourself and of teachers. But to show you that you actually have good luck (because never has such a bad student been lucky enough to find such a good teacher), I'll give you a whole five and this will also serve to remind you that the right answer is not four or six, but five."

Sitting in one of the booths in the lavatory during recess, I overheard the following conversation: "It's a scandal, a five for such an answer! Even Kaplan never got a five. Kaplan is a genius . . . Kaplan repeated the Pythagorean theorem right after the teacher expounded it, and he only got a four . . . That's some luck . . . ! No, it's a swindle, a scandal!"

But Gerasim Isakovitch seemed to have his own opinion about me. He called on me more often than routine dictated and posed the questions in such a tone and with such gestures that they evoked laughter even before I could manage to answer. It appeared as if he begrudged the good mark he had himself given me and had suddenly decided to compete with me for the class's laughter.

One time he called on me and, placing his black pointer on the colored map on the wall, asked, "What's the name of this sea?"

When I made a move toward the map, he pushed me back with the pointer and said, "If you're nearsighted, why don't you ask your father the millionaire to buy you a pair of glasses?" And he got his reward of thunderous laughter.

I waited for the laughter to die down, then blurted out, "If you believe that glasses can help me, I happen to have a pair on me." And I drew an old pair of glasses from my rear pocket and stuck them on my nose.

This time instead of laughter the class responded with a long drawn out "a-aa-ah" of astonishment.

The teacher bit the side of his lower lip, slammed the table with his pointer, and in a voice filled with amazement, embarrassment, and anger cried, "Listen here, young man, I'm losing my patience already with all those stunts. This isn't a circus, and I'll ask you to stop your clownish tricks and give me a straight answer to my question!"

I made a wistful face. "If Mr. Teacher won't be mad at me, I'll confess that I'm not sure. Still, I would say that according to all probabilities, that's the Black Sea."

Gerasim Isakovitch waved the pointer impatiently and turned to the class. "Would you be good enough to tell the small ignoramus the name of the sea?"

"The Red Sea!" some thirty-odd voices cried with smug satisfaction.

I endured the mocking gaze of the thirty-odd pairs of eyes for a moment, then put the glasses back on and said, "Now it's up to Mr. Teacher to judge which of us is right. All I can say is that through my glasses I can see that the sea isn't black or red but blue." The teacher grabbed me by the collar and heaved me in the direction of my desk.

Still, during recess that very same day, I heard the following conversation in the lavatory: "That trick with the glasses was a pre-arranged business . . . Gerasim Isakovitch is on his father's payroll."

"That's a lie!"

"My mother told me so."

"But a five for nothing?"

"He gets paid off in American dollars."

"Say what you like, if it was up to me I'd give him a five too."

"Me too!"

"Why?"

"I don't know why—but he deserves it."

This started an argument from which I gathered that some were for me, others against me, and that it would be better if I left the whole thing a mystery and didn't try to explain it. But they wouldn't let me. They cornered me during every recess and tried to drag the "truth" out of me—was I really a violinist, or a magician? It was just as if they suspected that my presence in school was somehow tied to a secret that I didn't want to share with them.

Once, when they pressed me against the wall to make me tell them where I had learned to speak so fancily, I boasted that I could speak English and Italian, too. Some of them had heard that my father was from America and therefore believed I might speak English, but they refused to accept the Italian.

"I speak French, too," I added.

"Cut it out, what do you think we are, idiots?" they said, ranging themselves around me with rising impatience. "Wait here a minute—"

I didn't wait, but tore loose from the circle, leaving them in a stew. Behind my back, I heard them mimicking me and even calling me insulting names, but their insults fell like paper arrows against metal armor, which only served to arouse them, and the more they tried to break me, the more invulnerable I became.

One time, as I was leaving the school, they drew me into a circle and began to taunt me. "What's your hurry? When are you going to America? Have you packed your things yet?"

"Yes," I said, "I'm leaving this coming Thursday." And I pulled a train ticket out of my breast pocket.

They were left completely flabbergasted. I went on, "And if you want to know the whole truth, I'll tell it to you, but you must promise not to tell the teachers."

They moved in closer.

"I'm a midget," I announced.

"A what?"

"A midget. And just a short time before I came to this school, I grew to my fullest height."

The crowd broke into resounding laughter and began to applaud.

Fired by their applause, I told them how a certain Gorodenko had ensnared me into a circus and how, cursing me with the foulest oaths, he beat me, bent me, squeezed and shrunk me, trying to transform me into a forty-five-year-old midget. Twisting and turning me this way and that, he crippled and crushed me so that I became half of what I had originally been. At first, I took this as a joke, but when I came home and rolled up my shirt and saw my tiny belly and shrunken backside, I realized that things were more serious than I had thought. I wasn't so frightened by the fact that a good half of me was missing as by the fact that the damned barker had squeezed all of the forty-five years into the remaining half. I felt very old and miserable. True, I slowly stretched back like a piece of compressed rubber and regained my former height, but the forty-five years remained stuck inside my bones. And now, "Whether you'll believe me or not, I am forty-five years old."

And from my breast pocket I took out a stamped birth certificate, which gave the year of my birth some forty-odd years before.

They were left agape and dumbfounded. It was clear that this was a fresh lie, but this time the lie was so daring, so astounding, that they were spellbound.

Suddenly someone cried from the rear, "Lampedusser," and soon all the others joined in. "Yes, yes, that's what he is, a lampedusser!"

This was a nickname I had never heard before, and I had no inkling of what it meant. Still, the moment I heard it I felt it go through my bones and nail me to the wall. It evoked a momentous reaction within me, as if I had been suddenly doused with some foul liquid.

To try to protest and stop them from using the name would have been impossible, for as far as I could tell, none of them knew where the name came from and who had used it first. And it wasn't so much the name itself as the enormous pleasure they derived from taunting me with it that hurt me. At times I felt that they were doing the same thing to me that I had once done to Berchik, namely, seeking to crush an enviable quality and to obtain dominance by using a mysterious factor—in my case the nonexistent Golem, in their case an inscrutable nickname.

Nevertheless, I comforted myself that I was someone who couldn't be described with any existing words but for whom special names had to be coined. There were wastrels, quacks, connivers, cheats, swindlers, and horse thieves aplenty, but I was the first of the lampedussers.

This knowledge gradually aroused within me a feeling of satisfaction, followed by a strong urge to be in fact a lampedusser both for their pleasure and for my own satisfaction; to become that from which both the caller and the called derived such gratification.

It happened when the winter melted into great puddles and began to race noisily through the crooked gutters and out of the city. The dozing rooftops awoke and playfully threw off their dingy snow blankets onto the heads of the passersby below. The returning flocks of birds plucked the dingy clouds away from the sun with happy cries, tore them to shreds, and strewed them over the city. The people swept the streets with huge brooms and discarded their heavy underwear and felt boots. Spring came.

But not for long—for presently, a premature summer seized the city in a hot grip more befitting the Sahara than Lithuania. Even the oldest people in town couldn't recall such a summer. The summer was even hotter for the students of the junior high school, since it arrived simultaneously with the year's final exams.

Those days were always considered pure hell for the students, regardless of climate. But when in addition to the tests a blaze erupted in my home, I tasted the flavor of the lime oven into which the patriarch Abraham had been hurled. And if old Abraham was the first person to emerge from a lime oven alive, waving a diploma signed by the Jewish God, then the lampedusser was surely the second.

A special examiner used to come down from St. Petersburg for the senior class examinations. He was the famous "Learned Jew."

Various legends circulated in the school about this examiner: that he was one of the most learned men in the land, a great historian, a great mathematician who spoke no less than fourteen languages. Besides, he was a very stern, bad-tempered man who took sadistic pleasure in torturing the students with extraordinarily complicated questions.

Even in the first class, the pupils drew pictures on the blackboard during recess of the dread figure whom they would be meeting one day. They represented him as a Chinese dragon with snakelike hands and sawlike teeth. In the second and third classes the pictures drawn of him were more restrained; they showed a half-man, half-wolf, or a man with the head of a cunning fox.

Only in the drawings of the fourth class did he emerge in fully human form with a large, professorial forehead and a thick mop of curly hair. By now, some positive traits were added to his awesome reputation. Notes were taken of his enormous popularity and the important connections that he enjoyed not only in the Jewish but in the Christian world as well. It was deemed worthwhile, therefore, to get to know such a person even if he did possess animalistic instincts and liked to bite a student and watch him squirm between his sharp teeth. It had happened that after the examiner had so severely chewed up a student that he had nearly broken a tooth, he then took him along to St. Petersburg and, through his great influence, obtained a false passport for him and enrolled him in a university—and that the bitten victim became a famous engineer, a lawyer, or even a doctor.

Maybe it was better, therefore, that the inspector wasn't a plain person? And if he did bite, he could possibly make up for it by falsifying a passport and then—St. Petersburg? University? Who could tell?

With this in mind the students worked during the terrible heat wave with utmost dedication.

I, too, sweated and tried to prepare myself for the examiner's sharp fangs. It was during one of these feverish days that I came home and heard strange, muffled sounds issuing from inside the house. I raced up the stairs and stopped at the threshold to the dining room where my father sat half-naked in the center of the room racked by a frightening cough. If I hadn't been standing in my own house I would have sworn that this wasn't my father but some strange figure composed of various colors and resembling the horrible monsters featured on the posters advertising penny-dreadful novels.

His normally pale, round face was completely brown, his lips were blue, and his eyes were like pieces of chalk caught up in a network of blood-red veins. The resounding blasts issuing from his chest were too explosive even for a man of his height and strength. His naked abdomen heaved convulsively in and out like a punctured bellows. His purple tongue trembled inside his gaping mouth and his nostrils flared like those of the famous horse in the Russian children's story. He seemed to be filled with gunpowder that exploded periodically with deafening blasts and threatened to blow off his head like a cork from a bottle. Only the ugly blue-green ropes straining under his neck kept the head firmly anchored to the shoulders. He gripped the edges of the big oak table with his mighty hands.

Two doctors hovered around him preparing to jab something into his arm. Pressed silent and frightened into a corner were my mother, the two servant girls, and a couple of neighbors.

Under the effect of the hypodermic, Father finally stopped coughing and began to wheeze in a whistling sound as if a rope were being tightened around his gullet. Later, he collapsed altogether. The two doctors carried him into the bedroom and put him to bed.

The next day, the same terrible scene was repeated. The asthma attacks didn't slacken on the third or fourth day either. The doctors tried desperately to work their way into his clogged lungs with all kinds of spells, pulmotors, and bellows, but to no avail. Father whistled frighteningly for help, like a racing locomotive just before it blows up.

In a few weeks, a consultation among no less than four doctors determined that Father was suffering from the worst kind of asthma, and that he must leave immediately for Germany if he wanted to save his life. The greatest specialists, hospitals, and clinics were found there, the doctors said, also insinuating that he should take along lots of money to meet the expected high fees. Hurrying as much as possible, Father packed a few shirts, took along all his bankbooks, and, accompanied by a local doctor, went off to Germany to consult the specialists.

This sudden, terrible illness distressed me so that even after he had gone I couldn't drive away the ghastly scene, the gasping and wheezing sounds that kept ringing in my ear. Naturally, under such trying circumstances and with the murderous heat besides, even the little bit that I wanted to remember of the Pythagorean theorem wouldn't stick in my memory, which normally sucked in the tiniest detail of everything. Now my memory refused to retain the things I had to remember and kept the things I tried to forget. So that when I came to the examination I was a raw, soft piece of flesh for the sharp fangs of the examiner, and I quietly slipped into my desk.

Soon, footsteps could be heard approaching. The students jumped to their feet and turned their heads toward the door. There stood a remarkable individual—resembling all the drawings and paintings made, from the first class to the last. His extraordinarily long and skinny arms and legs undoubtedly had something of the dragon in them, and there was something of the fox in his long, sharp face with the pointed jaw. But his bristly silver hair and especially his good-natured, squinting, smiling eyes, which looked out over a pince-nez attached with a silk tape to the right lapel of his uniform, partly reflected all the positive traits attributed to him in the senior class.

But a man's importance is judged mostly by the actions of those around him, and the teachers, who were now all dressed up in their holiday best and hovered about him with such rare politeness and respect, gave witness to the fact that this was indeed the famous man who could obtain big favors in the Christian world. And as proof that the picturesque allegations about both his biting and his magnanimous deeds weren't pure fabrication was the fact that a couple of teeth were missing in his smiling mouth.

"I wish you all the best, people," he said in a flat, prosaic voice.

"We're pleased in our efforts, your excellency!" some thirty-odd clear young voices responded in a metallic echo.

The inspector took the center chair before the long green table and, without even waiting for the teachers to settle down in their places, he raised his long arm, baring it nearly to the elbows, and pointed with a bony finger to one of the students. The test had begun.

One by one the students of the junior high school stood up before the examiner from St. Petersburg and virtually overwhelmed him with the agility with which they handled his questions and with the clarity of their answers. He kept on exchanging glances with the teachers and shrugging his shoulders and saying, "Ingenious! Ingenious!"

Fifteen, twenty, thirty times the Learned Jew had already pointed with the finger of one hand and marked a five with the other and, instead of torturing the students as had been expected, the dragon after several hours sat there weary and sapped as if the students had blown the breath out of him and it was now he who was anxious to slink back to St. Petersburg.

He sat there drenched in sweat and exhausted from the monotony of the obvious inevitability of it all. Who better than he, the Learned Jew, should have known that if the children of this Jewish school weren't something bordering on genius, what would be their prospects in the future even after finishing the four-grade school? Where could they go from here when everything was barred to them with a fence composed of a compound percentage quota that made a third out of a fourth out of a half-Jew? If the local teachers were modest in the estimate of their students, it was due more to the fact that familiarity breeds contempt. But to a stranger they could display all their magnificence, their entire inherited, two-thousand-year-old determination to overcome all odds, all restrictions—to transform their behinds into lead and their heads into iron with which to shatter the thick walls of the Pale of Settlement.

Fifteen, twenty, thirty times he posed his questions, and thirty times he got the well-prepared answers right back in his face with all the assurance and certainty of a foregone conclusion. This soon began to weigh heavily on the great mathematician. To hear the same correct, unmistakable, undisputable answer over and over again in the temperature of a steam bath became a terrible burden. For the hundredth time he tried to affix the impatient, capricious pince-nez onto his sweaty nose. He gradually unbuttoned his tight uniform and nonchalantly began to scratch behind the collar.

So that by the time the tired, indifferent finger pointed to me automatically, the frightful myth about the Learned Jew had already gone up in the steam of the sweat. His amiable, bored face no longer showed even a trace of the terrifying image that the students had ascribed to him through the years.

The only thing believable about him was that he was indeed a Jew, but as for all the other attributes—they were obviously slander. He wasn't bad-tempered or sadistic; his questions were so plain and simple that there was nothing even to indicate that he was a great scholar. And even if it was true that he spoke fourteen languages, he did speak Russian with a pronounced Yiddish accent. And if with everything said about him the only thing that was true was the fact that he was a Jew—what was there to fear?

Filled with these thoughts I came up to the table, drew myself up erect, and clicked my heels with all my might. The examiner recoiled from the unexpected sound and, trying to catch the pince-nez, which had again slipped off his nose, he caught his sleeve button on the silk ribbon that bound the pince-nez to his lapel. It flew into the air and fluttered between his hands like a frightened bird. A cool breeze seemed suddenly to permeate the classroom. Everyone breathed a pleasured sigh of relief. And when the inspector had the glasses back on his nose again, he fixed his eyes on me and cried, "God in heaven, how old are you?"

Even previous to this, he had asked several of the students their age and marveled that the oldest among them was barely fifteen, but looking now at my skinny little body whose waist he could have encircled between his thumb and middle finger, he put his pen aside, leaned back in his chair, and, fanning himself with the lapel of his unbuttoned uniform, observed, "It's a positively remarkable experience. Years back I recall that when I came for the exams the students in the fourth class were mature youths, nearly grown men with beards and mustaches, and now—look at him, will you? If it continues this way, in the near future we'll be testing nursing infants at their mother's breasts."

The class erupted into thunderous applause. "Bravo! Bravo!"

The students' spontaneous outburst blew like a cool wind over the steaming examiner, cooling, refreshing, and reviving him. If he had been pleased with the students before, he was now exhilarated with himself. He leaned back in the soft armchair. "Say what you will, but the present generations' urge for learning is something to wonder at. In my day, there were students in the university who were nearly forty, and some over forty. They were called 'the eternal students.' And I must truthfully say that many of them, including myself, knew less than these—"

He wasn't allowed to finish. The teachers and the principal had joined in the applause, along with the students.

The examiner rose from his chair, picked up the pen, ran it over the pages of his register, where he found the names of the four students who hadn't yet been tested, and put a five next to each of their names. And, turning to the teachers, he said, "I thank you, my colleagues. I have nothing more to do here. A foregone conclusion needs no proof. Especially in such a terrible heat."

The students leaped from their desks. "Hurrah, hurrah, for the Inspector. Hurrah for the teachers. And be what may, hurrah for the lampedusser too. Let him know and remember that it was our sweat and bitter effort that forced the examiner to give him a five. And no matter what secret powers the lampedusser used to get his generous fives, let him know and remember that the last and best five was *our* doing. So hurrah for everything and everybody!"

I stood before the green table and didn't move.

To me, the five meant nothing. I had *known* that I would get it.

Had the examiner conducted himself according to prescribed fashion and called the students by alphabetical order, I would have been the second to be called, but since he had called them by pointing with his finger, I knew from the outset that my luck would guard me thirty times from the pointing finger. The shadows that threatened me were those of the specialists in Germany, for if they weren't able to save my father's life there while I stood here before the green table, what good was the five to me? What would I do with it? Even under the best circumstances what could one do with a five from a Jewish junior school?

If I still nursed a dying hope that my father would again spend a fortune to break the bars of the Jewish quota and enroll me in the official gymnasium and that I would be able to face my archenemies in a uniform as an equal, now that he lay half-dead with all his bankbooks with him, this final hope too had been dashed. No, no, I wanted no gratuitous fives. Bite me or tear me to bits, but take me along to St. Petersburg as you already did to that other student or help me get into the gymnasium as you managed to do for someone else a few years ago . . .

And even before these thoughts had raced through my brain, the noise in the classroom stopped as if they had guessed that this wasn't the end, that they weren't yet through with me, that I had yet another trick up my sleeve. And they fell silent.

"I thank you, Honored Sir, for your generosity," I commenced. "On behalf of my colleagues, too, a hearty thanks. We assure you that we will try not to weaken your faith in us. I'd like this opportunity, however, to inform you that your anxiety about my youth is misplaced, since funny as it may sound, I was once forty-five years old." And I took out my passport.

The inspector looked at the teachers, who looked at the students, who looked at one another, then all together at me.

The great mathematician leaned toward me across the table like a big question mark. "I don't understand. When were you forty-five years old?"

"When I was a midget, the biggest midget in the world."

"You mean the smallest midget in the world?"

"No, I mean the biggest midget in the world."

"But that's an inconsistency . . ."

"Only from a mathematical standpoint."

This reply shook the room like an earthquake, as the students and teachers rocked with laughter.

"Yes, yes, the biggest lampedusser in the world!" a student piped up.

"Who is this lampedusser? What does he want? What does he say?" several other students demanded.

"Yes, yes," the class applauded, not realizing how greatly they helped me.

I acknowledged it, raised my right hand, and showed them the ring on my little finger. "Could this little ring on my digit of the left hand be replaced on the large thumb of the left hand? No." And I turned to the green table. "Could a corner of a forty-five degree angle be placed into a corner of, let's say, thirty-eight degrees? No! Certainly not! Could a cube of five centimeters go into a ball with a circumference of six centimeters? Absolutely not! Well, here you have the small ring of the right hand on the large thumb of the left hand."

The students were quizzically turning to each other. "How is that? How did he do it? Not so much the cheating but the eloquence . . . did he prepare himself or is it extemporaneous?"

But I stood facing the inspector, who was struggling with his pince-nez that were sliding off his perspiring nose and then, with plain annoyance, placed them on his ear as if he suddenly began to see with his ears and listen with his eyes.

I felt I was on the right road and proceeded. "The ring on the thumb is of course just an illusory deception, which I performed for your enjoyment. What pleasure would you derive had I presented to you a true mathematical formula as, let us say, thirteen times seventeen is two hundred and twenty-one and this divided by three would be seventy-three point six, six sixty-six, six hundred, sixty-six, six, six, six." (I just threw it out as fast as I could.) "I am sure that you will be much more appreciative when I pull an egg out of my left pocket and put it into my right pocket and ask you, 'Is it true that water brought up to two hundred and twelve degrees of heat disappears into the air?' Does it? Absolutely right, then permit me to ask you, 'What would happen to the egg in my right pocket if I heated it to two hundred and twelve degrees?'"

This time the suspense of uncertainty was on the side of the green table. The class thought it had once seen me doing it and, in a hurry to beat the teachers, shouted in chorus: "A small, little, live chick!"

I smiled. "I'm sorry, you're wrong. It will be a very, very hard-boiled egg." I knocked several times on the dais with the wooden egg. The reaction was as I expected. Silence. The principal at the right hand of the inspector was signaling me with a finger: Enough . . . go back to your bench. He was sure that in my fervent desire to please the inspector I went beyond permissiveness and might even lose the good note the inspector had awarded me out of sheer tiredness. But I felt differently: that it would be this learned Jew, who knew the fourteen languages, who might find the meaning of "lampedusser." But the "Dragon of Saint Petersburg" was ahead of everybody. He bent over the green table and gravely asked, "What is your problem, my little friend?"

And I blasted out, "Not one, your excellency, but ten—an impoverished millionaire. One mother sick after a Caesarian delivery, the second forced to leave the house because of an illegitimate pregnancy, a father in the grip of death, a couple of grandparents who died simultaneously, and if all that is not enough there are two students in the gymnasium who are after me—to kill me only because, as your excellency has heard it, I'm a lampedusser and a Jewish lampedusser to boot."

The great mathematician wiped the sweat off his nose and several times scratched the tip of his ear and the Adam's apple on his throat as if baffled by a mathematical dilemma. He then took the unruly pince-nez off his ear and saddled them back on his nose, and holding them with both hands pierced me with enlarged and stern eyes as if he saw me for the first time and made up his mind to remember me.

A few days later, I got a letter from the inspector general asking me to report immediately to his hotel. I found a second letter waiting for me there addressed to the principal of the gymnasium, which I was supposed to present in person. The letter began with the words: "Esteemed Colleague, this is the boy about whom we've spoken . . ."

The principal of the gymnasium gazed at me with a none-too-fond expression, handed me a paper, and said, "I hope that you'll be half as good as what I've been hearing about you."

The paper bore the date of the start of the term at the gymnasium, the kinds of textbooks needed, and an explicit description of the uniform to be worn.

Part Two

XVI

~~~~~

WHEN THE SUMMER vacation ended and the arched iron gates of the official gymnasium opened, the courtyard filled with the happy sound of students.

At the very entrance to the building stood a table where the students registered and at the same time selected their seats from a diagram hanging on the wall.

Romek and Sasha picked two adjoining seats on bench number six. They were among the first to register, and they had time for a quickly improvised game of soccer at the side of the courtyard.

When registration was over, the great bell hanging on a tripod in the corner began to toll. The students formed up in twos and marched off to the rhythm of the bell to their new classes where the aroma of the freshly whitewashed walls and newly lacquered benches lingered.

When Romek and Sasha came to their bench they found a youth in a brand-new, glistening uniform already seated there. Four question marks flashed like sharp sickles in the eyes of the two students.

"What's he doing here?"

"In our class?"

"On our bench?"

"Of all the damned gall."

"Dirty Jew!"

I drew myself up with military bearing and thrust out my chest with the gleaming brass buttons as if letting my uniform answer all the questions posed by the two pairs of piercing eyes. The uniform spoke its piece; we bowed to each other with assumed politeness and silently resumed our places.

A few minutes later, a group of teachers entered and lined up in a row against the wall and, soon afterward, a priest with a yellow beard and a thick braid down his neck came gravely striding in.

The students bowed their heads and listened to a long recitation of blessings and good wishes and, following a lusty rendition of "God Save the Tsar," the priest retreated toward the door, gesturing with three raised fingers from wall to wall and from ceiling to floor. Soon he backed all the way out of the room, followed by all the teachers except for the one who would give the first lecture.

The three students on bench number six fixed their blank faces on the teacher while mauling each other with invisible hands and silently haranguing:

"Are you the one we're after?"

"Is it you or isn't it?"

"And if it is, what of it?"

"By God, we'll heave you off the bench!"

"Try it!"

"Wait, maybe it's not him."

"Maybe it's someone else."

"Somehow his nose is more snub and the hair is combed differently."

"So how can we tell?"

"How can we find out?"

"You can't. I'm not here, it's only a uniform."

Bench number six trembled as if in a high fever. Still, when it came time to leave, the three of us rose and bowed with the same gallantry as before and quietly disbanded as if we had nothing further to say and no interest in getting to know each other better.

These formal bows in the mornings and afternoons continued for quite a while, but the silent, invisible war on the bench grew ever more brutal.

"By God, it's him! The American swindler!"

"He must pay with his blood."

"He insulted a defenseless woman. He deceived and seduced her."

"He should have his mask ripped off."

"He must be exposed."

"He should be stripped of the uniform and shown in all his nakedness."

"He should be dragged by his hair to Niura, so she can identify him and we can beat him to death."

"He's sly, he'll slip away."

"We must prepare a foolproof plan."

"Yes! A plan! A plan! A plan!"

Romek and Sasha crashed iron battleaxes against the armored

plate of my uniform, under which I lay constricted like a turtle and contemplated my own plan of battle. And before my foes could get together and decide which of their plans was better, I already had mine fashioned down to the smallest detail.

On a certain day when the students were getting ready to go home, I turned to my two benchmates and with exaggerated politeness said, "Gentlemen, I have a message for you," and, taking a bunch of green cards from my breast pocket, I gave two to each of them. Romek and Sasha fixed their eyes on the cards which read:

You are cordially invited to a concert to take place on
Sunday at 24 Boulevard of St. George.

A program of humor, magic, and music will be presented with
the participation of the world's greatest midget, Vaska Sibiriak,
and the greatest violin virtuoso, Paganini the Third.

Delicious refreshments will be served.

You are urged to bring along any member of your family

Admission is Free

Ladies admitted Free

They had probably never heard of Vaska Sibiriak, but the name Paganini did ring a bell. The main thing that struck their eyes, however, was the listed address. The house number was the same around which they had once wandered seeking Niura's vanished seducer, and they promptly accepted the invitation. What could be better than to corner the beast in its own lair?

Meanwhile I stood by the gate and distributed green cards to each of the departing students.

When Niura and the two bloodthirsty youths arrived quite late, they were met by my mother, who turned them over with pointed politeness to the maid, who was all dressed up in an embroidered, typically Russian dress and a garland of paper flowers on her head.

The maid led the three latecomers through the rowdy audience, which was already jammed to the rafters in the big room, and showed them to the places I had previously reserved for them.

Two-thirds of the room was taken up by long benches. The other third was occupied by the stage, which consisted of several doors laid on sawhorses and covered with two pretty blankets behind which, and off to the side, stood a phonograph with a big tin horn, playing a military air.

The moment I spotted Niura through a hole in the curtain, I shut off the phonograph and ran up to the mirror backstage to gaze for the last time at Vaska Sibiriak. The wide trousers and long black frockcoat with the high, stiff collar that swallowed the bottom half of my face, and the top hat that bit off the upper part of my head to the ears, gave me a very comical appearance. I gave the signal that the performance was about to begin and, presently, Vaska Sibiriak stepped out in front of the curtain.

Seeing Niura's face so close before me, I grew entranced and flustered and rushed to the main number of the first part of the program—the trick with the chicken and the egg. But I grew clumsy and lost control over the chicken: the frenzied bird tore loose of my fingers and flew out into the audience. The front rows sprang back, shrieking as if it had been a lion, not a chicken. The back rows ran to catch the bird, and a wild melee erupted. I promptly announced the intermission and at the top of my lungs enumerated all the delicious dishes waiting for them in the dining room.

Leaving the battered chicken hiding under a bench, the audience stampeded into the other room and like a pack of wild dogs vented the rage they felt against the chicken on the set table, which in minutes became a stained tablecloth strewn with empty plates and glasses.

I changed clothes in the greatest haste and, shrieking as if someone were holding a knife to my throat, begged the crowd to come back into the hall for the second half of the program. And before the unruly crowd could manage to sit down, the stage was already occupied by Paganini, wearing a wig of long black hair over a pale, powdered face and tragic, mascaraed eyes.

I announced the prelude, drew the bow briskly across the violin, and began to recite a poem describing the sad experiences and bitter misfortunes that befell the great musician during his visit to America, where he fell afoul of some "missus" of ugly mien and unhealthy passions . . .

And it happened that when he fled from America on a ship, it was attacked by pirates. In the desperate struggle, he used the only weapon at hand, his violin, as a club to smash the head of the vicious leader of the pirates, then leaped into the stormy sea . . . Here came another musical interlude, which described the maestro's struggle with the raging waves and his near demise.

How he subsequently saved himself wasn't clearly elaborated, but in the second half of the poem, Paganini already lay half drowned on a flowery bed on an island while a beautiful maiden sat beside him and used every conceivable means to bring him back to life . . . Another musical interlude and another surprise followed—for the girl, that dear and noble creature, turned out to be none other than the daughter of the bloodthirsty leader of the pirates.

For the first time, some people applauded.

I was certain that besides the three special guests no one in the room had the slightest inkling as to the symbolic allusions in the poem that suddenly silenced and enraptured them; rather it was the way in which Paganini captured the music that issued from the phonograph's large nickel horn and so cleverly incorporated it into a violin that didn't even have strings. But as if out of spite, some vicious demon brought the concert to a worse conclusion than I could have anticipated.

As I was nearly at the very climax of the poem, a senile, repulsive voice in the rear of the room shouted. "Bravo! Bravo! By God, the boy is an artist!"

The whole audience lunged forward like a rebellious mob rising to an insurrection and began to shout, "Bravo! Bravo!" Leaping over the benches as if over barricades, they stormed the stage, which soon buckled and crashed to the floor along with the phonograph.

Luckily, no one was hurt. But this final catastrophe was enough to make everyone clear out before anything worse happened.

The room was cleared, and I was left sitting in lonely despair behind the stage among the fallen boards and the crushed phonograph horn.

My face revolved in the mirror like a colored lantern, pale from fatigue and disappointment, red with shame, and green with rage. This was a blow I had never expected.

But soon the maid came up to me. "Two students and an older man want to speak to you."

I jumped up. "You mean two students and a girl?"

"No, two students and an older man."

"Yes, an older man," an echo resounded above the shattered stage. "Allow me to personally express my professional appreciation, young man. My name is Nazarov, a former actor of no small reputation, and let me tell you that I'm simply enraptured! My two friends and I waited for the audience to leave so that we could thank you for the great pleasure you've given us."

The man speaking had gray hair and a long, sweaty, pleated jaw like an old worn shoe. Next to him stood two students I didn't know, with lips stained by the chocolate ice cream on which they had been gorging themselves.

I quickly scrambled over the fallen boards, excused myself for a moment, dashed through the hall to the dining room, and from there raced down the steps leading to the street. But there was no one there.

Biting my lips in frustration, I came back into the house and ran up to the old man. "Was it you who shouted 'bravo' and ruined the whole concert? Why did you do that? Who brought you here? Were you put up to this by Voktuzen and Zavatski? Why did you do it, you horrible old man?"

"Calm yourself," Nazarov said, all the muscles in his face trembling. "The names you've mentioned mean nothing to me. I assure you that my outcry was provoked by genuine admiration. I have no words with which to express my revulsion at the vulgar undisciplined behavior of your colleagues. I'm even tempted to write a personal letter about it to the principal of the gymnasium—"

"Don't you dare do that. That's none of your business!" I exclaimed.

"On the contrary, it's *indeed* my business. I am an artist too, and I know how you feel. But this shouldn't concern you because it was all extraordinary, excellent . . ." And, seizing my hand, he kissed it fervently.

I grew ashamed and, wiping the saliva off my hand, I asked, "What actually do you want of me?"

"You would do us a great kindness by accepting our invitation to a fine restaurant."

"Thanks, but I don't believe my mother would—"

"Oh, if need be, we'll appeal to your mother."

"That won't be necessary," I said and, after brief deliberation, added, "All right . . . Wait till I wash up and put on my uniform."

When we came out on the boulevard, Nazarov took me by the arm and let the two boys, Petya and Volodya, trail along behind. He hailed a cab and told the driver, "The Eldorado."

Throughout the ride and even in the restaurant Nazarov didn't stop complimenting me, especially for the final number on the program, concluding each compliment with a tremulous, tearful, "An artist, by God, a true artist!"

The more he recalled the various nuances and temperamental variations of the recitation, the more his enthusiasm soared—until he could no longer contain himself and again seized my hand and gave it a long kiss with his trembling slobbery lips.

I grimaced with revulsion, but this didn't faze Nazarov and, stroking my hand, he went on. "You're tired and exhausted, aren't you, my dear? Who better than I who cut his teeth on the stage knows how a true artist feels after such a performance—after a moment of such creative exhilaration?"

I hung my head in embarrassment, and Nazarov seized the opportunity to grab my head in both hands and kiss it wildly.

"That's enough!" I cried. I pulled away and nervously rearranged my disheveled hair.

"No, not enough," he protested. "There isn't a thing in the world I wouldn't do for an artist! There's no more important duty or greater pleasure than helping a young artist . . . Isn't that so?" he asked, turning to Petya and Volodya. The two students smiled in fatuous agreement.

By that time, a waiter in a red frockcoat had brought a big brown fish with two large human eyes, garnished with a garland of paper flowers. A second waiter in a black frockcoat brought a bottle of wine wrapped in a basket. I announced in a firm voice that this was my first time in a restaurant and that I didn't drink wine. The two boys promptly admitted that they didn't drink either, but the old connoisseur revealed a few yellow fangs in a smile and observed, "I'm against drunkenness too, which is only too common among the current generation of actors. It's true that you're still young, but you're old enough to know that a banquet without wine is like a violin without strings. It doesn't play, but you made it play. That's where your talent lies. But why did you bring wine when I ordered champagne?" he asked the waiter in the black coat.

Soon, the red-coated waiter put four quarters of a goose doused in a thick brown gravy on the table and garnished it with a whole garden of yellow potatoes, green peas, and red carrots. Later he brought big saucers of applesauce and, finally, Turkish coffee.

Throughout the meal Nazarov didn't cease describing the deep impact I had made upon him. He spoke with tireless enthusiasm, gesticulated, and drowned out the mandolin orchestra, the gypsy chorus, and the dancing couples in the room.

When the meal was over and we left the restaurant, Nazarov again took my arm and hired a droshky with two horses for a two-hour ride outside the city.

He didn't stop raving with the same emotional fervor, but the loud hoofbeats on the sandy highway, the quiet rustle of the cool breeze among the trees, and especially the rocking of the carriage finally lulled him to sleep. He babbled a few more words and gradually dozed off. But before dropping off completely, he muttered, "An artist . . . by God, a true artist . . ." and managed to plant a last kiss on my ear.

XVII

~~~

THE FOLLOWING DAY, when I came to the gymnasium, I was surrounded at the gate by several students. One pressed my hand firmly
and shook it, a second gave me a good-natured shove into a third,
who—trying to stop my fall—tore a button off my uniform. I responded to this somewhat emotional reception with a mute smile
and walked quickly into the classroom.

As usual, I was the first to bow "good morning" to my two
benchmates. They sat with heads bowed, picking at their fingernails,
and didn't respond. I looked at them for a moment, then addressed
them in my mind: Well, stand up. Now you know who I am. That
was me who stole your sister's love. So you know what you can do
about it, you cowards. Yesterday after the concert you ran away.

I bowed to them again with calculated reserve and whispered.
"Why did you run away?"

They looked up at me with glazed eyes.

"Excuse me if I alarmed you, but I'm very much interested in your
opinion of yesterday's concert."

Romek fixed me with an icy stare. "What concert?"

"Paganini's concert."

"Which Paganini?"

"Paganini the Third."

"Never heard of him."

"Excuse me . . . weren't you at the concert yesterday?"

"Don't you understand Russian?" Romek exclaimed angrily and
let Sasha conclude. "If we tell you we weren't there, we weren't
there."

"You mean . . . I don't understand. I gave you an invitation, and it
seemed to me—"

"We threw the invitation away. We didn't hear the concert. Be so
good as to stop annoying us." And they both grew absorbed again
in their nails.

"You mean to say that you weren't at Twenty-four Boulevard of St. George yesterday?"

"We don't know what concert you're talking about," Romek hissed, jumping up from the bench with indignation.

"We weren't there!" Sasha said.

"Then who was that with your sister on the left side of the audience?" I suddenly felt myself losing the assurance in my voice.

"What sister? I have no sister," he replied with a perverse, irritating smile. "You dreamed the whole thing up."

"You mean to say Niura isn't your sister?"

"No."

"You don't live on Pilna Street?"

"No."

"Wasn't I at your house once?"

"No."

"Didn't you go looking for me once?"

"No . . . what kind of dumb stunt is that anyway?" Romek said and they both displayed white, triumphant teeth.

Even earlier that morning on the way to school I had been tormented by a bothersome premonition about the upcoming encounter with my two archenemies. I had weighed every kind of possibility and tried to guess the manner in which they would greet me.

I expected them to grab me the minute I showed up, take me out to a corner of the yard, slap me once or twice, and that would be that. I was fully prepared to accept this punishment, because if this was the only way to once and for all end this long, drawn-out, painful, silent war on the school bench and, above all, to come back to Niura, what did a few slaps mean? I had even stopped on the street a few times and tried to assume the attitude of true forbearance with which I would react to their blows. But that they would completely deny having seen the performance, that those for whom I had arranged the concert would not even have been there . . .

The walls began to reel as if made of calf's-foot jelly, and the students trembled like shadows on water. I dashed from the room and, straining to control my hand, rapped on the principal's door. Under the pretext that the direct light from the window was too strong for my sensitive eyes, I asked permission to change my seat to a back bench where there happened to be an empty seat.

When the lessons were over, I quickly gathered up my books and was the first out of the room. I stood at the side of the gate waiting for the students of the fourth class to come out, and when I saw Petya and Volodya, I ran up to them as if we were the closest of friends.

The day before, in the restaurant, I had completely ignored them—nor had I said a word to them in the droshky—so my sudden friendliness was probably a puzzle to them. Still, it must have been a pleasant surprise, for they promptly invited me to join them for butter cookies and hot chocolate. I seized upon this as if I were starving. Petya hailed a droshky and ordered the driver to take us to the Café Bon Bon.

This café was famous for its outstanding pastry, torts, and cakes, and particularly for its rich ice cream. Besides, it had a back room with the largest billiard parlor in town and a special card room where an intense game went on without interruption day and night. The Café Bon Bon was the gathering place for the rich ne'er-do-wells, the so-called golden youth of the city. Its high walls and round ceiling were decorated with large, colorful murals. On one wall, a naked fleshy woman reclined in a bed clutching at the loincloth of a fleeing, frightened youth. On the other wall, an emaciated, headless figure lay sprawled on the stone floor while an attractive woman with a sword and wild, cunning eyes stood alongside, staring at the bloody head she held on a silver platter.

Petya and Volodya noted the deep interest that these pictures evoked in me, and they explained their meaning with the importance and the familiarity of old and seasoned habitués.

After we had finished the hot chocolate and butter cookies, Petya ordered double portions of ice cream, a syphon of soda water with special lemon syrup, and, on top of all that, three extra dishes of cherry jam.

During the whole time, the two boys tried to amuse their new friend with suggestive observations about the other patrons, about the paintings on the wall, and particularly about their own extravagant gluttony. But when it came time for the jam, I hiccuped, pushed the dish away, and said, "That's enough." And with unexpected gravity I leaned over the table and asked, "You're in the fourth class, aren't you?"

Petya stopped laughing.

"Why?" Volodya put down his spoon.

"Because I'd like to know if you know a Sasha Voktuzen in the fifth class."

"No."

"And Romek Zavatski?"

"Him neither."

"Did you happen to notice two students and a girl sitting on the left side of the room during yesterday's performance?"

"We don't know which two you mean."

"Two who looked like this and this . . ." I quickly described the height, width, and coloring of Voktuzen and Zavatski.

Both boys thought it over a moment.

"I can't say for sure."

"It seems to me that there wasn't anyone like that there."

"For God's sake, don't say that it *seems* so!" I said, seizing their hands in agitation. "Think harder."

"We did see two students in the audience, but it seems they looked somewhat different, not as mean and snotty as you describe them."

"Try to remember. Two students with a girl . . . Yes, a girl." And I began to describe Niura.

For the first time I grew tongue-tied, as if unsure myself of the size and coloring of the person whom I had seen at full length only once in my life, and long ago at that. But soon, a fountain of words began to erupt from me as I described a sleeping princess, a lonely Cinderella, an Arabian beauty in *A Thousand and One Nights*.

The two boys sat with mouths agape. Now they were positive that such a girl hadn't been in the audience.

"That's a lie! You're just as big liars as they!" I shrieked in wild rage and slammed the table.

"Why do you call us liars?" the befuddled boys wondered.

I drank up the remaining soda water and, somewhat calmer now, said, "Forgive my temper, but it took nearly half a year to prepare for this concert and now if what you say is true, then the whole thing was a total bust and I really am what they say—a dreamer and an idiot."

"We aren't liars, it's you who are the liar. There was no girl such as you describe. And why do you use such flowery terms and such fancy words? And why such a fuss about a concert when you can't even hold a violin in your hands?"

"Volodya and I," Petya took over, "came to the concert, as you call it, because we found a few green cards on the school steps. Knowing that our old friend Nazarov is a former actor, we showed him the cards, and it was more because of him than because of our own interest that we came. Nazarov says that you're an artist. Maybe you are, we don't understand much about such things—"

"Why are you making such a fuss about some Paganini the Third?" Volodya picked up again where he had been interrupted. "You gave out free tickets. You didn't make any money out of this. And who is this Niura anyway? Don't get mad, but the way you describe her I'm not sure that you yourself know such a person. Tell the truth—did you ever see her? Did you ever speak with her? Or did you just make her up like your stupid poem about the pirates?"

For a while I sat there crushed, then I clutched both their hands on the table and said, "I like you guys! You're right . . . I only want you to believe that everything I told you, even the poem about the pirates, wasn't something I made up. Maybe I didn't tell it well. There are people who can lie so neatly, plainly, and simply that it sounds as if they are really speaking the honest-to-God truth. As for me, I can't free myself of the damned weakness of speaking the simplest truths in such a way that they sound like the greatest lies. Maybe it's all because I'm a lampedusser."

The last word of my confession evoked no reaction at all.

"I'm a lampedusser," I reiterated.

"So what? We're lampedussers too. We're all lampedussers. Here's another lampedusser." They pointed to a person passing by.

"How can you say that? Do you know then what 'lampedusser' means?"

"Of course, we know. Lampedusser is the same as piladusser, rakedusser, shmatgedusser, and kockedusser."

I gripped the edge of the table. They proposed that we forget the whole stupid conversation and renew our friendship over a fresh portion of ice cream.

"Tomorrow, tomorrow . . ." I stammered and begged their pardon. I couldn't return their graciousness in the same generous fashion, since my father lay deathly ill in a clinic in Germany and the weekly allowance I received from my mother was very modest, and I could rehabilitate myself only by inviting them for tea and rolls at the Turk's.

It seemed that this simple confession made more of an impression on them than my passionate exposition of pirates in uniform. They each offered to lend me a few rubles. I quickly and categorically refused, but when we met after school the next day and I proposed to take them to the Turk's, they persuaded me to go back to the Bon Bon again, where they reordered the same delicacies in the same sequence as the day before.

After the jam, Petya asked if I played lotto, if I smoked, if I was interested in cards, and if I would care to accompany them to the card room and risk a few rubles at twenty-one. I hesitated a moment. I hadn't touched a card in three or four years, although I had once been famous in the old marketplace as a whiz at twenty-one.

"They won't let us near the table, we're not old enough," I warned them.

"They know us here already. We've lost a good bit of money," Petya boasted, taking a pile of silver out of his pocket. "Come, come, you'll draw the cards!" And, pushing me ahead, they steered me into the card room.

We squeezed through the crowd around the cardtable. Petya put down a whole five rubles—until I yelled, "Banco!" and lost, and within five or ten minutes they were already down fifteen rubles. Still, for the next few days they insisted I keep drawing the cards.

Between the snacks and the card playing, the two boys continued their daily efforts to reform me and demanded that I stop bothering them with stories about some Niura, who was "nothing more than an Indian spirit coming out of a bottle." A few times I rebelled. Although they had already obliged me by a lot of cake and tarts and jam and I had squandered a considerable amount of their money at the cardtable, I still tried to stand up to them. After all, I was a student in the fifth class and they were only in the fourth. But they would stop me and demand that I speak plainly and to the point, so that they could understand me better. And when I tried to speak the way they asked, I had to shut right up since I didn't remember what it was I wanted to say.

One day after I already had more than sixty or eighty lost rubles on my conscience and the two friends began to drag me once more to the Bon Bon, I refused to go on the pretext that too many sweets upset my stomach. Volodya proposed that the three of us should go to his house instead and play lotto.

Volodya's father—a bald-headed bureaucrat in a worn uniform—

greeted me in military fashion, laid his finger on his forehead, and clicked the heels of his battered shoes. I examined the small rooms with the faded wallpaper, on which could be clearly seen the stains of crushed bedbugs, and studied the moth-eaten velvet draperies on the windows and the old-fashioned, creaking chairs. The bald-headed bureaucrat apologized—the mistress of the house was unfortunately out and he could, therefore, offer me nothing but tea without sugar, since the lady of the house kept it locked in the cupboard and always carried the keys with her.

A day later, Petya contended that it was his turn to invite me to his house. He opened the door, and a nauseating stench of cooking cabbage assailed my nostrils.

The father—a broad, husky man with a stern upturned mustache, wearing a train conductor's tunic with a red string around his neck from which dangled his professional whistle—promptly apologized for the fact that there was nothing in the house to offer me except a few green apples that he actually brought to the table.

I sat down in a wicker rocking chair and, choosing the smallest apple from the bowl, began to chew.

The conductor sat down alongside me and began to tell me about his experiences on the long trips that he made twice weekly and about the various interesting people he met, including some spicy anecdotes he had heard in the men's room about Jewish traveling salesmen.

I sat rigidly in the chair and gnawed the raw green apple. Suddenly I felt a terrible pain in my intestines. The day before yesterday I had feigned an upset stomach to get out of going to the Café Bon Bon, but now I actually felt my guts rising up to my mouth and drops of cold sweat broke out on my upper lip.

The pain that slashed along the length of my body didn't stem from my stomach but from a sudden resentment against my two friends who had so grievously insulted and deceived me. Who was this conductor boring me to tears? And who were my two friends in whose impoverished homes all you could get was bitter tea and a raw apple, while at the same time they indulged themselves with double portions of ice cream at the Café Bon Bon?

And if I hadn't pulled them away from the cardtable, they were ready to lose even more than eighty or a hundred rubles . . . A woman who kept sugar under lock and key surely wouldn't treat a son to licorice jam at the Café Bon Bon, where a glass of plain water cost more than a whole samovar of tea in her house. Where in heaven's name did these two penniless boys lay their hands on the piles of silver that they slung around with such abandon, as if their parents were bankers or big industrialists? What kind of secret were they concealing from me? I would have sworn that this conductor with the frayed elbows had never seen a hundred rubles at one time in his whole life. What kind of a strange, mysterious business was this?

I looked with pointed suspicion and contempt at my two friends, who calmly fumbled in the corner trying to fix the old-fashioned wall clock.

Dozens of gnawing question marks began to skim through my brain: Who are you? Did I really come to you so that you would draw me out of a dream? Was it for you two slobs that I unbuttoned my uniform and shook out my deepest secrets while you poisoned me with double portions of ice cream, stuffed my mouth with jam, and even robbed me of my nickname "lampedusser," my identity, my whole self, and transformed me into a straw figure in a uniform?

How dared they teach me to use simple words when their own plain talk concealed a lie that was a thousand times bigger than my vision. How dared they tear the tender web of my dream with their filthy fingers when they themselves lay entangled in a dark web of sordid mystery? And even if it was only my dream that Niura had come to the concert, I wanted to remain in this dream because, who knows—maybe my honest dream was the reality, while their cunning reality was a nightmare.

I stood up, wiped the sweat off my brow, and started edging toward the door, but Petya and Volodya dragged me back into the room. I looked at them for a moment and opened my mouth to blast them with the monologue I had so clearly prepared in my mind, but the fear that they wouldn't understand me and would again order me to speak plainly and simply sealed my lips, and I barely managed to mumble: "I can't . . . stay. The stomach . . . is churning. Churning . . ."

The conductor quickly brought me a glass of salted water and told me to make a hearty belch, then sat me down again in the broken rocking chair and began to regale me with a fresh anecdote about a "scurfy zhid."

A few weeks later when I again met my two friends at the gate of the gymnasium, I led them off to the side and said, "So that every-thing should be straight between us, I'll ask you for the last time. Do you believe that a dream can ever congeal into concrete form and become as real as a cardtable, a piece of butter cake, or a double por-tion of ice cream?"

"What? What dream, what butter cake . . . ? What are you talking about?" they mumbled.

Instead of answering, I took a letter out of my breast pocket with a trembling hand and began to read:

Most Esteemed Paganini the Third!
    I heard you at the concert on Sunday.
    I recognized you immediately.
    I was simply enchanted by your playing and reciting.
    My escorts were in a hurry to catch a train.
    I don't know if you are aware that we moved out of Pilna Street and that we now live in the suburbs, which take a whole hour to reach, that's why I couldn't come backstage to congratulate you.
    You are the first person I'm inviting to my birthday party. I would be happy to see you and particularly to again hear your splendid recitation.
    I beg you not to disappoint me as you did once before.

Yours,
Niura Voktuzen

XVIII

༼ၿၿ༽

BENJAMIN CAME BACK with the same suitcase and the same few sets of underwear he had left with for Germany. He brought back everything—his illness included. The only thing he didn't bring back were his bankbooks.

He had squandered a fortune on a whole army of famous German specialists, clinics, hospitals, and spas—and the result of it all was that on the second day after his return he suffered a fresh attack that was even stronger than any of the previous ones.

The local doctors came again and availed themselves of all the old methods, but by now it was already obvious to everyone—most of all to the patient himself—that nothing would help him anymore and that the next day or the day after that he would surely choke to death. The stricken bruiser who until the time of his illness hadn't experienced so much as a toothache now suffered not only from the pain but even more so from the fear and vexation. To feel so choked and shattered from a pair of insignificant lungs, when until a short time ago he hadn't even known on which side of his body they were located, left him wildly furious and resentful. He slammed the table in his bitterness and cursed all the doctors and specialists who had taken his "millions" and, instead of curing him, left him on the verge of death. With every cough he spat out his anger at the medical profession with all its specialists and famous professors. He forbade the local doctors to come into his house and "practice their barbering on his beard."

Relatives, friends, and acquaintances from the old marketplace, particularly those who had always enjoyed his benevolence, came to comfort him and to advise him not to drive the doctors away even though they were ignorant quacks, for even if they knew nothing, they would keep trying until they finally came up with the right thing to do. But the patient responded to each effort to calm him with a choice epithet dripping with sarcasm and directed at those who lived off his charity . . . and at the doctors who milked him for his money, and at himself for wasting his fortune.

The proud paupers from the old marketplace resented the insult! His sickness was given by God as had his money been taken by God, for wasn't it written that God giveth and God taketh away? To this the irritated patient replied that he had no quarrel with God, since the list of those who had taken his money included no such name, and that it was sheer abomination to make up sayings in His name and to attribute to Him such a vulgar canard as "Charity delivereth from death" in order to wheedle money out of a doomed benefactor.

Singly and in chorus they strove to convince him that they were ready to give him their own lungs if that were possible, but Benjamin remained adamant, for the facts were clearly on his side.

If the patient's bitterness had no bearing on his physical condition, it radically altered his spiritual state. He suddenly grew loquacious and began to use words and express ideas that as far as the market people could recall he had never uttered before.

It seemed as if he had grown somehow exalted by the illness, as if in place of his clogged lungs there had suddenly opened within him a source of remarkable wisdom. He began talking as if with a borrowed tongue, like Balaam's ass when it saw the knife blade at its throat.

At first his friends came to see him out of duty, but presently they came to provoke him into a conversation since they were no longer as interested in his health as in what he had to say about his illness, about himself, about the world, and even about God.

They had known him when he was still a young fellow, a poor cap maker. They used to call him Handsome Benjamchik. Almost every market person had a nickname, but most were as fitting as a fifth wheel on a wagon. For instance, Pinie, who was lively, spirited, and agile, was called "the Turtle," while Haim, a tiny fellow with a button nose, was called "the Elephant." But Benjamin was really handsome, far too good-looking to be a simple cap maker. Sitting around their stoves on winter evenings, they had speculated as to whether he wouldn't be better suited to be a banker or a millionaire. But that the millionaire should suddenly lose his millions and turn into a sage just like old Job, who was also a simple middle-class man who, thanks to his horrible afflictions, became a world-famous sage—this was intriguing, this merited a closer look, this justified getting into a discussion or even a debate about higher matters with that new fellow "Job."

Sarah would place a large bowl of cooked chickpeas on the table (a snack befitting a broke millionaire) and, chewing the chickpeas, the market people tried to convince the sage that he wasn't completely right. But the sage used his biting scorn like an ax to hack away at the polemicists so that they could only shrug and admit that although he didn't let them conclude their thoughts and finish what they had to say, he was nevertheless right.

The only thing that stood in his way was his constant coughing. Some of his opponents would take advantage of this and, the moment the patient stopped in mid-argument to catch his breath, they would jump in and present their views. The patient would wave his hands for them to wait for his rebuttal, but the opponents used this opportunity to outshout the cougher. The moment he regained his breath, he would fix them with his bloodshot eyes and angrily say, "We won't settle anything this way. We're not fighting on equal terms. Go and catch asthma first, then come to me as equal to equal and we'll finish the discussion."

Although the visitors didn't take this proposal too seriously, it put an end to the discussions.

The incessant coughing burst the patient's eardrums and subjected him to a new source of intolerable anguish. It was difficult enough for him to speak, and now it became painful for him to hear as well. His only source of comfort, the discussions, had to be abandoned.

Only one person was still welcome in the house and treated with a measure of patience and tolerance by the invalid, and that was Barve's Son.

Whether this was because this gentle soul was himself a victim of consumption and thus an equal, or whatever the reason, he was the only individual permitted to come to the bedside of the lonely and condemned man and talk without interruption.

In the last years, the historian had changed almost beyond recognition. He was lean as a spider, with sunken cheeks overgrown with the curly moss of a worn brush; the only things left him from the past were the bland, velvety voice and the eyes that still glowed with the reflection of the burning braziers around which he had once lectured the market people on world affairs.

Although Barve's Son had in his time also partaken of the millionaire's bounty, he never tried to deceive his benefactor with extravagant promises from the holy books, and he richly earned whatever money he accepted.

Even while Benjamin was still living on Market Street, it would often happen that on a cloudy Sabbath or holiday he would lean out his window and hiss up to an attic window in the building across the way, where the tousled head of the educated young man would promptly appear.

"Tell me," Benjamin would speculate, "why is it hot in summer and cold in winter? Is it that the sun is closer to Earth in summer and farther away in winter?"

"Just the opposite," the scholar would shout down. "The sun is farther away in summer and closer in winter."

"How can that be?"

"That's how it is."

"Can you explain it?"

"Of course, but it's too complicated for you."

"It doesn't make any sense to me."

"The world isn't made according to your reason. If you want, I'll come down and try to explain it to you."

"If you say it's that way, that's how it probably is."

"Not probably, but certainly. In summer it's farther, in winter it's closer. And don't ask any questions." And the head would vanish under the roof.

Benjamin would stare up toward the attic room for a long while with the greatest delight, then take a ruble from his pocket and send me with it up to Barve's Son since it was no secret that the educated youth froze and starved there under the sloping roof.

Thus, Father could hold no resentment against Barve's Son. First of all, Barve's Son always was and had remained an enemy of millionaires and had always contended that money was the curse of the world. In his view, the fact that Benjamin had now been left a complete pauper was only just and proper. Besides, he scoffed at God and at the holy books. He felt that the saying "Charity delivereth from death" was an old wive's tale thought up not by the paupers but actually by the millionaires themselves, who didn't want to die. Even Napoleon, who was nothing but a piece of matter that had destroyed six million other pieces of matter, had to die.

His eyes closed, his head hanging low on his heaving breast, the patient listened to the soft, velvety voice drawing a parallel between the end of the great emperor and that of an ailing furrier.

A pleased smile would crease his swollen face, as if he were accepting this comforting prospect with joyful resignation—to disintegrate as a piece of matter, like a second Napoleon . . .

He looked down at his big body as if seeing it for the first time and wondered: had he been smaller and leaner, he would probably have it easier now—the more body, the more matter, and the more matter, the more death.

If he were a worm, he surely couldn't cough so hard, so painfully, and he wouldn't need so much air to fill such a big reservoir as his chest. He even envied a worm momentarily. What more did man know about the secret of death than a worm knew?

At the same time, he reminded himself that years ago he had had a rare opportunity, one that comes along perhaps once in a thousand years, to discover the secret of all secrets—death.

Serving in the army deep inside Russia, he had befriended a young man in his regiment, a yeshiva student who out of grief and pain over having his earlocks trimmed and being forced to eat nonkosher food had contracted consumption and within a short time expired. Benjamin felt guilty since it had been he who with a large shears had trimmed off the earlocks that the fanatical youth had tried to hide behind his ears.

What was even worse was that one time, seeing the youth twisting with hunger pains and still refusing to touch the bowl of *tref* food, Benjamin, more out of fun than malice, had sneaked up behind the youth and smeared a piece of greasy pork across his lips. The youth had actually licked his lips with great relish, but a while later he had vomited green bile. The other soldiers, Benjamin among them, had been convulsed with laughter but, when the youth died shortly afterward, Benjamin felt deeply disturbed.

Several weeks later, Benjamin was standing guard on a cold, rainy night outside the barracks. Suddenly, he felt someone pull his mustache from behind and, when he looked around, he saw the yeshiva student dressed in a shroud.

"How are you, Benjamchik?" the corpse asked with a smile. But instead of answering, the terrified soldier began to shriek for the dead man to leave or else he would shoot him.

The yeshiva student didn't move, and Benjamin fired at him.

He didn't know what happened to the ghost because he fainted, and when he came to, he was surrounded by a group of soldiers who rocked with scornful laughter that such a big, healthy bruiser should be frightened by a corpse. The sergeant scolded him for wasting bullets on ghosts and put him on bread and water for a whole twenty-four hours.

Sitting there on the stone floor of the guardhouse, he shook off the whole incident and forgot it completely, but now in his downy bed, it implanted itself with strange clarity in his memory and evoked dreadful pangs of regret that he had been so foolish and thoughtless as to drive away the gentle youth, thus losing an opportunity to learn something about death and about the other world that surely existed—since where else could the dead student have come from?

He could find no justification for his stupid and brutal behavior toward his pious comrade. True, he had shot at a ghost, but the question then arose, why hadn't it shown up again? The answer could only be that he had actually killed it. That meant that after the youth had died a natural death he had still remained in some form resembling life, but after he had been shot he had been transported out of this world and out of the other world as well. Dead as man, and destroyed as matter.

This strange speculation spread through his ailing body with a seething sensation of inexcusable sin and guilt. But at the same time a kind of odd, trembling joy fluttered beneath his heart.

He leaped out of bed, ran into my bedroom, woke me, and told me to fetch Barve's Son that minute.

When the sleepy scholar appeared in the doorway, Benjamin put his arm around him and, instead of taking him into the room, said right there on the threshold, "A few days ago, you told me about the death of Napoleon. But you haven't told me anything about what happened to him after he died!"

Frightened and dazed, Barve's Son began to rub his sleepy eyes and, in a raspy tone, as if all the velvet in his voice had been rubbed away, said, "Nothing . . . Napoleon's history ends at the moment of his death. What does history have to do with a corpse? History only deals with living things, history has no interest in the dead."

"But don't you know that I'm already more dead than alive myself, and the history of a dead Napoleon is more important to me than that of a living one?"

"I know nothing about the dead Napoleon," the scholar blurted out in confusion.

"If that is so, then here's the final ruble for all your troubles and don't come here anymore!" And stuffing the banknote into the hands of the bewildered historian, he shoved him outside and slammed the door soundly behind him.

With this, the patient knew that he was saying farewell to the living world. Now he knew that there was no one left who could either help him in life or inform him about death. Now he was left completely isolated, estranged, dangling somewhere in limbo between life and death.

Having driven off the living and murdered the dead, he strayed through the large apartment in a darkness that was darker than night.

Thus, roaming from room to room, he wandered into the small side room seldom visited after Grandfather Moshe and Grandmother Liba Number One had died. Their beds still stood in the same place, as did the prayerbooks, psalm books, and Gemaras grown worn and spotted from snuff, also the prayer shawl, phylacteries, Liba's Sabbath candlesticks, her Yiddish Pentateuch and prayerbook stained by dried tears—all left untouched in their places. Even the windows were draped as they had been on the day of their deaths. It was as if the two old people had gone on a vacation and had left death lying in their beds, waiting for them.

For a moment, Benjamin had the sensation of seeing and feeling the still darkness and velvet softness of death. For a moment he stood poised, afraid to take a step, to move and shatter the peaceful, mysterious stillness and tear the delicate, shadowy web that enveloped the room.

He strained with all his might not to trigger the raspy grating in his torn, tired throat and cough so as not to disturb the somnolent and caressing aroma of the ancient volumes.

He paused for a long while motionless on the threshold, then slowly, carefully shuffled over to the edge of Moshe's bed and sat down in a waiting position as if almost certain that at any moment now the two old people would step out of the misty darkness and ask him, "How are you, Benjamchik?" But by now he knew that he would no longer be the fool he had been. He wouldn't shoot and drive them away. Now he would sit there calmly, listen and answer, and if necessary even follow them, for if he was already fated to go to his death, what better company could there be than these two gentle souls to whom death was an old story? Why hadn't it occurred to him during his long and arduous travail that right here ten, twenty paces from his room was a doorway to a world about which history had nothing to say and about which one would learn only through personal contact?

How was it possible that he should think so much about that former yeshiva student and never remind himself of these two dear people? Maybe this was because in life they had been nothing more than a poor, sick father-in-law and mother-in-law? And who loved a mother-in-law, even a healthy one? And what possible interest could he have had in a father-in-law whose thoughts were always more in the other world than in this? Maybe this was the reason he had known them so little and had so quickly and totally forgotten them.

And just as he had cursed himself for having murdered the dead yeshiva student before, he now began to curse himself for so carelessly and frivolously destroying the memory of the two such fine, tender souls.

Man dies twice. Once when he leaves the living and the second time when the living forget him. If all that remained of Napoleon was his history, it meant that all that was needed to destroy him completely was to forget his history. To forget the history of those two people meant to erase them completely, to root out even the last particles into which they had shattered.

With this fresh sin on his conscience, he stretched out on Moshe's bed and with his waning willpower resolved that if he could no longer do anything about the yeshiva student, he might still rescue his last two victims and thus cleanse himself of a guilt that had now planted itself like a fresh stone upon his sick lungs.

He closed his eyes and let himself be enveloped by the warm, soothing darkness. He soon sank into the depth of his memory, where he began to gather up the bits and pieces of past events in order to reassemble Grandmother Liba Number One and her husband, Moshe, who had lived so humbly, suffered so patiently, and expired so silently.

He lay in bed with a smile like that of a child who has been roused from a deep sleep and sees its mother standing over its crib with her arms outstretched like an eagle over a nest. For the first time in months he drew an easy, deep breath as streams of air began to course in and out of his trembling body. He grew alarmed and began to cry.

What had happened? What had he done? Had he crawled inside himself and with his own hands torn open the clamped doors of his lungs? How was this possible?

This was and remained a secret to everyone, especially to the invalid. It was one of those miracles. From that afternoon on, from the moment he stretched out on Moshe's bed, Benjamin ceased to cough, began to breathe, and commenced to live.

Next morning my mother summoned me with a silent gesture and in a trembling voice asked, "Do you hear something?"

I shook my head in perplexity. "No."

"What can it be? What can this strange silence mean?"

Holding hands, we tiptoed into Father's room, but he wasn't there. Nor was there anyone in the third or fourth rooms.

Where was he? Had he jumped in his despair out of one of the windows?

Sarah was ready to scream for help when I stopped her. I had heard a rustle from behind the door that we hadn't even thought to open.

With the greatest care we parted the door a crack and peered inside. In the corner stood a large figure wrapped in Moshe's prayer shawl and phylacteries, swaying quietly.

XIX

~~~

WALKING DOWN the boulevard with my books under my arm and
Niura's letter in my breast pocket, I looked around to see if anyone
was watching, then stopped to rehearse again the words and manner
with which I would greet her at her birthday party a month and a
half hence.

My imagination, over which I had never had much control, seized
me now and, riding a streak of lightning, bore me to the front of
Niura's new house.

Through the high windows came the sound of gay, laughing
voices. Waltzing shadows were circling across the drawn draperies.
It was clear that the party was already in full swing.

Among the waltzing shadows, I recognized people whose por-
traits I had once seen in Niura's house on Pilna Street, the same
proud, erect generals, the same bristly, side-whiskered barons.

I edged toward the stairs and rechecked my freshly polished shoes
and the newly shined buttons on my uniform, patted my stiffly
combed hair with the sharp side part, then pulled the doorbell,
which rang with the long, deafening peal of a great church bell on a
Christian holiday.

The laughter ceased, the music stopped, and the door opened to
total silence. Niura stood on the threshold.

Behind her, cheek to jowl, crowded the generals with their bemedaled chests out and the barons with the red, green, and violet
sashes across their starched shirt fronts. They peered with bated
breath at the tardy guest who, as it was known, had been the first to
be invited to the affair.

I bowed, and when Niura held out her hand to me, I serenaded
her birthday with several of my homemade rhymes. She came up
very close and thanked me heartily, and when I tried to take this
opportunity to whisper something in her ear, she winked at me as if
to imply that it wasn't necessary, that she knew all about it and

understood everything. At the same time she took my arm and escorted me through the hall to where a sturdy stage had already been set up with a plush curtain in front . . . I quickly jumped up onto the stage and, without any ado, recited the poem "Paganini the Third."

From all sides, with enthusiastic hands, people clutched at me, but Niura ordered everyone off to the side and taking my arm again led me up and introduced me to her honored father and aristocratic mother. Then, avoiding her brother Sasha and his bosom friend Romek, who like the other guests stood watching with greatest respect, she took me to the very center of the hall and swung me into a dance . . . Well, my mastery of the violin and of recitation had already been acknowledged and lauded by experts, but as to dancing? I had never had any experience at this, and I had to be careful since it would have been an unforgivable error to allow the dance to mar the success I had achieved in the first fifteen minutes.

That's why it was so fortunate that I could practice now on the hard cobblestones of the boulevard the dance that I would eventually perform on the gleaming parquet in Niura's house . . .

And so, whirling and twirling my feet, I danced into my house. I had barely managed to put down my books when my mother whispered into my ear that my father wished me to come to his room, and I went right in.

He spoke with the facility and ease of a completely healthy person. He opened with an apology that he didn't know how to begin, since a person had to at least know to *whom* he was speaking in order to know *how* to speak.

"For me, it's never been clear who you are," he said. "At times, I was under the impression that you're too old and too serious for your age. Other times, I watched you jump over your own shadow like a small child. I have actually wanted to talk to you many times before, but I simply didn't know how . . . My parents never gave me an education. I was already working a full day when I was a boy, and I earned a reputation as a first-class cutter of women's furs. I managed with my own hands to save up a whole ten thousand rubles. And though the poor market people in their gratitude greatly overestimated my worth and dressed me in the frockcoat and top hat of a millionaire, I never lost my respect for those who carry a book under their arm. And when I began to meet you along the boulevard with a whole stack of books in your hands, I tipped my hat to you and bowed as if it was really an honor for me to know you.

"To be a real millionaire I only lacked nine hundred and ninety thousand rubles. Still, I never dared open my mouth when others spoke of loftier things—such as, for instance, the sense of the world, the puzzle of man, the mystery of God. I felt the same toward you. I was always under the impression that you were growing up a second Barve's Son, and therefore out of sheer respect didn't dare get close to you.

"But lately it so happened that I was condemned to go through seventy universities in a short period of time, and I must tell you that, as excruciatingly painful as this was, I'm happy to have come out of them with a diploma and with the feeling that I've learned something. And this feeling now gives me the courage to speak to my educated son as equal to equal . . .

"I was a strong, healthy man. I used to bend a silver ruble between my fingers. I never even knew what a headache was, and if someone had told me then that I would soon die, I would have spit in his face . . . Suddenly, the doors to my lungs closed shut. I had never in my life seen a lung, nor had I the slightest notion where and what for I needed them. In my ignorance, I connected the word 'lungs' with the roast lungs served in Jewish restaurants. Well, I was, after all, as I said, an ignoramus. But imagine that among all the dozens of educated doctors and professors I couldn't find one who knew much more than I. The funniest thing about it all was that while in Germany I ran from one great specialist to another, and when I was finally recommended to the oldest and greatest of them all and through great effort and much money was brought to him, I found him coughing and choking himself, and all he could do for me was take my money and show me how to cough and choke in German. That was the end . . . Nothing remained for me but to take Barve's Son's advice, lie down in bed, and die—disintegrate like any piece of matter.

"Yes, that's what he said. Napoleon was the greatest, the mightiest. By himself he brought death to four, five million lives, but when death faced him personally he behaved like any other simple man, just lay down and even forgot to say good-bye. Therefore I must stop wasting my last few coins upon the doctors, who are, as far as death is concerned, as ignorant as myself. 'Be a man!' Barve's Son demanded. 'Don't leave your wife and children penniless with a big bundle of debts. I understand,' he said, 'you have a few silver pieces, a gold watch, a ring with some diamonds. You'd better hurry up with a will, because if you die . . .'

"'Now wait a minute,' I grabbed his arm, 'you mean I should stop resisting and rush myself into death?' I felt like jumping out of bed and kicking him out of the house. Yet in my helpless rage his comparison with Napoleon had a peculiar consoling effect on me. To die like Napoleon is something one cannot spit at. I suppressed my anger and asked, 'Had Napoleon ever had asthma?' 'Perhaps,' he answered. 'With these people you never know. Besides, to get rid of him once and for all he was forced to move to an island and die in seclusion. But one thing is sure one hundred percent. He left to his son an even more deadly sickness than asthma, of which the son died in his adolescent years.'

"This remark cut me to the quick. I don't have to tell you that Barve's Son, whatever he is, is certainly not a liar, and the thought that the sickness of a father may be inherited by a son, that a few seeds of my sick lungs may have been replanted in my offspring, is probably more than possible. This would mean that before anything else I've already supplied you with asthma. This was more than I could take. Yet Napoleon stood before my eyes.

"Had I been able to leave you in my will instead of an old watch at least one sizable bankbook, I could comfort myself that together with the affliction I provided you with some help. But as things were I had to go to the grave with the feeling of foul play: I gave you a sickness and no means to cure it. As ridiculous as all this may sound to you, for me it was an unbearably painful stain on my conscience. I refused to lie down. Why Napoleon? What have I in common with that wild emperor? Why do I have to die like him and be proud of it, when he himself did not die of his own will but was forced to it? Nobody forces me . . .

"In my early years as a soldier, standing guard in a dark and drizzling night, I saw a shadow of a dead friend approaching me. I shivered in my pants, and I let my rifle fire. My conscience tormented me all my life. I said to Barve's Son, 'Now you tell me to leave the world with the idea that I may have killed my own son . . .

I've never been a Napoleon. Nobody wants to get rid of me, and I am not going to move. Get out of here!'"

My father stood up strong, tall, and healthy. He wiped the fury out of his eyes and, measuring me up with a look of commiseration, continued.

"You know I never paid much attention to God. He didn't bother me, and I left Him alone. I was a simple furrier and I didn't need God's help to cut a woman's chinchilla coat. Why bother Him with prayers and blessings and other such stuff? What good am I to Him? And what good could He do me? Besides, listening to Barve's Son all these years I even strongly doubted if there was such a thing as God. But lying there chained to my deathbed, isolated from the world and from everyone including Barve's Son, I wondered who it was that had so easily created so many millions of people with so many millions of lungs while all those dozens of doctors and professors couldn't fit a single set of lungs into me or fix the old, broken ones. Wasn't this in itself a sign that there is someone who is immeasurably, inconceivably, wiser, stronger, and greater, One who is far, far above the patient and above the doctor?

"I know that Barve's Son is probably right when he says that summer is hot even though the sun is farther from Earth and winter is cold when the sun is closer to Earth, but who pushes the sun here and there? For whom and for what is it being pushed? Who needs it? And why would it be necessary if man was only a thing and there was no God? Day falls and night comes, trees bloom and trees wither, plants sprout and plants die—for whom? For what? I no longer speak about who makes these things: I only ask for whom are they made? And if it's true what Barve's Son says, that millions of stars are similarly pushed here and there and don't crash or get mixed up, doesn't this show that someone wants it this way? Someone needs it, someone holds it. So if someone has to be—there is no doubt that someone is.

"Yes, there is a God. The only question is who needs Him. A stone, a fish, a bedbug, a lion doesn't need a God. Is it then possible that God should create so many things from which there wouldn't even be one that needs Him? That's absurd. God needs man, man needs God, and you too will need Him.

"Who God is doesn't concern me. I only know that my father and mother were Jews, and if their seeds are within me, they are undoubtedly Jewish seeds. And if it's also true that I passed along to you, as Napoleon to his son, the kernels of my Jewish lungs, your remedy must be the Jewish God.

"Don't listen to what Barve's Son says. Because what good is his truth when he himself spits blood? Truth is only that which is good for me, for you, for everybody, and what is good for everybody is the truth.

"That's why I want you to learn to pray, put on phylacteries, go to the synagogue, observe the Sabbath, avoid *hometz* on Passover, and fast once a year. But above all—to believe that you aren't a thing created in the image of Napoleon but in the image of God and that in your lungs you bear the breath of the Jewish God."

At this, he again stopped for a while and, as if anxious to illustrate his remarkable lecture with an irrefutable fact, he raised his head and with proud assurance drew in a great breath of wonderful air and with an expression of "What do you say to that?" in his beaming eyes went on: "All that I've said to you isn't just random philosophy. I'm not a philosopher or a rabbi, and if the foolish market people in their exaggerated enthusiasm adorned me with the crown of a sage, you should know that I'm nine hundred and ninety thousand miles removed from this. Everything I said to you has to do with simple, concrete matters—as, for instance, rent money . . .

"Early this morning I made the last payment on our apartment, and this is actually the last because we'll soon have to move out of here. As you know, I've been left without money. I can't and dare not work yet since the smell of fur isn't good for me. Until I can switch over to something else I'm not able to keep paying for such an expensive apartment. So it's entirely possible that we'll be moving back to Market Street, where apartments are considerably cheaper.

"As for you, even though your education isn't too costly so far, I can't even meet this modest expense. Any further education such as a university or the like is naturally entirely out of the question. Therefore, I feel it would be practical that you should stop studying altogether and learn a trade, and the best would be the fur trade.

"I'll teach you the secret of how to be a good craftsman and, having God in your lungs, you might even become a millionaire someday, if not with a whole million, then at least with ten thousand rubles.

And believe me, coughing and bringing up blood like Barve's Son, who doesn't even have ten groschen, or a rich man to help him, or a God to heal him, is seventy times worse than the deadliest death."

The whole time he was speaking I stood with my head bowed. A few times I glanced up to see if it was the same father talking whom I had known for years as a simple man who liked a good meal, a drink, a game of billiards or cards, and about whom it was gossiped that he had had some strange dealings with some whore in America, and who had later been transformed by his terrible illness into an ugly curser. How was this possible? Could an ass turn overnight into a lion?

He now stood tall and healthy with the pride of a knight who has just returned from a bloody encounter with death and keeps it cringing at his feet like a dog on a chain.

Furrier or knight. One thing was clear—there stood a living miracle. And what can one say when a miracle speaks? But silently and submissively accept such a terrible, unexpected sentence—No! Make peace with the old God of the mournful Jewish cheder from which I had escaped long ago? Become a furrier and wait for asthma to strike me? Leave the gymnasium? Forget about the party? The dance with Niura? No! No! No! Such a demand was too cruel even if it came straight from God. And after a long silence during which I mustered all my spiritual and physical strength, trembling from head to toe, I replied more or less like this: "I know that I'm a Jew, and God doesn't have to give me asthma just so I'll need Him. He can keep his favors. I don't need any of His cures or His sicknesses. There's no doubt in my mind that God can perform miracles and that He proved this with you, but I believe that not only God but man can perform miracles too. I myself have already performed a few. This uniform that I wear now is one of them. And so long as my lungs are still healthy, I won't take it off and exchange it for a furrier's smock.

"This uniform is my armor in which I fight, and so long as I wear this uniform I won't move out of this house. I won't go back to the old marketplace, because I have an invitation to a house which I've dreamed of entering for almost a year. I was invited to this house as a gymnasium student from the Boulevard of St. George, not as some

Jewish furrier from the old marketplace, so I can't give up the gymnasium now and take off the uniform even if there is a God in heaven, because one thing is certain about God—*He* won't pay the rent, but I will pay it. I'll get the money and I'll pay both for the apartment and for my tuition too!"

And, breaking out in a fearful wailing, I ran out of the house.

XX

∞

THE VERY NEXT day I waited at the gymnasium gate for Petya and
Volodya and promptly proposed that we go to the Café Bon Bon.

Once there I commenced: "Listen here, friends, you once offered
to make me a loan. I didn't need it then. I desperately need it now.
I beg you, if it's at all possible, lend me a hundred rubles."

"A hundred rubles," Petya repeated. "When do you need it?"

"My father was so impoverished by his terrible sickness that he
can't pay the rent or even my tuition at the gymnasium. I want to be
sure that I won't have to take off my uniform and give up my
education."

"We can't allow this to happen!" Petya slammed the table.

"We'll get the money for you."

"You don't have the money yet?"

"No, but we can get it."

"When?"

"Let's say—six, seven . . . in seven weeks."

"Maybe even a bit sooner . . . You needn't worry."

"Don't you trust us?"

I threw down my napkin. "Lately, I've been very disappointed in
you. At this very same table I revealed to you all my secrets. I told
you about Niura and about the invitation to her birthday. Not only
didn't you respond in kind, you even tried to make fun of me in a
nasty way. It's not enough to help me out with a hundred rubles,
you must also tell me where you're going to get this money."

The boys laughed uneasily.

"Damn it, what a strange guy you are! You make a mountain out
of every molehill. We were sure you knew that Nazarov is our pal
and that he is loaded."

"You never mentioned that before."

"We don't consider it important."

"You say he is loaded. Where does he get it?"

"His father or his grandfather was a rich landowner."

"But why does he give it to you?"

"He'll give to you too."

"How?"

Petya wiped the chocolate off his lips and in a sobered voice said, "Come along with us. But we must warn you—you talk very nicely, but much too much. You must keep your lips buttoned."

"Why?"

"Because it can be dangerous," they said in chorus. To ease the tension, Petya ordered three dishes of pistachio ice cream.

"Maybe you're right in not trusting me. Maybe I do talk too much . . . Maybe it would be better if I didn't go with you to Nazarov's. It would be safer if I didn't."

The two boys grew pale with rage. "What kind of crap is this? We're trying to keep you from being thrown out of school. All we ask of you is to keep your mouth shut!"

"I see your concern for me, and I promise I'll return the favor in whatever way I can."

"Why thank us? Come along and earn your own share. He hasn't stopped raving about the 'artist' and even insisted that we bring you along. Now that we're ready to help you, you should be willing to help us."

As usual, our conversation ended with my wholehearted admission that they were one hundred percent correct.

On Sunday we took a droshky to the Antokol suburb where Nazarov lived in a one-story brick house. The shutters were closed and a half dozen cats scampered about on the balcony. Nazarov met us at the door in a ragged cotton bathrobe and promptly led us into a large room.

From the musky, putrid air it was obvious that the house hadn't been aired in years. The faded walls were covered with old photographs. The sharp beams of light that tore through the carved hearts in the shutters slashed through a dense cloud of dust and came to rest on a large spiderweb with the spider dozing inside.

Nazarov greeted us with his customary nervous enthusiasm. "Ah, here come my children, my artist, my past, my youth, my hope!" And he gave each of us a long, resounding kiss on the lips.

"The lotto is all ready," he said, pointing his sharp, blue-tinged jaw at the table where the cards and markers were already set up.

"Did you explain to our new friend how we play lotto here every Sunday?"

Petya gazed down. "Not yet."

"Oh, that's not good!" the old man said, embracing the new guest. "But we'll enlighten him in a moment. I still haven't forgotten the deep impression you made on me, young man. I kept asking about you. I was angry at my two little friends for not bringing you. You see all these things in this room? This is only a small part of the trophies from my past when I myself was an actor. But you mustn't think I'm as old as I look. I'm still a boy at heart. That's why I love to be friends and play with boys. Every Sunday we play here. We play lotto . . . If I lose, you can ask whatever you want of me, and if I win, you have to satisfy my demands—ha, ha, ha!" He hopped from one leg to the other.

"But Mr. Nazarov, if our friend the 'artist' wins, will you give him a hundred rubles?" Volodya asked in a direct, businesslike tone.

Nazarov sucked in his lips between his toothless gums, dropped slowly into a chair, and, scratching his bluish jaw, mumbled, "A hundred rubles is a lot of money . . . You know, after all, that the highest I pay is ten rubles for the two of you. But a hundred for one person—that's a bit steep. To win a hundred rubles from me, a person must be a good player, a very good player."

"How can you be a good player in lotto?" I asked.

"Usually, artists are great fools, but this boy manages to have talent and a little gray matter besides. Such a combination is rare . . ." He grabbed me by the rump and dragged me to him. In my embarrassment, I tried to pull away, but the skinny claws dug themselves into the cheeks of my behind like a pair of metal tongs and wouldn't let me budge.

"If you'll be a good boy, you don't have to play lotto—I'll give you the hundred rubles," he whispered feverishly.

"You're hurting me!"

"I'm willing to let you repay the favor," he said, rising from the chair and tremblingly removing his bathrobe and Turkish slippers, leaving himself completely naked. "Well, boys, show him what you can do," he said, turning to my two friends.

Petya and Volodya removed their tunics with remarkable calmness, rolled up their shirtsleeves, and, after Nazarov had stretched out face down on a nearby sofa, commenced to tickle him on the back of the neck, under his arms, and all the way down to the soles of his feet. His face buried in the sofa, he pleaded under his breath, "Harder, harder!" and soon afterward lifted his head with his contorted face and winked at me to join in.

For a moment, I felt the urge to grab my cap and run. Still, despite all my revulsion I couldn't abandon my two friends, who were trying to get the hundred rubles for me. This would have made me lower than Nazarov himself.

I quickly slipped off my tunic, ran up to the prone figure on the sofa, and with a full swing landed a blow on his backside. Nazarov sprang up as if he'd been burned and cried hoarsely, "What's this?" Petya and Volodya motioned mutely to me that my first move had been a mistake, that it wasn't as simple as it appeared, that my hundred rubles was in danger. But I pushed them aside, ran up to the sofa again, and began to pound both my fists on Nazarov's shoulder, gradually increasing the tempo and finishing up with a tremendous blow. To the surprise of the two professionals, Nazarov moaned with great delight, "That's good, that's the way!"

By now I no longer cared whether I got the money or not. At that moment I even forgot what I had come here for. I became fired with a terrible urge to be even crazier than the madman.

I seized him by a leg and dragged him down from the sofa, then took a few steps backward and with a flying run kicked him with all my might as if he were a football. He shuddered, his tongue fell to the side of his mouth like an old hound's and, upturned eyes lolling, he tossed several times from side to side like an epileptic before coming to rest in a swoon on the floor.

The boys grabbed my arms and dragged me off into a corner, where we waited pantingly for the body on the floor to move.

Gradually, Nazarov came to and with an exhausted but satisfied smile got to his feet. He huddled inside his bathrobe, wiped his jaw with a side of the robe, then said in a shattered voice, "The boy is extraordinary. A bit more polish and refinement of manners and he'll grow up one of the best artists, an artist par excellence . . . I haven't the slightest doubt about this. And now, my children, you'll amuse yourselves for a while with the lotto while I lie down for a little nap, then I'll get dressed and we'll go down to a restaurant."

"No, I don't have the time," I said, putting on my tunic.

Nazarov stopped me. "I realize that you need a hundred rubles, but as I've already said, I never paid your two friends more than five rubles each. I concede that you alone are better than the two of them put together, and I insist that from now on either all three of you come, or none of you. Your fee will be ten rubles. As to the hundred rubles, I'll give you an advance to cover the next ten visits. But from the way you're trying to run away without even a good-bye, who'll guarantee me that you'll come back again?"

"We'll guarantee it!" both boys shouted in unison.

"In that case, all right. Hand me my jacket!"

Petya brought him the jacket and Nazarov took out a wallet and counted out ten ten-ruble notes. "Boys, I demand respect toward this young man. He possesses something that neither of you has, and that's the thing I've always been searching for—talent. When I came to the concert at your house, young man, your mother gave me to understand that your father was very ill, and if he still isn't well, take this money and use it to help him. I don't know you too well yet, but the word of honor of my two honest friends is good enough to guarantee that you'll visit me again this coming Sunday."

With these words, he handed me the ten banknotes and gave to the other boys five rubles each; then, rubbing his loins and mumbling, "That was good, good . . . That is what I call talent," he shuffled off on wobbly legs to the bedroom.

XXI

WE SAT BEFORE the emptied saucers of jam at the Café Bon Bon and didn't speak.

In order to convince my friends that I could keep silent, I had clamped a lock on my lips. They seemed to be pleased that I had been silenced. I knew that I was in their hands more than they were in mine. Because no matter how dangerous a careless word of mine could be for them, my own situation was ten times more dangerous. If, for instance, someone at the gymnasium were to find out about our despicable actions, we would all be subject to punishment. We had sinned equally, but when it came to paying for it, mine would be the greater share of retribution. At worst, they would each receive a punch in the jaw from the principal, but I would be expelled— because, to begin with, I was in a higher class, and second, what was forgivable for a son of a Christian train conductor was inexcusable for a son of a Jewish furrier. There was nothing I could do about this. I rolled the money up in a rag and stuffed it in a crack of a tree in the Botanical Garden, so that in case I was questioned I could deny the whole thing and wouldn't have the bills on me to incriminate me.

But this wasn't enough. My greater responsibility in the affair diminished my faith in my two co-conspirators. I tried to comfort myself with the reverse logic that the fact that my partners weren't Jewish might serve to cover up the affair, but I had serious reservations about their loyalty. I therefore tried to become closer to them. Day after day I went with them to the Café Bon Bon and stuffed myself with cloying concoctions, then dragged along to their homes, where I played lotto and patiently listened to the long, boring anecdotes of the conductor.

One evening, Petya got the urge to smoke a cigar. The three of us went into a dark alley and each smoked a long, black cigar. We promptly felt nauseated, and we vomited in concert.

I sought every opportunity to be with them, to lose myself between them, so that the three of us should become two ones-and-a-half. Nothing should be left of me.

Thus the uneasy days dragged on until the long-awaited week of the twelfth arrived. Days before, I had prepared fresh shoe wax for my boots, pomade for my hair, and polish for the brass buttons on my uniform. Only three more days remained until the fateful Sunday.

During recess, I stood in the noisy corridor leaning against the wall and nibbling a few sugared nuts remaining in my pocket from the Café Bon Bon. Suddenly, I felt a hand on my shoulder. "I'd like to talk to you, young man," Sasha Voktuzen whispered over my shoulder. "Be so good as to come with me."

The unexpected, grim, and forceful request made me immediately uneasy. I wanted to ask, "Why?" But my long self-enforced silence now caused decided results—I wasn't able to open my mouth and silently followed my escort.

Voktuzen snaked his way through the throngs in the corridor, sped across the courtyard, and, motioning to me, soon turned a corner and walked down brick stairs into the school cellar.

I stayed close so as not to lose him in the dim light that managed to enter through the single, dusty, mud-spattered little window under the ceiling. We walked past a long row of wooden doors from behind which wafted a damp stench of sawed wood, chopped cabbage, pickles, tar, lime, and rusty iron.

Voktuzen waved his hands in the dark as if he were swimming. Several times I banged against his heels, Suddenly, I stopped. Over Voktuzen's shoulder I saw the gleaming buttons of another uniform shining in the dark like wolves' eyes in a forest. For a moment I thought to turn and run, but quickly decided to do the very opposite.

Forcing total indifference, I asked, "What do you want of me?" But instead of answering, Romek pushed open the door nearest to us and indicated with his hand that I enter.

Shuffling along gingerly on trembling feet in the dark storeroom, I fingered a mound of sawed planks and some sticky tar barrels and came up smack against the awesome shadow with the gleaming buttons. Voktuzen followed and, closing the door behind him, began right off: "We found out that you got a letter from my sister . . ."

"We demand you hand over this letter right here and now."

"And don't you dare come to my sister's party."

"Let me," Romek pleaded. "If you come to the party this Sunday, we'll split your skull open with this pipe and sling you out of the house!" And he brought a piece of metal up to my nose so that if I couldn't see it in the dark, I could at least smell it.

"But we want the letter right now!" Voktuzen demanded. "You dare not walk around with my sister's letter on you."

"She's my girl! She's his sister. And you're nothing but a scruffy Jew!" Zavatski said, and poked me with his elbow.

I slipped, fell against the barrel of tar, and landed on the pile of sawed wood, which fell on top of me with a clatter.

The two waited until I was standing again and, without wasting any time, laid the cold iron against my fevered brow and asked the curt and simple question, "Well?"

I drew myself up and mumbled, "Gentlemen, I don't know why you needed a pipe for this. I didn't ask your sister to write me. I never acknowledged that I even accepted the invitation . . . I got the letter, I read it. I wasn't even going to answer it."

"But you did!"

"More out of respect for you. I assumed that the invitation had been issued with your consent. The fact is that I don't even know your sister, I barely remember her, having seen her only once in my life. If you insist, I'll run home this minute and bring you the letter here."

"You don't have it on you?"

"You can search me and see for yourselves," I said, taking a terrible chance.

"We have to run back to class now. Remember, in the classroom you don't know us and we don't know you. Bring the letter with you tomorrow here to this same place so no one will see you or find out anything about this."

"No one will see," I answered in a broken voice.

"And don't you dare come to the party." A hand seized my hair from behind, a second hand seized my ear, a third waved the pipe under my nose. "It just might occur to you that if you give us the letter, the matter is settled and you can go to the party. Don't make that error. We'll turn you away, but minus your hair, ears, and nose." And the three hands roughly jostled the three mentioned features on my head.

After a short pause, the low, resigned gasp of a dying dream pierced the silence: "No, I won't come."

We left the cellar together but, once in the courtyard, we parted. The two students ran quickly into the classroom and I went to the lavatory.

I took off my uniform jacket and tried to wash the grease off the elbows, but the tarry stains had worked into the fabric and the more I rubbed the more they seemed to spread. I couldn't under any circumstances show up in class in my soggy uniform. I decided to stay in the washroom until classes ended and then, when everyone was gone, to grab the books from my bench and run home.

The next day the stains were even more apparent, but I went to school a whole half-hour earlier than usual. After a long, sleepless night I could no longer curb my impatience. I was the first to enter the classroom and took my place on the rear bench. When Romek and Sasha appeared in the doorway, I gestured to them that I had the letter . . . We would meet in the same place where they had taken me the day before. Then I raised five fingers, which meant after the last class was over.

When the gong sounded, I packed my books and was the first out of the room.

I waited for a few minutes in the dark cellar until Zavatski and Voktuzen came groping in.

"Are you there?" they asked.

"Yes," I replied and, opening the door of the alcove, politely and submissively let them enter first. The moment they were inside, I slammed the door shut in a wild rage and rapidly threw the bolt to lock them in.

For a while, a murderous stillness reigned in the cellar, but soon a banging on the door could be heard and two desperate mouths crying and cursing the lousy Jew—but the Jew didn't answer, for he was already in the courtyard mingling with the students joyously skipping on their way home for the weekend.

One student slapped me on the back. "Hey, when are you going to hold a second concert?"

Another poked me in the rear. "I hear you can lay eggs. How about selling me some—I'm hungry."

I ignored them all. I knew now that I must remain silent forever. No more concerts. No more highfalutin' talk. No more rhymes for

Niura's party. No party for me, but no party for anyone else, either. It would be a party without guests, a dead party in which she would dance a lonely *danse macabre* in an empty ballroom. As for me, I'd have to hide—maybe here, maybe there, or perhaps at that madman Nazarov's house. I'd beat him to a pulp and get enough money to buy a new uniform. Monday morning, perhaps even Sunday late in the evening when the party would be over, I'd let the boys out of the basement.

Just then I reached the edge of the boulevard. There, leaning against the lamp post, I saw the squat, grotesque figure of my Uncle Abrashka. His head withdrawn into the collar of his tattered jacket, he chewed on a matchstick.

He ran up and embraced me. "Hey, my little brother, how are you? Remember how I once grabbed you on this same corner and took you to Gorodenko's carnival? I haven't seen you since . . . And now I've come to say good-bye to you. I've left Gorodenko . . . Let him go to hell, I'm going to Odessa . . . Oy, Odessa—Mama! Odessa is a big city, lively, gay, with many circuses. They're looking for talent, and I know a whole bunch of new tricks. All I need is the chance and I'm sure to become a headliner."

"I wish you luck," I mumbled with dry indifference.

"But Odessa is far," he complained in a petulant tone, "and a train ticket costs eight rubles. I need a suit or two, a pair of shoes . . . I figured I would go to Mother's, I mean your grandmother's. She hadn't seen me in almost a year . . . but all I could get out of her was three rubles. And I have no heart to go to your father. I've heard he's mostly sick. You're the only one who can save me."

"But I don't have any money. When father used to give me an allowance—"

"All I need is twenty-five. If that's too much, I'll make do with twenty . . . You must help me. Because if I have to go back to Gorodenko I'd rather slit my gullet." And he drew his finger across his throat in the old melodramatic fashion. "You must save me . . . now that I'm on my way to success. Maybe I'll become famous not only in Odessa but throughout the world—that I should lose such a chance over twenty-five rubles, oy, oy, oy . . ." He wrung his hands, holding back his tears.

I looked at my little uncle, and my chilled heart began to melt in the sweet warmth of pity. Before me stood a lonely, broken soul with an imaginary invitation to be a star in Odessa. Should I push aside the outstretched hand? Should I suppress the fact that I had a bundle of money stuffed into a tree somewhere and thus sever the thin thread of the tightrope on which this pathetic clown would walk to his imaginary circus in Odessa? Should I now deny him, deceive him, betray him, drag him down into a dark cellar and pluck the dream from his heart and take away the invitation to Odessa?

Those who had done the same to me only yesterday had been strangers, after all.

More alien than strangers . . . They hated me before they even knew me and had a virulent abhorrence after they had met me.

But this pitiful, amiable, good-for-nothing was an uncle, a blood relation, godfather to the midget, a partner in my uniform. So why shouldn't I put a parasol in his hand and let him walk the thread to the source of his dream? Why not, like Nazarov, help out an artist in need? Besides, what did a hundred lousy rubles mean to one who could earn it with one slam? Why keep the damn money hidden in a tree when only a half-hour before I had been robbed of my greatest treasure?

"Hold my books," I said in a dark but firm voice and raced off toward the Botanical Garden.

I came back in a hurry and, wiping the sweat off my brow with one hand, I used the other to stuff the ten-ruble notes into my uncle's hand. Abrashka leaped backward as if a burning coal had been thrust under his nose. His whole body trembling, he sputtered, "Is this true? I mean, are you really giving it to me? Real money? A hundred rubles? Where did you get it?"

"Don't ask."

"And you're giving it to me?"

"You've got it coming."

"Why?"

"For the uniform!" And I burst out crying.

"What uniform are you talking about? Why are you crying? I'll give you back the money, I swear—I'll pay it back . . . The train to Odessa leaves in a half-hour. If I hurry, I can still catch it." And, tucking the money under the sweatband of his hat, he started to take his leave. But he hadn't taken twenty steps when he looked around and exclaimed, "Hey, write me a letter. You promise?"

"I promise," I blubbered. "What's your address?"

"Odessa, Odessa."

"Odessa is a big city."

"All Odessa will know my address. You'll hear from me." And he was gone.

Monday morning, on my way to school, I saw in the distance my friends Petya and Volodya running toward me. They were waving their arms, signaling to me to stay where I was. And when they came up closer, they pressed clenched fists against their cheeks to muffle the excitement in their voices. "Go back! Go back! You can't go to the gymnasium anymore. It's terrible there! They found two boys unconscious in the cellar . . . They said that a Jew did this to them. And everyone knows it was you. They're looking for you! They've sent for the police! Run, hide—disappear somewhere."

I stood petrified.

"Why, why did you do it?" the two boys pleaded. "They say that you wanted to kill them. Like Beilis, who killed a small boy in a cellar. This could be very dangerous for you and for all you Jews. You must run away . . . Maybe you can go to another city temporarily? What do you say? They're liable to find out that you used to spend time with us at the Café Bon Bon . . . We were good to you. We treated you to cakes, we gave you money to play twenty-one, we took upon ourselves the responsibility of a hundred rubles . . . We'll pay the debt, but you mustn't drag us into your trouble. You must say you don't even know us, that you never spoke to us, you're in a higher grade, you're a Jew and Jews are only friends with other Jews . . . Will you say that—will you?"

"I'll say it, but would they believe me?"

"That's why we tell you to disappear."

"Wherever I'd go they'd find me."

"Try! Try!" they pleaded.

"I can't do it. Because I'm a Jew, you understand." I let my books fall to the sidewalk.

They seemed stunned by my last remark. Was it some sort of self-pity? Or that, being Jewish, I felt no responsibility toward non-Jews?

"Don't just stand there—run! Hide!" They pushed me, but I didn't budge.

Where could I go? Where could I hide? The times when I could enter a mirror and call on the mighty Golem to protect me were long gone. I was now a little man of flesh and blood that no mirror would accept any longer. But if not in a mirror, where else could a Jew hide?

It wasn't the fear of punishment nor the vexation that I couldn't protect these good friends with whom I had played, snacked, and debauched that distressed me, but the sudden realization that with my revengeful act in the cellar I had placed all the Jews of the city in great danger. Two locked-up Christian boys in a cellar a few months before Passover would only mean a second pogrom in the market-place. I still recalled the destruction after the little Christian girl had come to shave her beard at the barber's. And if that had brought down such a terrible tragedy upon the people of the marketplace, what would their punishment be for my present crime?

What could happen to Petya and Volodya even if it came out that they had eaten ice cream and played cards with the filthy Jew who had committed that foul deed? A strong dressing down or, at worst, a few slaps in the face. For this I should run away and leave the marketplace unprotected? If I ran away now or denied that I had done the deed, the blame would surely fall on the market people.

That would be the real crime, the only crime. After all, I had acted in self-defense. I had locked up Romek and Sasha for a day in the cellar so that they couldn't go to the party on Sunday. First thing Monday morning, I would have released them. What did one night in a dark cellar mean in comparison with the darkness into which they had plunged me? If there was any criminal here it wasn't me, and even they weren't criminals because we had fought like three equal knights with three equal suits of armor—they with iron pipes and I with my strategy, and in an equal struggle the winner is not a criminal. If I had actually done any harm, it was only to the inno-cent market people. If I had made them pay for my sins then I was really the worst criminal in the world. No! I dared not and I would not run away. I would stay and if necessary give myself up, because no matter that I might be a criminal, a lampedusser, a horse thief, or an artist—I was first, last, and utmost a Jew.

Again and again my two frightened friends tried with both kind and angry words to drag me away from the boulevard, lest some-body see us together, but I stood nailed to my shadow on the sidewalk.

For a moment, they glared at me the way they had used to when I nagged them about Paganini and Niura. But now, seeing who I actually was, they considered themselves lucky to be rid of me, and they raced off to school.

That same day, Benjamin took one of his suits from the closet, quickly tore it apart, and cut it down to my size.

The following morning when he received an order to report to the gymnasium in order to hear personally the sentence the school board had issued against his son—namely, that he be expelled permanently from the gymnasium—he replied in a very respectful letter that he had just gotten up after a very serious illness and was therefore in no condition to come in person. At the same time he thanked the honorable board of directors for the mild and just sentence with which he was in total agreement and assured them that from now on he would watch over his son with particular care and would see to it that he learned a trade quickly—possibly the fur trade. He would also make every effort to make an honest and useful citizen of him.

Several weeks later, father and son helped move the contents of Number 24 Boulevard of St. George into Barve's big moving wagon, and that's how Benjamin and his whole family went back where they had come from, to the house facing the old marketplace.

Part Three

XXII

⟨≈⟩

FROM THE THIRD-STORY window the old marketplace seemed smaller and quieter, and the people older and sleepier.

A flock of crows was gathered around the green garbage bin, and the moment I showed up at the window, they lifted with a frightened impetus and scattered over the rooftops cawing wildly.

These black birds never brought any luck to the marketplace, and their cawing always presaged bad tidings. I used to chase them with a stick, but now I gazed out at them like a prisoner from behind bars and would have been glad to be one of these ugly but carefree creatures.

I put the textbooks, notebooks, the library I had accumulated when I had my own room in the big apartment on the boulevard, under the sofa and behind the kitchen shelves. Dumas, James Fenimore Cooper, Edgar Allan Poe, Jules Verne—all that was good for a gymnasium student, but for a furrier? Out of habit, I still glanced occasionally into the series called "The Conqueror of Death" that were sold in five-groschen weekly installments at the newspaper kiosks and that described the extraordinary adventures of a French doctor, one Chantille Jeantaigne Delacroix. This mysterious individual, who fought for the oppressed, the poor, and the ill, and thus won for himself the nickname "The Conqueror of Death," had been sentenced four times to life imprisonment and six times to death as a swindler and sorcerer.

Although the ploys that he used to save himself (one week from the gallows in France and the third week from the polar bears at the North Pole) were even too fantastic for a boy who could sometimes picture himself as a black crow flying over the rooftops, they somehow struck a familiar chord and evoked within me a genuine sentiment and a deep sympathy for the persecuted Frenchman.

Besides, I knew that this was the last book I would be reading, for immediately following Judgment Day on Yom Kippur, when the fur season began, I would be apprenticed to Reuben Buchalsky, thus concluding my own series of adventures.

On the Day of Atonement my father would take me to a synagogue where I would present myself to the Creator, repent my past deeds, and beg a measure of good fortune for the furrier. A midget, a lampedusser, and a gymnasium student could live without a God, but a furrier couldn't.

And so it was. On sundown on the eve of the holiday, Father came up, put his hand on my shoulder, and said "Go eat a decent meal, for tomorrow you must fast."

Later, we left the house together, walked past Tartar and Glass streets, and soon turned into Jewish Street. Father stopped just once. He leaned against a wall, raised his head, and without effort or sound drew in a few deep breaths of cool evening air, then slowly and with great pleasure and frank pride exhaled them again.

I trailed along behind and observed with wonder his erect back, which had straightened like a wilted flower stem that had been doused with fresh water after a long dry spell.

When we came out on Jewish Street, the blue of evening already stretched over the gray, peeling walls. Gnarled beggars with dusty beards and ashen faces filled the sidewalks. They looked like piles of bricks that had crumbled off the walls. Palms outstretched, they promised the donor a year of plenty and blessings of good health, good luck, and other good things for only a groschen.

The dirty, gray, moss-covered arches spanning the street (a remnant of the medieval ghetto) didn't admit much light even on a sunny day. You had to be careful, too, of the rotted boards in the sidewalks that sprang and vengefully splattered mud on any intruding stranger.

We crossed the street and stopped before the iron gates of the great Synagogue Complex.

This monument to a two-thousand-year-old wonder consisted of a group of hoary buildings with crooked roofs and dark, winding steps within which were secreted dozens of Talmud Torahs, synagogues, study houses, charitable societies, cheders, schools, and yeshivas.

More than a hundred prayer houses were piled here one on top of another. Every trade, every line of business was represented. There was a house of worship here for tinsmiths, glaziers, bookbinders, printers, coachmen, sawyers, cap makers, furriers, black-bread bakers, white-bread bakers, water carriers, wood turners, painters, carpenters, chimney sweeps, shoemakers, lacemakers, quilters, coopers, tanners, gravediggers, and musicians. Every house of prayer had its carved plaque on the wall and its old book of records listing its past benefactors, rabbis, teachers, saints, and plain righteous Jews, with dates going back to the 1500s. Every house of prayer was also named after some remarkable legendary figure, as for instance the prayer house of Reb Joshua who, although blind from birth, had memorized all the sixty thick volumes of the Talmud. On the old, rusty plaque you could still clearly read the blessing that this blind saint had offered for the famous English Lord Moses Montefiore when he had come for a visit.

Wandering through the dozens of prayer houses and synagogues, we passed the Great Synagogue that had been built underground to circumvent the law that it couldn't top any of the city churches and which (according to Barve's Son) Napoleon himself had visited on his way to Moscow.

"And there, there . . ." Father said, pointing upward, "in the attic of this synagogue, lies the Golem that the famous Gaon formed out of clay into a living creature of flesh and blood by placing a piece of paper with God's name into its skull, and when he took it out, the Golem became a mass of clay again covered with dust and spiderwebs."

I stood there with my head cocked upward and wiped the tears from my eyes. "Ah, my good, old friend the Golem, what have they done to you and to me?" I silently lamented.

By now, my father had already gone inside a small, dusty room with long, narrow windows and peeled, corroded pillars beneath heavy, half-arched vaults. This was the prayer house of that famous Gaon.

The gloom and silence were suddenly shattered by a heart-rending cry from two desperate women who burst inside and fell upon the holy ark, begging and demanding that the Gaon report immediately to the Throne of Glory and, in a private conversation with the Almighty, arrange a cure for one of the women's sick husband, and something similar for the other woman's dying child before the Day of Atonement sentence was carried out.

This pitiful lament penetrated through the walls and windows of the synagogue and drifted into the courtyard to mingle with the chants carried there from above and below and from the various corners, nooks, and crannies of the great complex. From one side came the drawn-out, haunting chant of a solitary yeshiva student swaying over a flickering candle; from the other a rousing hymn from a group of aged scholars. And as the melody died down in one corner, it was picked up in another by a new quorum, by another recluse, and it evolved into an endless, remarkable, unique chant.

The second part of the synagogue complex was separated from the first by a thick stone wall with a rounded entranceway called the Archway. Above it hung two large clocks.

"These two clocks are here," Father said, "to notify the people when to stop working, cooking, worrying and put an end to all the weekly routine and begin the Sabbath. One clock tells when to make the benediction over the candles and greet the Holy Day—and the second, when to say the *Havdalah* and usher out the Sabbath. But soon, soon now all the clocks in the world will come to a stop for one day and one night and it will be neither weekday nor Sabbath. Time will stand still and not stir until judgment is pronounced for the coming year."

With these words he stepped through the Archway into the back courtyard.

Several huge barrels stood there as repositories for all the hundreds of worn-out, sweat- and snuff-stained pages from the prayerbooks, hymnals, penitential prayerbooks, Pentateuchs, Scriptures, Gemaras, Midrashim, Commentaries, *Shulhan-Arukhs*, Talmud commentaries, commentaries on commentaries, Books of Morals, Cabala volumes, and rabbinical interpretations by the Tannaites, Gaonim, and sages.

The huge barrels of pages served as a soft sleeping place for the two town idiots, Moshe Governor and Artche Onionstalk.

Moshe was a short creature with bowed legs and a head three times too large for his tiny body, resplendent in a cracked top hat and varicolored rags pinned up with hooks and nails. His consort, Artche, was a long skeleton draped in yellow, parchmentlike skin and featuring dirty, bare feet. They raced from one end of the courtyard to the other, proclaiming to everyone with professional assurance that this Yom Kippur would be the greatest and most important of all the Yom Kippurs ever. Foam speckling their lips, eyes burning, they pounded their breasts and swore on the lives of their unborn children that they had received positive tidings that the Messiah was already on his way and would surely be here soon. The world would be redeemed and this would be the last Yom Kippur— they therefore harried the crowd imperiously to hasten to their respective houses of prayer.

People jostled each other on the hunched stairs and pushed through the crooked doorways of the stacked synagogues and houses of prayer. The words, the sermons and chants, flowed like unruly streams through all the doors and windows, then mingled in the courtyard into a raging torrent that carried to the Great Synagogue below, which was already flooded to the brim with waves of white prayer shawls and veiled in a mist that rose from the overheated mouths and bodies.

Deep within this mist the holy ark flashed with hundreds of candles like a fantastic lighthouse on some distant, unreachable shore.

Suddenly, the waves of prayer shawls began to sway and toss in resounding song: "Help! Help!" But the outcry broke against the stone walls and fell back in pieces with a sigh upon the prayer shawls.

"Come under my prayer shawl and join in the chant," my father said, drawing me to him.

"How can I sing to a God that I cannot see, in a language that I don't understand?"

"Well, then, close your eyes and sing without words," Father urged.

"What shall I sing?"

"Sing that we should have enough to pay the rent. Sing that the heart shouldn't stop beating, the stomach should keep working, and the lungs shouldn't become clogged. But above all, sing that we shouldn't be drowned or burned or torn to bits by wild beasts." And taking me around, he swayed in rhythm with his chant: "Praised be the Lord Almighty who has created the world according to His will and created us in His own image . . ."

I drew one edge of his prayer shawl over my head, and with the other wiped away the tears that dampened my closed eyes, and quietly chanted, "Why . . . why judge that which You created in Your own image with thousands of parts and thousands of aches and pains in every part? Why judge and condemn Your own image?

What's the sense and meaning of it all?"

Suddenly, the whole crowd swayed in my direction and broke out in a mighty cry: "Yes, yes, that's the way!"

"Sing to the Almighty!"

"The Awe-inspiring!"

"The All-avenging!"

"The Merciful!"

"Because Whoever He might be, He is here—forever after."

"Sing that He might remember that He forged an eternal covenant with our ancestors so that what is good for Him will be good for us, and what is good for us will also be good for Him . . . That He is together with us in the world in the same marketplace and the same synagogue courtyard, from which He cannot escape and is bound up with us in His own creation for better or worse!

"So let us sing out together in unison, like one mouth, like one heart, like one world for one God, who created a world where you can breathe and sing, and even more for the fact that the Almighty and eternal God bears a Jewish name. This alone is sufficient guarantee that His judgment this Yom Kippur will not only be just but merciful as well."

The next day, after Yom Kippur was over, when we walked tired and hungry through the Archway, Moshe Governor and Artche Onionstalk lay peacefully dozing inside the barrels of torn holy pages. They surely didn't know that from that day on they were no longer the only town idiots, that on that Yom Kippur it had been proclaimed in heaven that the whole world should go crazy, and that events were about to happen that would defy all normal human understanding. True, their announcement about the Messiah's coming had actually been nothing more than a vision in their fevered brains. Still they had guessed correctly that this had been the greatest and most important of all Yom Kippurs since this was the Yom Kippur of the Jewish year 5675, which coincided with the non-Jewish year 1914. On that Yom Kippur, the judgment over the people of the old marketplace and over those in the synagogue complex and those in the whole world had been proclaimed not only for one year, but for a hundred and perhaps a thousand years to come.

Several weeks later, my father escorted me to Reuben Buchalsky's shop and arranged for a year's apprenticeship for me, which would cost him twenty-five rubles. I sat down in a corner on a pile of furs with the resigned grimace of a convict condemned to life at hard labor.

"Get to work," Buchalsky grunted.

"What shall I do?"

"Sweep out the shop."

"Where shall I get a broom?"

"Look, you'll find it."

I went off to find a broom. On the way, I took an installment of "The Conqueror of Death" from my back pocket and reread the last few pages. I felt better because the French doctor, Chantille Jean-taigne Delacroix, had again (until the next installment) wriggled out of the dreadful danger that threatened him.

"Take out the chamber pot," Buchalsky ordered me later.

I went out with the slops and bought another installment of "The Conqueror of Death."

One time, as I sat engrossed in a fresh installment, Buchalsky tore the booklet from my hands. "What is this, a library?"

"What shall I do?"

"Nothing. Watch me and you'll learn how to hold a needle in your hand."

For a few weeks I sat with my eyes glued on him and wondered why he never took off his hat. In the mornings, when I came in, he would be parading around in his drawers but with his hat already firmly on his head.

But one day he ran into the room without his hat on. "A fire on them, they should only burn! He should croak altogether, the tsar! How do you like that—they shoot a prince somewhere and I have to take his part and report for mobilization tomorrow. The shop is closed! Go home and tell your father to dun the tsar for the money he paid me."

I ran from the shop without so much as a good-bye and, almost dancing, ran up to a kiosk where I bought up all the installments of "The Conqueror of Death" that I had missed during the weeks I had been staring at Buchalsky's hat.

That same evening as I sat deeply engrossed in the new, fantastic adventure of Dr. Delacroix, I heard a terrible commotion outside and ran to the window.

The marketplace was filled with strange, unfamiliar people who had assembled from the farthest corners and deepest holes of the city. Leaping about and waving their hands in the air in insane fashion, they roared in wild voices, "Hurrah, hurrah, hurrah!"

One lunatic stood on the great garbage bin holding a big portrait of the tsar and shrieking hysterically: "Listen! Listen!"

"Hurrah! Hurrah! Hurrah!"

"Let me talk!" the madman with the portrait pleaded.

"Hurrah! Hurrah!" the other lunatics shouted obstinately.

"They've shot a crown prince, Francis Ferdinand!"

"Princes, crowns . . . Hurrah! Hurrah! Hurrah!"

"Austria-Hungary . . . ultimatum Serbia!"

"Multimatum, Bessarabia, hurrah, hurrah!"

"Bel, bel, bel, bum, bum, bum! Hurrah, hurrah!"

"Idiots, let me talk!"

"Hurrah, hurrah, hurrah!"

"Go to hell!"

"Hurrah, hurrah, hurrah!"

"Kiss my ass."

"Hurrah! Hurrah! Hurrah!"

The lunatic toppled off the garbage bin in an epileptic fit, still holding the tsar's portrait.

Later that evening, two orchestras assembled in the marketplace. Someone had supplied the even wilder mob with burning torches. The long shadows of madmen danced for hours with their feet in the marketplace and their heads jostling against the buildings of the surrounding streets, then stretched in a long procession through the city. Leading this procession and leaping along with wild enthusiasm were Moshe Governor and his adjutant, Artche Onionstalk. Saluting the puzzled spectators in the windows and on the sidewalks, they commanded the marching madmen behind them: "Bel, bel, bel, bum, bum, bum . . . !"

XXIII

⁓⁓⁓

A BUNCH OF the market people gathered on the corner of Market Street. "What's this? What does it mean? What happened in Bessarabia or Serbabie or whatever it's called?" they asked each other.

The only one who could have explained it to them in detail was Barve's Son, but they knew that he had lain for weeks in bed spitting up blood.

"Maybe," Hershel suggested, "it's time for us to go to him."

Notte quickly confessed that he had been to see the invalid a few days ago and had found him more dead than alive.

"What is it all about?" they wondered.

"The end of the world," Barve's Son's deep velvet voice suddenly answered from behind them.

He looked dreadful. The sharp contours of his skull jutted out from his shrunken cheeks, and the withered lips drew back to reveal big teeth.

"Why did you get out of bed, and in such a threadbare coat at that?" Notte asked. But the ailing historian pushed his way into the center of the throng and in his usual fashion promptly began to paint with a shaking finger in the palm of his other hand. "These are the Balkans. Here is Serbia, Yugoslavia, Croatia, Macedonia, Herzegovina, Bukovina. Here is Russia and here is Germany . . ." He clutched his heart and grimaced.

"Go, go back to bed," several voices urged him.

But the living skeleton stubbornly shook his head: No, no he had to stay with them, now that the end of the world was imminent.

"Why do you think that the world will end?" Notte asked.

"Is it possible that the world would end over one dead prince?"

"The hell with the prince, my heart bleeds for you!" Barve's Son shouted in rage. His legs buckled. Notte helped him up to a wall.

"All I can tell you," Barve's Son went on, "is that whatever existed before the prince, will no longer be after the prince. The times you stood warming your hearts and souls with sweet stories around a burning brazier will be like a dream gone by. Great tragedy is coming. The world will explode and the city and the marketplace along with it, and none of you will live out your years."

Notte wiped away the gloomy prophecy with a wave of his hand. "That's silly. A whole world can't go under because of some little war about some silly prince. All we need do is pray to God that just as He made the war He should stop the war."

"God didn't start it, nor will He end it."

"Who then?"

"It's the end of the world."

"But that prince is already in the grave."

"The trouble is that he will drag everyone along to the grave—the Germans, the Russians, the French—and he won't forget you either."

"You mean to say the whole world will disappear?"

"Would God allow some dead prince to destroy the living world that He created?"

"That's the tragedy, that He *didn't* create it."

"Who then created it?" Hershel shrieked. "He created it with one word. As it's written in the Torah: He said, 'It shall be' and there was a world and there were people . . .'"

"Nonsense." The sick man spat into his handkerchief. "God never said it. To whom would He talk if there were no people yet and He was all alone? Stupid! It was only when the first two people met that they got to talking and created the world."

"You mean to say that two people—"

"Yes, yes, two and three and a thousand . . . glass, paper, ink, fire, bread, a wheel, a kerosene lamp—all that didn't come down from heaven. Human hands made it."

"If people are so smart that they could create such beautiful things, why do they want to destroy it now?"

"Not only will they destroy the world, they'll tear each other's guts out and that will be the end of them all."

"You mean to say that some people, not God, created the world?"

"Yes, the world and everything in it, even God was created by men."

"What's he babbling about?" the crowd looked at each other. "Is he serious or just fooling?"

"Man made a kerosene lamp, and the same man made God, too."

"You mean to say there's no God up in the clouds?" Notte demanded in a rage.

"There isn't! There isn't! Neither in the clouds nor in the moon. And you should thank God that there is no God, otherwise you'd be in a hell of a fix. If there was a God and this world was His doing . . . Man can be made over and with the better man will come a better world, but what can you do with a God that's almighty, invisible, and beyond reach and a bungler besides—can you make Him over?" And he wiped a speck of blood off his lips.

The market people huddled together like sheep facing a vicious wolf. Shlome the phylactery maker looked as if he expected lightning to strike the blasphemer at any moment.

They had been listening to this fellow for so many years, he had cleared up so many baffling things for them, but now his brains had grown definitely addled and he had ceased to make sense. People would destroy the bad world they had once made? The re-created world would then re-create the man, and this better man would produce a better God? It didn't stand to reason. That comes first, what comes next?

There was one consolation in all this complexity: the destruction of the world wasn't their fault. This prince—he had been no Jew, nor had any Jew killed him. Therefore, whatever happened to the world, the marketplace would somehow be spared. But when this once beloved youth in whose name they had used to bless each other now took away their only support, their only consolation, their only possession—their God—he suddenly became worse than the prince over whom the war had started. It wasn't enough to shoot him once, he should be beaten long and hard, because if it was really true that this was the end of the world, there would certainly be no more history, no further need for any of his explanations and interpretations. So why not give it to him now good and proper?

But how could a Jew hit someone who could barely stand on his feet . . . someone spitting up the last drops of blood from his wasted body? No. A good smack in the face was all right, but then again that would kill the invalid. No. He first had to be cured, then dragged out of bed and beaten to a pulp, then thrown back in bed. The first thing was to stuff a few good lunches down him so that he would put some flesh on his bones and be able to stand on his feet and take a good hiding. And holding out the same hairy paw with which he had been ready to slug Barve's Son, Notte now turned to the crowd and whispered peremptorily in everyone's ear, "Fork over a little change. He doesn't know a thing about God, still he told you where Serbia is, in the *balconies,* so be so good as to hand over a few groschen."

Holding the pile of coins behind him, Notte leaned toward the invalid and, to conceal the fact that he was stuffing the money into his pocket, he said with assumed good humor, "Go home and go to bed. Believe me, you can still be helped, and I'll bet you'll outlive us all."

"Of course I can be helped," the sick man said, raising his eyes from under his bowed head, "but not by God, just by a good doctor, and for a good doctor you need good money. So go home and lie down in your bed and bury your head in your pillows and weep because I'm better off than you are. I believe that I can still be helped by a good doctor. Somewhere there is such a doctor. But you depend on a God who doesn't exist now and who never did."

Hershel protested.

"Let him be! His sickness has gone to his head."

"Along with his blood, his brains have run out."

And soon they dispersed in the surrounding streets.

I remained standing, crushed by the tragic sight of the mocked, rejected, dying idol of my childhood.

It had been Barve's Son who with his speeches in the marketplace first roused within me the curiosity to know, to communicate, to paint with a stick in the sand the beauty and wonders of the world. How could I abandon him? Abandon the one who had once been the inspiration for the blessings repeated by my mother: "May he grow up another Barve's Son." How many times had I envied his fluttering eyes, his glib tongue, his beautiful words, even his long, green faded coat? How could I abandon one whose blessings had come true?

Now I too wore a long patched coat, now I could talk rings around him, and if I had a stick in my hand, I could now draw a bigger map of wonders on the pavement than he had once drawn in the snow. I could paint for him the miracle of my father and show him how wrong he was; prove that there was a God who both created the illness and provided the cure; prove that the world wouldn't go under; and that in the end lay the beginning; and that the bullet that had killed the archduke in Serbia had passed through the hat of my boss, Buchalsky; and that I was no longer a furrier but a free spirit; and that I had come back to my beloved Market Street, to the same place where I had played the "Perpetuo Mobile" with Paganini the Second for the Golem . . .

Yes, I knew that this scholar who "knew every book in the world" would jeer at me the way he had jeered at the common market people who didn't know who the Duke of Serbia was or where Bessarabia was—yes, I knew that he would mock me and rightfully so, because what did the twenty- or thirty-five-groschen booklets, the weekly installments of "The Conqueror of Death," mean in comparison to "all the books about Alexander the Great and Emperor Napoleon"? But who knows, maybe these childish stories about the French doctor provided me with more solace than all his thick volumes gave him. Maybe it really was true that just when the executioner raised his ax to chop off the Frenchman's head, it started raining and the ax slipped out of the executioner's wet hands and he cut off his own foot? And that when the noose was already tightened around the condemned man's neck, the rope burst, a fire broke out, and an earthquake erupted? If Barve's Son would only let me talk, if he would just listen to me, I could help him—either through an inscrutable God or through that weird French doctor . . .

With a suddenly uncontrollable impulse of daring, I approached the sick man:

"Why did you scare those poor people?"

"I told them the truth."

"What for?" I asked with a strange feeling of confidence in my powers.

The invalid flung my hand off his arm and gritted his big, angry teeth. "Your father, that ignoramus, caused me a lot of grief too. He also began to babble about God in his older years, but I always considered you an intelligent boy, a gymnasium student . . . I saw you with books under your arm. What did you learn from all those books? What do you know about the world? Do you know that there's a war on and everyone in the world will be killed including you?"

"Not me."

"Why not you?"

"When it comes time to shoot me, the gun will break, the powder will get wet, or the war will end."

"Where did you get that information?"

"A famous doctor told me."

"The doctor who helped your father?"

"Only God helped my father."

"Which God? Why are you running on about a God that never was? Let me alone, you boring pest."

"My father is completely recovered. All healed. Healthier and stronger than he ever was," I said with sly perversity, trying to pierce the sick man's obstinacy.

"A rich man's luck." Barve's Son spat through his teeth. "He brought thousands from America that he embezzled from some whore. Here in town, he also sucked a fortune out of a female—General Renenkampf's wife. And when you have money you can cure the worst sickness." And he slid to the ground with a deep sigh of envy.

He reached his hand into his pocket and his face suddenly twisted in a queer smile. "Look here, what's this doing in my pocket?" And he pulled out a pile of coins along with some paper rubles. "This money isn't mine. When did I ever have so much money? Unless I've put on someone else's jacket," he joked in a weak voice.

I feigned ignorance. "What's the difference? If the jacket is yours then the pocket is yours too, and if the money is in your pocket—it's your money."

"But I can't remember . . ."

"Maybe you've forgotten. You haven't left the house in the past two weeks, haven't worn your jacket, haven't looked in your pocket. Maybe someone sent it to you. Maybe someone lent it to you." I was hammering away at the invalid's confused brain.

He stared goggled-eyed at the money in his trembling hand: "Maybe you're right . . . maybe I've forgotten. My memory is getting weak. I don't remember . . . maybe someone actually gave it to me. Your father used to help me out quite often. He is a good-hearted person, and you say that he has been cured. . . . So you see I'm right—all you need is a good doctor. I remember how your father used to run to Germany from one doctor to another. Do you know which German doctor helped him? Maybe that would be an idea . . . Maybe I should too—I mean Germany . . . I don't know what I'm talking about—there is no more Germany."

"The doctor isn't a German but a Frenchman."

"A Frenchman? Where does a Frenchman come to—the market-place, I mean—in Germany? Oh, I don't know what you and I are talking about." And he grimaced as if about to faint.

I caught him under his arm. "I'll take you home, then I'll go get the doctor."

"From France? Oh, it's growing dark before my eyes." He stretched out his trembling hand with the money, as if offering it to me for carfare with which to go to France and bring the doctor.

"Put it back in your pocket, the good doctor cured my father and didn't ask a kopeck for it. My father is now healthier than he was before he got sick," I said with a strength I never knew I possessed.

"Why not? A good doctor can help."

"He can help you, too."

"Can we go to him now?"

"I can bring him to you."

"Does he live far from here?"

"He's in town by chance."

"What do you mean?"

"They're after him."

"Who is after him?" Breathing with effort, the sick man reached for support. I began to tremble all over, as if I had caught his fever, and spoke with the speed of a racing train: "He escaped from France. The police are on his trail. He's in hiding—by chance, he came to our house, and when he left, he took my father's sickness with him. My father was cured as if he had never been sick at all."

"How is that possible? Why are you plaguing me? What do you want from me?" And he began to vomit green bile.

But I didn't let up. "I'll bring the doctor to you, and he'll cure you without money, only on your promise that you won't tell anybody, because if they deported him to France he'd lose his head on the guillotine."

"I'm sick. Help me!"

"He cured my father."

"Where is this doctor?"

"He's a Frenchman . . . He speaks French."

"What's his name?"

"Monsieur Chantille Jeantaigne Delacroix," I said gravely.

Barve's Son used both hands to straighten his head, which dangled on his shoulder like a torn puppet's, and sighed. "Ah, but I know him . . . I know him well."

It appeared that the two liars had finally come to an understanding. All that remained was for the first to take the second by the arm so that the second would let himself be put to bed so that the first could bring him the imaginary doctor that the second knew so well . . . But not yet. Barve's Son suddenly gathered his last bit of strength and, gritting his teeth, cried hoarsely, "Get away from me, you filthy ignoramus! Why are you annoying me? I don't need a doctor. I know that French charlatan, that swindler. He's a first-class phony. I read about him someplace . . . He calls himself 'The Conqueror of Death' and peddles black magic or hypnosis, or some other nonsense. Get away, you little idiot. I don't believe in that crap—beat it!" And he clutched his breast to contain the terrible pain that now twisted him into a human corkscrew.

"This is the end, I'm dying . . ." he whispered in dread and stretched out on the pavement.

I quickly crawled underneath him and, wrapping his flaccid arm around my neck, half-dragged half-carried him to his attic room and to bed.

For a while he lay there with a terrible strain in all his tissues, his eyes turned up, his lips twisted, his delicate hands clutching the edge of the sheet, like a woman in the final stages of labor. Gradually his strained limbs relaxed and a gentle, weary expression settled over his face. He opened his eyes and, looking up at me with the smile and vacuous blankness of a newborn baby, he mumbled, "Pardon, Monsieur. I know you . . . I've read about you . . . But I don't remember. Your name is . . ."

"Chantille Jeantaigne Delacroix," I prompted him. "In forty minutes you will be cured. Do you have a watch? You don't have one, neither do I . . . I ran out of the house without it. Here's a little water and, in the meantime, I'll run home and bring the watch."

XXIV

A GREAT SHOCK of brown hair over a high forehead made Sarah seem taller than she was. From her mother she had inherited her wide blue eyes and the dimples in her downy cheeks. From her father's side came the humble, optimistic smile and, just like him, she could count the number of words she uttered in a single day on the fingers of her hands.

When she was still a girl, Itzik the bookkeeper fell in love with her. A good provider, pious, a former yeshiva student, he never held a card in his hand, never smoked a cigarette—in short, a youth without a fault, as the saying goes, but not good-looking. Red-haired with jug-handle ears and, like most redheads, his nose and hands sprinkled with freckles. In a word—ugly. And this one fault outweighed all his positive traits in Sarah's eyes.

One time he brought a box of candy and promised her the life of a princess. He showed her letters from a wealthy bachelor uncle in America who promised to leave him a large fortune in his will. Since this uncle was already in his sixties and constantly complained in his letters of a weak heart, the bookkeeper reckoned that he couldn't live much longer and that the inheritance would come to some hundred thousand dollars. But Sarah was a woman to whom a hundred thousand dollars wasn't enough to make up for the freckles on the bookkeeper's nose. Had she told him this at once, perhaps the thing would have ended right then and there, but in her usual fashion she kept silent, and he didn't know whether she didn't respond because she couldn't grasp the enormity of the sum or whether she doubted if the uncle would be dying so soon.

In order to pry open her mouth, Itzik once threatened to poison himself. This led to both his parents and hers taking a hand, and a match was imminent when by chance Sarah happened to meet Benjamin—and when she saw his black mustache over the blood-red lips within the clear face, she opened her mouth and in uncharacteristic, clear diction and firm voice she cried, "No!" Itzik's fate was sealed. Now, even if the American uncle were to die as promised and instead of a hundred thousand dollars leave a hundred million, it wouldn't stop Itzik from taking a dose of poison.

But to his good fortune, the conscription was ordered. Itzik wormed his way out of the draft by giving himself a rupture, but Benjamin was sent away deep into Russia for a whole four and a half years. This was a good opportunity for Itzik to try his luck again with Sarah, and now his chances appeared better than before. First of all his uncle had already died and left him actually not a hundred thousand dollars as he had hoped, but just two thousand. However, according to the reckoning of this specialist in arithmetic, a couple could live on two thousand dollars for a hundred and forty years in relative comfort and respectability. And who lived that long anyway? So it would be possible to leave a big inheritance to several children. Second, Benjamin had been sent off to Russia, and a man of his character who was capable of stealing a bride from under a wedding canopy would surely come back married.

But Sarah, who lacked education and didn't understand arithmetic, trusted only the one whom she loved. She let her heart do the reckoning and the account came out right. Benjamin *did* come back five years later, still a bachelor, and they were married.

Itzik felt very bad. But figures are figures, and the accounts were clear: since he could live on his inheritance for a hundred and forty years, he would surely outlive Benjamin. And since he could no longer take Sarah as a virgin, he would get her as a widow.

That his reckoning wasn't as foolish as it sounded was proved by the facts when, a few years later, the Russo-Japanese War broke out, and since Itzik was already deferred because of his rupture, his reckoning left two possibilities: Benjamin was a trained soldier and would probably be sent to the front in the first draft; second, no one came back from the first draft. This meant that there was a good chance he would get Sarah a lot sooner than he had expected. That Benjamin could make himself a rupture of his own was something Itzik was sure couldn't happen. He knew Benjamin only too well. He, Benjamin, loved himself too much to let even a tip of his mustache be trimmed to save himself from possible death.

It looked as if Sarah was in Itzik's pocket, but Benjamin now played him another dirty trick. Instead of going to war, he ran off to America. This was something Itzik hadn't counted on. Still, it represented a big victory for him. And as soon as Benjamin had gone off, he got himself all togged out in a high collar and an expensive dickey, put on cuffs and chamois gloves to hide the ugly freckles on his hands, and each Monday and Thursday he knocked on Sarah's door to see if he could get a glass of tea on the strength of their old friendship.

One warm evening when he had filled himself with tea, he wiped his sweaty brow with a yellowish handkerchief and proposed to Sarah that they take a ride in a droshky in order to catch a little breeze. When in her terse fashion she replied that she was a married woman and that it wasn't proper before God and man, he countered that it said in the Torah that it wasn't right for a man to covet his neighbor's wife, but there was nothing written about a man's wife taking a little ride with her husband's best friend.

Sarah was more than sure that what the Torah did not specifically forbid was permissible, but she couldn't see why she should take a ride when it represented neither sin nor enjoyment. But the book-keeper had the patience of Job, and by quoting the Torah he finally managed to persuade Sarah to take a ride with him.

She put on her large hat with the black ostrich feathers, padded herself in front and back with several cushions, took out her special fringed parasol, and even let him hold her arm as she got into Fat Eunuch's droshky.

In the droshky he started telling her that actually he had two uncles in America, not one, and if the first had died, the second had sent him a treasure a thousand times greater than that which the first had left him—namely, a letter containing a bit of evil gossip: that Benjamin had gotten involved with a whore in America and was laughing at his wife, Sarah.

Whether Sarah believed this or was hurt by it was something that couldn't be determined since, as usual, she smiled more than she spoke. But when a few days later she heard that Itzik was going through the marketplace showing the letter to everyone, and when on the following Monday Itzik came to beg a glass of tea again, she met him at the door with an unexpected look of anger on her face and with such language that if the bookkeeper had added up and measured the words she threw in his face in the course of five minutes, it would have come to more than he had heard from her in the course of their years-long friendship.

Before him stood not the mute Sarah he knew, but one great big mouth spraying fire. And, finally, she slammed the door in his face.

When he came downstairs he nearly tore the hair from his head—how come, how come? The fact that she hadn't believed that he had an uncle in America who would leave him an inheritance—that was quite understandable. But how could she possibly have concealed her gift of gab from him all these years and deceived him into thinking that she wasn't capable of uttering more than two words a day? And all of a sudden—such a mouth! This couldn't be determined even with mathematical logic.

In a state of shock he reminded himself of a passage in the holy books: "From love to hate is a single step." And he actually decided to take this step. And just as he had sought for years to make her happy, he now decided to destroy her.

As soon as Benjamin came back from America, Itzik waited for him on a quiet street and there, under the guise of devoted friendship, let him know that it was a good thing he, Benjamin, had come in time since Sarah had enticed him and nearly forced him to break the commandment of coveting his best friend's wife. Benjamin, who at that time set no store in the Torah, seized the bookkeeper by the throat and in a moment he would have broken a commandment himself—but luckily for the informer, who was about to breathe his last, the Karaite policeman came by just then and, as is often the case with policemen, scolded the innocent and rescued the guilty one.

But a word is sometimes like a disgusting fly that will neither fly away nor be waved away. The broken commandment wouldn't stop dancing before Benjamin's eyes or buzzing in his ears until he finally decided to subject his wife to an inquiry. But since even in the best of times Sarah barely uttered a word, it was quite natural that in her astonishment over this unexpected investigation she should lose her tongue altogether and emit only these few words: "not true, false accusation, a lie."

These words, which never sound convincing to a jealous mate, had the same contrary reaction as usual and served only to arouse the inflamed husband even more. Certain market people who had known Sarah since childhood tried to intercede and testified that the bookkeeper had flaunted the accusatory letter from America, but this merely added fuel to the fire. Benjamin maintained that America was only being used to expose his sins *there* to conceal her crime *here,* and the more the market people shouted, "No, no!" the madder he got. It appeared that until he found a witness to say "Yes, yes," he would crack up altogether and, God forbid, lose his mind. And soon he found just such a witness in the person of his own son.

I, naturally, meant no harm by this, I hadn't the slightest desire to cause my mother any grief—all I wanted was to appease my father. And when he locked himself in a room with me and began to pose one clipped question after another, in order to satisfy him I said "yes" to everything he asked.

"Bookkeeper?"

"Yes."

"Evening?"

"Yes."

"Droshky?"

"Yes."

How could I possibly have known that whatever I said would have made no difference at all to my father—all he wanted was confirmation of his suspicions. And since Fat Eunuch's droshky was known as a conveyance for illicit couples—then it had to be true, after all.

"Yes."

"Then I am right?"

"Obviously."

A fiery surge of justified rage flared in my father's eyes. He dashed from the room, ran in to my mother, and a loud slap and the thud of a body falling to the floor resounded through the house.

For a while she lay there sprawled on the floor. Among the stars she saw now, she probably saw Itzik soaring on white wings and winking to her with the two thousand dollars. But soon she got up and wiped a drop of blood from her silent lips. Better a slap from a handsome hand than a pat from an ugly once. Once in love, always in love. And she therefore kept silent, forgave—and, that same night, forgot the whole incident.

And she proved to be no fool. The same hand that so unfairly insulted her brought her not two but a whole ten thousand dollars with which she could live in contentment and satisfaction five times a hundred and forty years. But, as the saying goes, it wasn't fated. Benjamin caught the asthma, and the ten thousand dollars were squandered in a hundred and forty weeks.

Each time he got an attack and the doctor stuck him with the poisonous needles to put him to sleep, she would stand by his bedside and hold his convulsive hand to her heart, for she loved and trusted the hand—the hand that had slapped her and the hand that had fondled. And again the hand didn't fool her. In a manner that no one could understand, Benjamin pried his own lungs open again with his own hands and took out the sickness from which no doctor could cure him or even ease his suffering. This was considered by the doctors and professors and by the whole world as a miracle from heaven. But if it isn't fated, even a miracle can turn to a tragedy. The World War broke out and Benjamin again received notice to report for military service.

Day and night Sarah exerted her powers to rework the miracle and stuff up his lungs again. But it wouldn't work. Once a miracle always a miracle. She raced with him through the streets, jumped off stairs, gave him fur to inhale, cigars to smoke, fed him salty, peppery, and sour foods—but as hard as it had come to him to open his lungs, it proved completely impossible to stuff them up again. And when on a certain morning Benjamin reported to the town hall and presented himself to the medical commission, they clapped him on the back and assigned him to the Twelfth Company of the 275th Orenburger Regiment, which was the first to be hurled into the fire.

XXV

As the first and largest population center near the border where the tsar's downfall began, the town quickly became the vortex of a terrible commotion as well as the main point from which masses of troops left for the front and to which they then fled in retreat or were transported on stretchers directly from the battlefront. In a city of only two hundred sixty thousand inhabitants, hundreds of quickly improvised hospitals and field stations sprang up to accommodate the nearly two million casualties that sent a bloody stench over the whole region.

From Church Street poured an endless procession of mounted Cossacks carrying black lances. The horses, clip-clopping nose to tail through the narrow streets, poked their rumps into the windows of the stores, shattering the panes. Converging to meet them from Tartar Street marched a never-ending column of dust-covered infantry. Licking their cracked lips with parched tongues, they still made an effort to keep their weary legs in step with the mournful song:

> Sparrow, sparrow, little bird
> The canary sings so sad.

Along the parallel Seminary Street rolled long rows of high wagons with noisy iron wheels, enormous soup kitchens trailing behind. The vats swayed, spattering the gutters with stale stew.

The marketplace was thronged with squatting, newly mobilized troops loaded down with field packs, blankets, and kettles and waiting to be issued uniforms and told where to go. Some played sad tunes on harmonicas, others got drunk, danced, then fought. These were peasants from the neighboring villages who were alien to the marketplace. Most of the regular market people were no longer there. When the war first broke out, the city garrison had been the first to be thrown into battle. The hastily assembled regiments of the city garrison were made up of fifty percent Jews, so that many of the market people were the first to be consumed by the hellish fire. And those who remained now marched along Tartar Street in a freshly mustered column. Running after them were their wives and children, who wrung their hands and cried, "Mendel, for God's sake, where are they sending you?"

And Mendel, hopping from foot to foot to keep in step with the blaring military band, pleaded in embarrassment, "Go home, woman, I'll be back soon."

"See that you're careful!" the wives admonished their husbands.

From the depot trundled hundreds of little carts with bloody wounded, their bodies still unbandaged, groaning on the straw pallets.

At the same time, hundreds of youngsters, mostly gymnasium students wearing Red Cross armbands, carried stretchers on which lay soldiers missing a quarter or even a whole third of their bodies. From all sides came a terrible groaning and cursing: "In the blood and bones and marrow of the fathers and mothers and sisters and brothers and, especially—the Jews!"

The most tragic procession, however, emerged from Glass Street. These were the refugees from the towns and villages lying near the front—the spies and the traitors, the despised, cursed, damnable Jews. Children, women, the old, the sick, the lame, most of them barefoot, tearful, ragged—they supported one another, toting pillows, teapots, pots, and toys on their shoulders. In front of the pitiful procession walked a skinny horse pulling a small peasant cart with a cloth-covered holy scroll that the refugees had managed to rescue from a synagogue damaged by a shell. On each side of the wagon walked several gray-bearded men intoning prayers from small prayerbooks.

In great despair over the incredible catastrophe that he had suffered at the front, the tsar turned for comfort to his hysterical mystic of a wife and his long-legged and tiny-headed uncle, Nikolai Nikolaevich. The tsarina proclaimed the cause of the military calamity to be a "finger from God," but the uncle—a more cultured person and a composer of verses—didn't completely agree with his niece. It hadn't been a "finger from God" but the "hand of the Jews" that had sold Russia out to the Germans . . . And it was promptly decided to sweep the entire Jewish population from the towns and cities along the front and to throw those Jews who were no longer useful out of the army and the hospitals for the wounded. Thus a number of dismissed military doctors, nurses, and typhus victims trailed along behind this procession along with a sizable number of Jewish soldiers lacking arms or legs and, oddly enough, sporting medals for valor on their chests.

The Christian onlookers lining the sidewalks spat upon the passing "traitors," and pails of slops descended on them from several windows.

My mother sat brooding at the window and gazed at the Armageddon below. But beneath her gloom glowed a measure of pride. If not for her intervention, the bones of her beloved husband might now be rotting in some forsaken field of battle. The Orenburger Regiment, according to some of the returning wounded market people, had been "blindly led into a meat grinder and hacked to pieces." They hadn't even gotten the chance to take their rifles from their shoulders.

"If that old drunk, General Renenkampf, had kept pace with General Samsonov, who commanded the right flank, the tragedy wouldn't have occurred," the witnesses claimed. "But the two generals were bitter enemies from their younger days when they had fought over a game of cards, and now each had played his own card separately so that both had suffered a devastating rout. But Samsonov had at least behaved like a proper gambler so that when he saw his three hundred thousand men shrink to less than ten thousand within three weeks, he had the good grace to leave the card table, go to the toilet, and put a bullet in his head. But that lousy sot of a Renenkampf simply got drunk and went to sleep."

Some of the speakers tried to minimize the general's guilt and to place it on the shoulders of his wife, who "wore the pants in the family and had had a hand in drawing up the plans for the catastrophic offensive . . ."

"Where does a woman come off to wage war at all?" they seethed. "What did she think, that just because she could throw the old stinker out of her bed and take in his adjutant, young Kaverin, this meant she could do the same with the Germans? A plague, a cholera, a calamity on her head."

Sarah didn't want to listen. Because even if it was true that Madam Renenkampf had destroyed the Orenburger Regiment, she had managed to rescue her Benjamin.

It was only a few days before the doomed regiment marched out of the city when Sarah, dressed in her holiday best, which she hadn't worn throughout her husband's lengthy illness, went to the general's white palace in the Botanical Garden. She didn't have an interceder, a paper, a document, or a letter of introduction. All she had was her delicate and disarming shyness and her strange charm.

Madame Renenkampf received her graciously and offered her a glass of wine. She remembered the one-time guardian of her costly furs. She was under the impression that he had been terribly ill and passed away, and she was very pleased to learn that he was still alive. Mainly, however, she was pleased to hear that despite his poor health he had patriotically volunteered for the army.

"The thing is," Sarah explained, "one day he may appear healthy and the next suffer an asthmatic attack and become a near corpse. If he were allowed to go to the front, he'd have to be brought back the next day. In his patriotic fervor he'd probably run to the front again, take a few shots at the enemy, and again collapse. This would mean that the government would need a special wagon to take him back and forth between the front and the hospital."

The general's wife burst out laughing. She knew that the furrier's wife hadn't come to burden her with a tactless request to have her husband released from military service. On the contrary, a living corpse that volunteered to do its duty for the Fatherland—that was so splendid, so commendable . . . Then what was it she wanted? A coach to take him to and from the front? That was surely a good joke. "Speaking practically, what can be done for a soldier who is sick one day and well the next?"

Replying in the same good-natured vein, Sarah proposed that her husband be transferred to a hospital where he could do his military duty on the days he was well and be treated as a patient on the days he was sick. And since the Honored Lady supervised the biggest military hospital in town, could she not manage to again have her former subordinate under her supervision just like the good old days?

The droll, intimate conversation served to elevate Madam Renenkampf's spirits, and she proposed a second glass of wine, but Sarah knew when to stop talking. She thanked her hostess for the wine and said no more.

Early the next morning, Benjamin was summoned from the barracks in the Antokol suburb and transferred to the Zoo suburb where the main hospital was located. Once there, he was handed a ring of keys, a white smock, and made overseer of provisions for the hospital. At the end of the week he was allowed to see his family and even bring along a sack of groats, a piece of beef, or a few loaves of bread. Did Sarah have any cause then to curse the despised commander-in-skirts?

When the relatives and neighbors learned of Benjamin's lucky break, the house quickly filled with brothers and sisters, aunts, uncles, sick cousins, and near and far acquaintances who well remembered the generosity of the American millionaire who had now become something more than a mere millionaire because, in such times, a few loaves of bread were worth more than a million rubles.

The happy Benjamin sliced the bread and measured the groats, distributing them among the recipients, who heaped blessings upon him befitting the Messiah himself. As usual, Sarah stood off in a corner in silence. It never occurred to anyone that she had some thanks coming to her, too. But Sarah, who firmly believed in divine justice, knew that if she lived and stayed well, she would eventually receive all the gratitude that was coming to her.

On a certain day, the director of the hospital called the heads of the various departments and announced that, a week hence, His Imperial Majesty the Tsar of all the Russias, King of Poland, Prince of Finland, etc., etc., would visit the hospital, and he outlined for them the procedure to be followed during his visit.

First, the tsar would pass through the wards—therefore the wounded would have to be rehearsed on how to answer in case he asked them a question. Those who couldn't talk because they had lost the lower parts of their faces needed only to nod. Those with only one leg didn't have to march, only stand in the courtyard and, the moment His Majesty appeared, shout "Hurrah" and keep it up as long as their breaths lasted. His Majesty would also deign to taste the food. And the director fixed a stern gaze on Benjamin and his head chefs. Then he turned to the doctors, medical assistants, and pharmacists and issued them all instructions, concluding that a special stand was to be erected in the courtyard for the wives and children of the personnel. He had only to tell them how to dress and how to curtsy and bow when His Majesty passed by.

Following a long wait, the tsar showed up in the courtyard surrounded by his entourage. A group of priests in gold and silver garments came out to greet him carrying a diamond-encrusted icon. The sickly hysterical hurrahs made the tsar's pale face recoil even deeper within his beard, and he clutched the icon closer to his breast. He then handed the diamond-studded portrait to a Circassian with a great, wild beard and a bemedaled chest, who carried the holy picture past the row of kneeling soldiers. Those who could not bend their knees, or needed their arms for their crutches, fell face-down on the ground.

In the meantime, the tsar came up to the long table around which Benjamin and the chefs were gathered. A great bowl of black buckwheat stood on the table next to another filled with chunks of fatty meat and big platters of sliced bread. The director bowed deeply and handed the tsar a small silver spoon. The tsar fished out a drop of buckwheat that he put to his lips and smiled. He liked it, but didn't utter a word. The chefs, with Benjamin in front, legs trembling and bellies cramped, shouted the rehearsed "We wish good health to Your Imperial Highness!"

The tsar quickly walked away from the table and strolled over to the stand where the group of ladies stood around all perfumed and smiling coquettishly. The group included the director of the Red Cross, the nurses, the wives and children of the doctors, and Benjamin's wife and son.

Approaching the stand, the tsar seemed to be sad although his little blond beard showed something resembling a smile. He stretched out a pale hand to the ladies, Sarah included, with a quiet "*spasibo*—thank you."

And so Sarah received the highest possible human thanks for her love and devotion, for the insults and blows she had borne, for her silence, and particularly for her heroic rescue of her Benjamin from the Orenburger Regiment.

XXVI

⟡

THE FRONT MOVED even closer to the city. Big birds with black crosses on their white bellies often appeared in the sky and spewed down their deadly eggs on the morbid city below. They were promptly driven off by cannon fire that spattered the sky with whirls of silver smoke.

The black specter of hunger spread over the poor sections of town. Certain streets were sealed off where the yellow plague of cholera and dysentery had made sudden inroads.

Endless columns of retreating troops slogged through the center of town. In the Jewish streets, bands of embittered soldiers broke into the food stores and plundered the last of the provisions.

Military police lurked behind every corner ready to seize every passing young man by the collar and demand proof of why he wasn't in the army. Even if it turned out that he had been exempted, he was still capable of digging trenches behind the city.

With the need growing, Benjamin had to increase the size of the food packages that he brought home on his weekly twelve-hour leave. These packages now sustained a troop of approximately forty people—relatives and close friends. But, as if out of spite, the hospital director was replaced by a new military doctor who happened to be a decent but very strict man. Under his new regime, Benjamin was now allowed to come home once every two weeks, and for six hours only. The worst of it was that a special guard was posted at the hospital gate, and it was no longer possible to walk past him carrying packages. All that Benjamin could bring home was a few handfuls of groats in his pocket and two chunks of meat concealed under the armpit of his greatcoat. The forty recipients cursed the new hospital director heartily and, while they were at it, heaped a few curses on Benjamin's head as well.

One evening, when he came home, Sarah met him at the door

and whispered that Rabbi Isserson was waiting for him in the dining room.

"What does that madman want?"

"I don't know. He'll only speak to you. I told the Saint that sometimes you come late, but you know how he is. He's been waiting three hours already . . . I was afraid to argue with such a lunatic."

"Saint" and "lunatic" were two parts of one nickname by which Rabbi Isserson was usually designated. Which of the two names actually fitted him was difficult to determine.

Once he had been a respectable preacher in a prayer house within the Great Synagogue complex, but his intractable fanaticism and vituperative diatribes had so antagonized the elders of his synagogue that he had become the center of a furious debate.

He didn't preach piety—on the contrary, his words often smacked of heresy. He hurled the vilest abuse at the rich, whom he compared to the Jewish kings who had been "a gang of idolators." The poor, however, were no bargain either.

A tall man, bubbling with energy, with fire in his eyes and even more in his tongue, he carried a big stick and cast fear upon everyone he disliked, and he disliked almost everyone. But even those who privately cursed him wished him a long life, for they knew that after he had laid them low, he would do the same to their enemies.

This was the Isserson who had now come to visit.

First, Benjamin went into the kitchen and emptied his pockets of the little food he had managed to spirit out of the hospital—only then did he go into the dining room.

Isserson sat at the table, his hands leaning on his stick, his chin on his hands, letting the long beard doze lightly atop the cane. The moment he sensed someone in the room he sprang to his feet, shook his head, rousing his beard from its nap, and said in a commanding tone, "Be so good as to close the door, I must speak to you in private. I would have waited for you the whole night, but what I have to say can be said in just five minutes!"

Benjamin shut the door.

"I want the food package that you brought home today for the Jewish orphans."

"What package are you talking about?" Benjamin was trying to play dumb.

"A new group of Jewish refugees has entered the city. There are some hundred and fifty orphans among them, hungry, weak little lambs who must have food, food, food!" The rabbi struck the table three times with his cane.

"Calm yourself," Benjamin said. "You'll break the table—and why shout when you yourself asked that the door be closed so that no one would hear? I beg you, speak as man to man."

"Mad dogs can't speak like men, mad dogs bark, and you can't bark quietly and calmly!"

"Believe me, I have nothing to do with that crowd that's giving you a hard time," Benjamin said with a weak smile. "To me, you were always a saint and not a mad dog."

"The military commander of the city thinks the reverse, and since he's a general and you're only a rank above a private, his opinion is the one that counts."

"I don't understand."

"A few days ago I went to the commander to beg a little food for the hungry Jewish children. He cursed me for annoying him and said, 'Don't you know that all the roads to the city are blocked by armies concentrated around it for a decisive battle? No food can be brought in. Everyone has to suffer from the shortage alike and no exceptions can be made.' When I brought to his attention that the situation wasn't exactly the way he explained it, that a certain amount of food was being brought to the non-Jewish orphanages and for free at that, he told me to get the hell out. I turned tail and got out."

"How then is it my fault?" Benjamin complained. "I didn't send you to the commander."

"That's right! I shouldn't have begged a gentile general for something I could get from a Jew."

Benjamin's legs shook from anger and indignation. "I have no food. People exaggerate! I sometimes bring home some groats or a few loaves of bread that I give to the needy in my family, that's all."

"All Jews are one family—a lousy family, true, but a family nonetheless. If you help one, you must help all, and the orphans come first."

"It's shameless to libel me this way. It's damn dangerous, too. Who is the informer who told you? Who?" Benjamin demanded hotly.

"Tell me the name of the man who spread such terrible lies about me. After all, I'm a soldier. I can forfeit my life . . . Tell me who and I'll push his ugly face in."

"I did that already," the Saint replied. "I gave him a good once-across-the-whiskers so he won't be doing any more talking. Now I'm the only one who can inform on you, therefore you have to understand that since I'm here, I won't leave without the food." And he slapped his own beard to emphasize his demand.

"I haven't got much. A little I can spare."

"A little is not enough—I need a lot."

"Where shall I get a lot?"

"The same place you got a little."

"How can you demand this of me? Each time I take out a handful of groats I risk my life."

"You must take it out gradually—a little today, a little tomorrow," the rabbi advised with the air of an expert.

"How can a pious Jew like you propose such a thing to me? This is simple theft, after all. What about the commandment 'Thou shalt not steal'?"

"First of all, you've been stealing right along. Second, if you had asked me I would have told you to go right on stealing, because when the Jews went out of Egypt, God Himself told them to steal and He was right, because when Jews suffer as people, they must guard against breaking the Ten Commandments with the greatest care, but when they are placed into the category of dogs, the laws of the Torah no longer apply to them. The Torah was given to people, not to dogs." He suddenly lost his patience and slammed the stick furiously against the table. "Besides, what's one sin? I have, they say, six hundred and six sins on my conscience and I'm not afraid to stand in judgment before the Almighty a hundred and twenty years from now."

Benjamin realized that all further argument would be futile and that the next blow of the stick was liable to fall on his skull. To be rid of the madman, he showed him all he had brought home, with a promise to bring more in the weeks to come.

As Isserson was about to leave with the package under his arm, he stopped at the threshold and said, "Oh, I nearly forgot. I want a personal favor from you. If you have an extra slice of bread, I'll borrow it for my wife. As for me, the devil won't take me, but she is weak. She hasn't had a bite of food yet today. And if she should pass away prematurely, God forbid, they would excommunicate me again, and the worst of it would be that at my age and in these terrible times, I'd have a hard job finding a fourth wife."

After the lunatic had left, Father turned to me and announced that from now on I'd have to go every day to the hospital where he would fill my pockets with chickpeas, groats, or lima beans, which I would then bring home and pour into a special sack that I would take to Rabbi Isserson at the end of each week.

And that's how I became a daily visitor to the Zwerinitz Hospital. I would come in the mornings and wander around the large court-yard until Benjamin winked at me from behind the storehouse. My pockets stuffed, I would wait patiently until the guard at the gate grew drowsy from boredom, then carefully and swiftly slip out into the street.

Between Benjamin's wink and the guard's yawn, long hours often went by, so that the hospital employees got to know me and some-times even asked me to lend a hand carrying pillows or blankets from one part of the hospital to the other. I soon gained the status of a regular errand boy.

One day, they tied a Red Cross armband around my sleeve and sent me to the depot reserved for military trains. I accepted the as-signment eagerly, since it gave me the opportunity to pass the guard openly with my pockets bulging with lima beans. The depot was filled with peasant carts carrying the wounded who had been brought from the front, which was now only miles from the besieged city. Most of the wounded were carried on stretchers borne by hundreds of young volunteers wearing the same armband as I.

The hospital was filled to overflowing. Bed after bed held crushed, groaning, cursing bodies that spilled over into the corridors and an-terooms. I had to point out the corners where the fresh arrivals could be put until the doctors sorted them out.

My swift orientation drew the attention of the new director of the hospital, and he entrusted me with another responsible assignment: to register the number of the wounded and of those who had died on the way and to check off those who would have to be transferred to other hospitals.

I was obliged to run with a stack of papers under my arm from the depot at one end of the city to the hospital at the other—a considerable distance—three times a day. And in the very first week the soles separated from my shoes.

When the director noticed me straining to keep my flapping soles together, he ordered his adjutant to take me to the supply sergeant to be fitted for the smallest pair of army boots.

A few days later, with the director's permission, my father pulled a greatcoat, a tunic, and a pair of breeches from a shelf full of uniforms and personally patched the bullet holes in the coat, shortened the sleeves, cut down the breeches, and outfitted his son in a complete miniature soldier's uniform. At the same time, he didn't forget to sew a couple of extra large pockets into the greatcoat.

With my peculiar ability to adjust to a garment and to become what that garment represented, I soon managed to be included among the military personnel of the hospital, to receive the same pay of twenty-four kopecks a month, and even to be issued the same weekly packet of tobacco given to the regular soldiers. Although everybody knew that I didn't make even half a soldier, I saluted the hospital officials, who were all reservists or privileged military personnel, with the assurance and nonchalance of a full-fledged officer.

More than anyone, I made sure to befriend the director, who often praised me publicly and once, remonstrating with a young, inexperienced doctor, even mentioned how quickly "the little stinker—excuse me," he apologized, "I mean the captain," had managed to catch on to the routine and suggested that the doctor follow my example.

My father was deeply gratified each time he saw the guard at the gate draw himself up to attention in mockery when the "little captain" passed by with pockets filled to overflowing.

Not that it went altogether smoothly. There were a few uncomfortable moments, as for instance when I encountered a drunken lieutenant and failed to salute him. The tipsy officer chased after me and, measuring the puny soldier, broke into laughter and kicked him soundly in the rear end. But besides this and several similar unpleasant incidents, there was no doubt that my uniform and, especially, the praise of the director lent me extraordinary prestige among the employees and guards at the hospital and particularly among the civilian volunteers at the depot.

One cold, rainy morning as I wandered with my papers through a freight train that during the night had brought a transport of damaged goods from the front, I glanced into the empty wagons to see if any of the wounded had been left behind in the rush. And, as it turned out, one was indeed sprawled in a corner on a pile of rotten straw. His head was bandaged. His dark green officer's uniform was slit at the shoulder, indicating that he had been seriously wounded there as well. When I began to climb into the wagon, the policeman came up. "Hey there, little captain, be careful. He's dangerous. He'll tear your nose off."

"What's wrong with him?"

"A madman . . . Better take him out of there."

"There's no designation on my list for madmen."

"Who then will take him?"

"That's not my business." And I crawled under the wagon and skipped over the rails to a second train.

A while later I heard wild screams, and I crawled back to see what was happening. Four youths were struggling with the madman, whom they had managed to bind with a rope to a stretcher that they bore on their shoulders. The bound man roared in an insane voice, demanding that he be freed because he was completely well. He didn't want to go to any hospital but to go after the Jews—the betrayers of Russia who had shot off his leg and now wanted to cut off his head and arms as well.

"Bring me some Jews and I'll kill them all," he pleaded aloud. And when the youths (all four of whom happened to be Jewish) ignored his request, he kicked one of the forward bearers in the head with his remaining good leg and with such force that the youth fell and the stretcher tilted to the side. The madman rolled off and slammed his bandaged head against the rails. He twitched a few more times, then grew still.

"Hey, what's going on here?" The policeman came from the other side of the train.

"He jumped off the stretcher. Looks like he's dead."

"A dead man doesn't jump off a stretcher." The policeman rudely pushed aside the volunteers, and in a loud voice demanded, "Passports! Documents!"

The four youths stood there with faces pale as corpses.

"Documents!" the policeman persisted, holding out a fat, hairy paw with dirty fingernails. The four youths began to rummage in their pockets.

"Where are your documents showing your exemption from military service? And where are your documents freeing you from digging trenches?"

"We're volunteers in the Red Cross," one youth said, pointing to his armband.

"Red Cross—Jew Cross," the policeman grumbled. "Come with me."

"But our duty is to bring him to the Antokol section," the frightened volunteers said, trying to hold on to the corpse.

"Where is the madman?" I interjected as if I didn't know what was going on.

"There he lies, dead . . . This gang did him in," the policeman said, picking his nose as he was coming toward me.

"Oh, if he's dead, then he belongs to me. I do have a listing for corpses. Let me check him off," I said with authority. Then, to the trembling volunteers: "You follow me to sign the necessary papers."

They drew themselves up erect and respectfully put their fingers to their caps—a thing they wouldn't do even for a full general.

My new military clothes brought me not only prestige but extraordinary good fortune as well. On the long walks to the hospital I once found a silver watch and, a second time, a wallet containing thirty-five rubles. And, as if this weren't enough, I was once saved from certain death.

One evening, two German planes flew over the depot and dropped two bombs. One of them hit a railroad car around which several volunteers were fussing with the wounded. The wagon and people promptly went flying into the air. Even the policeman lost a hand that day. I was the only one to come out of it in one piece. No one could explain the remarkable luck of the "little captain" except my father, who knew that the same God who had favored me with the silver watch had now also protected me from the exploding bomb.

But I didn't make too much of all this luck. I knew full well that it wouldn't last.

In the evenings on the way to the hospital, I could hear the muffled thud of distant cannon just behind the horizon and see the red reflection from the fiery tongues that already licked at the out-skirts of the beleaguered city. Soon, soon, I would have to cast off these lucky clothes of mine, since they belonged to the vanquished, routed Russians. While it was true that to these Russians I was a Jew, a traitor, a Christ-killer, and a mangy dog that they would have loved to slaughter in their wild rage, they were still the only ones whose bloody wounds were familiar to me, whose groaning out-cries I understood, whose bitter curses I had learned in my cradle. But who were the Germans? What kind of people were they? What did they look like? How did their language sound?

From the accounts of the wounded in the hospital, I couldn't for the life of me put together a clear conception of a German. Ninety percent of the Russians were illiterates and couldn't even pronounce, much less write, the two-syllable word "Ger-man." They often begged me to write letters to their wives and children, in which they swore that they had seen a German with horse hooves for feet, a tail, and horns on his forehead.

One second lieutenant with a shattered hand provided a more human description of the enemy, but even he didn't know the name of the German capital, and therefore one couldn't place much cre-dence in what he said. But whoever these Germans were, devils in human form or men in devil form, one thing was clear—the fiery strands that they were already throwing around the horizon and that would shortly be tightened around the throat of the dying city would, as Barve's Son had predicted, end everything that ever was, that ever lived, that ever dreamed—it would be the end of the world and, with it, the death of the old city.

But along with this gloomy prediction, I soon reminded myself of the remarkable scene with the sick historian and the French doctor in the attic room. This used to flash in my memory with a phos-phorescent brightness that lit up the lonely street and momentarily blinded my dark, brooding thoughts. Before my inspired eyes would spontaneously appear a big picture in which the whole city was sud-denly transformed into a large attic room, and the street into a long bed in which the sick historian lay and with joyous, grateful eyes gazed up at the little Frenchman in the military greatcoat who, smil-ing proudly, stood at the edge of the imaginary picture. This vision filled me with a strange kind of faith that I was really the only blessed person who stood outside the condemned city, and that I was the only doctor capable of stopping the death that approached it from over the horizon.

I would draw myself up with military pomp and stride forth, clicking my heels with precise rhythm over the slippery cobblestones.

The black and yellow shadows of the sick and hungry streets would scatter before the pounding of my boots. The chickpeas and groats in my pockets would ring to the beat of my marching feet like tiny silver bells. I didn't march now like just a simple captain, but like a full major general . . . What general? Phooey on the generals! What did conquered generals mean, anyway? The lucky greatcoat concealed the greatest victor of all—the Conqueror of Death himself, Chantille Jeantaigne Delacroix . . .

And as I marched along thus with the vision of the French doctor in my head and the package of chickpeas under my arm on my way to Isserson's, a bearded man stopped me and asked, "Weren't you by chance a student at the junior high school?"

I was in no rush to answer.

"You don't recognize me," the man said with regret. "Have I really aged that much? The beard of course adds at least ten years to my appearance, but take away the ten years," he put his hand over the light brown bush on his jaw, "and you'll see that I'm the same Gerasim Isakovitch Dalski, your former geography teacher."

I opened my mouth, like a fish, in a dumb "o."

"People tell me the beard makes me look like a Mephistopheles. But these days, even a devil's beard is a blessing. My papers are in perfect order, but the beard makes me feel more secure walking the streets. And what are you up to? Ha, ha, ha! I ask just as if I didn't see that you're a soldier. And what can a soldier do these days but shoot or be shot?"

"I'm just as much a soldier as you are a Mephistopheles. The greatcoat is *my* beard," I said.

"Ha, ha, ha. Well said, well said . . . You remind me that you always had a sharp tongue. Tell me, do you know *The Inspector General*—Gogol's Inspector General? The swindler from St. Petersburg who poses as an inspector general, embezzles a lot of money from the city officials, and, in addition, seduces the mayor's wife and daughter? If you were a bit older and a bit taller, you could possibly play the inspector general. You probably know that the Jewish refugees are in a terrible plight; money has to be raised in their behalf. In relation to this, several worthwhile performances are being planned. I'm not by nature a community worker, but in this instance I took an interest since this is an opportunity for me to become involved in a theatrical effort. You, of course, know me as a geography teacher, but the truth is that if my parents hadn't been against it, I would be a great actor now.

"To make a long story short, I've assembled a fine company of which I'm the director, so to speak, the Stanislavsky of the group. To tell the truth, there are no great talents there but even a bear can be taught to dance. The main difficulty was to get a place in which to perform because, naturally, this would have to be on a side street to avoid a raid by the police. But we have Tanya, who's a dynamo, and she found us a hall with a stage at the Chorus Hall. She arranged for a curtain and also assembled real sets and costumes—wonderful! I wanted to do *Hamlet* first, but unfortunately I couldn't find the right person for the part, since this isn't merely some prince who sits in the palace and eats bread and butter, but a prince who poses the question, 'To be or not to be.' Are you familiar with that monologue?

"But that's not important . . . because I gave it up anyway and decided to substitute *The Inspector General* for *Hamlet*. In our times with people being grabbed in the streets each day, *The Inspector General* is more apropos. First of all, there are two leading parts—the inspector general and the mayor—so if one actor is no good, the other can cover up. Besides, we have a fellow there, Ziskin, playing the mayor's part. By trade he's a carpenter, but if you looked at him you'd swear that this was the real mayor. He has the bulbous nose, the pig eyes . . . the only trouble is, we're still missing an inspector general. Unfortunately, our group is made up of elderly people, and the inspector general must definitely be a young man of twenty-one, and this is a rare article these days.

"I strained my brain for where to find someone like that. I even found someone; he limped a little and this, I thought, would protect him from the police—but not so. They grabbed him coming to rehearsal, and he's already digging trenches . . . A shame, a shame . . . If you were a bit older and a bit taller, maybe you'd be able to fit in.

Although, on the other hand, if you were taller and older, you'd probably be digging trenches too . . . What's to be done then? What time is it?"

But before I could manage to take out my watch, he took my arm and said, "Come with me."

XXVII

⟨≈⟩

"PASSPORTS! DOCUMENTS!" The ex-teacher cried as we entered
the small foyer of the Chorus Hall. "I've brought a gendarme to
arrest you all."

About a dozen men and women were gathered inside the hall.
The men, with the exception of one with a cataract in his eye, were
all middle-aged or older. The women seemed a bit younger but were
already saddled with billowy breasts and wide, sagging hips.

The ex-teacher's joke frightened them at first, but as soon as they
saw the "gendarme" with a package under his arm, a greatcoat that
was a bit too long, and the cap falling over his ears—giving the impression that he had wandered in from a fantastic children's land—
they relaxed.

"He's a former student of mine," Gerasim Isakovitch announced,
throwing off his hat and coat. "I met him by chance and brought
him here to see how I work . . . Get to know each other . . ." And
then, grabbing me with two fingers by the collar, he pushed me
toward the group. "This is Kagan, Shapiro, Lapides, Badaness . . .
And this is our good Tanya." He pointed with particular emphasis
to the small stage where stood a woman with an exceptionally pale
face, one of those faces on which a person's life history is pictured.

Her hands were smeared with paint, and with a scraggly brush she
painted the final words of a poster:

> Sunday evening the 22nd
> At the Chorus Hall
> Under the personal supervision
> Of the famous theatrical personality
> Gerasim Isakovitch Dalski
> Will be presented
> Gogol's *The Inspector General*
> A Comedy in Five Acts.

It was immediately apparent that Tanya was no spring chicken, that she came from a poor home, that she had—as the saying goes— a golden heart and silver hands, and that she was undoubtedly a member of some half dozen welfare, cultural, and fraternal organizations. In all these organizations she wouldn't be the chairman or secretary or treasurer, but merely the one who set up the chairs for the meetings, decorated the halls, and guarded the door. And although deep pouches already showed beneath her drawn and pale cheeks, a childlike enthusiasm and inspiration still glowed in her chaste eyes.

Dalski turned to Tanya. "Where is Ziskin? I bet he won't come again today."

"He'll come, he'll come. His wife assured me that he'll be here. Yesterday, he had a toothache."

"What do I care about his teeth? I've seen actors play with a fever, with a headache, even with gallstones. A dilettante remains a dilettante!"

"He'll surely be here soon," Tanya said. "In the meantime, let's start the rehearsal." And she began to drag a table toward the stage.

"What rehearsal? With whom shall I rehearse?"

"We haven't even held our first rehearsal yet," Tanya reminded him. "Let's rehearse with whoever is here."

"No one is here!" the director said, waving his hand along the length of the wall where the group was sitting. "I have nothing to shoot with. You can't make a bullet out of cheese."

This crack evoked no reaction at all from the group, as if they were already accustomed to hearing worse things from their excitable director and were content to be compared to nothing smellier than cheese.

"Gerasim Isakovitch, I've already sold nearly half the tickets. The poster is already prepared."

"In God's name, why must you always butt in? How many times have I told you that you understand theater matters like a cow understands algebra. Please be a little more tactful and not give our guest the impression that you, not I, are the director here . . . The mayor didn't show up and we don't have the inspector general— with whom shall I go to the table?"

"Maybe you could play the inspector?" Tanya said, speaking to me, but Dalski stopped her again.

"The question of whether he could or couldn't play the part is something I'd like you to let *me* decide. The inspector has to seduce a mother and a daughter on the same night and for that you need a man in the truest sense of the word—and you, my dear lady, you are not enough of an expert in *such* things."

Tanya's pale face screwed up into a network of red threads, but even this didn't deter the aroused director. "If we can't find the right man, we'll have to cancel the show."

"How can you say that," Tanya pleaded, clutching her brow in alarm. "The tickets are nearly gone. You took half the money."

"Took it? I get paid for my work. For teaching bears to dance, I should be paid three times as much."

"Yes, but there are only nine days left until the performance."

"Tanya, my patience has definite limits," the director said, hurling a chair to the floor. "You have plenty of your own things to worry about—costumes, sets, props, posters . . . and the floor has to be washed, too."

"Mr. Dalski, I assure you everything will be in order."

"Three times already you've promised to get me an inspector general."

"I've talked to twenty people, but you know that these days—"

"Then what do you want from me?"

"Why can't you yourself play the inspector general?" The suggestion roused the group by the wall, and the one with the cataract even stood up and in a tinny voice predicted the great sensation that would erupt in the city when it was announced that Gerasim Isakovitch Dalski himself would play the leading role. But the ex-teacher suffered a sudden weakness of the knees and sank down in a chair.

"The matter is settled—let's rehearse!" Tanya said, and again began to drag the table toward the stage.

The director jumped to his feet. "Wait, wait, let the table be! I don't deny that my appearance in the role of the inspector general would cause a sensation." He wiped a bit of saliva from his bespattered beard and paced through the room in deliberation, then turned toward me and snapped his fingers as if some fresh thought had suddenly struck him: "Be so good as to get up on stage. I want to see how you look from this perspective."

The whole troupe groaned in disappointed chorus.

"What for?"

"Who needs it?"

"We want you!"

"Why lose any more time?"

"With you in the part we could put on a performance tomorrow!"

"It would be a sensation!"

The director stuffed up his ears, turned away from them with his nose averted as if they were really made of bad-smelling cheese, and imperiously waved at me to do as he ordered.

I languidly made my way toward the stage. On the way, I stopped and handed Tanya my package. "Be so good as to keep an eye on this. It's very important."

She threw it under a nearby chair, raced past me onto the stage, and, pointing to the poster, said to the director: "Gerasim Isakovitch, tomorrow morning I must put up the poster. If you're going to play the part I must paint over it and add in big letters, 'The famous Dalski in the role of the inspector general!'"

"For that, we've got plenty of time yet," the obstinate director replied. "I only want to conduct a little experiment . . . From the first row, naturally, the figure on the stage appears bigger. But let's just see how he would look from the last row." He strode to the very end of the hall and put his fists to his eyes as if they were binoculars.

"Let me hear your voice," he said. "Say something, recite something. It doesn't matter what . . . one of the fables from school. Don't be ashamed. I know you're not bashful . . . Let me hear Krilov's fable—*Demian's Fish Broth* or the other fable, what is it called? Oh, yes, *The Swan, the Lobster, and the Carp* . . . Louder, I can't hear what you're saying." And he placed his hand to his ear.

Tanya stood behind me with the poster in her hand. When she saw me look at her, she shouted to the director, "Gerasim Isakovitch, he doesn't remember!"

"Tanya, for God's sake! I want to hear his voice, not yours."

I was in no hurry to open my mouth. I stood half-turned toward Tanya. From the first moment I saw her I liked her—with her strangely weary face, her childish voice, and smiling eyes even when in anger. As for the fables, I could have recited them backwards, but the moment Tanya said that I didn't remember them, I knew that I *must not* and I *dared not* remember them. I had to wait until the forces that wrangled here grew exhausted, and I never doubted that it would be she who emerged triumphant.

I walked up to the edge of the stage: "Excuse me, but it's a long time since I read those fables and I no longer remember them."

"Maybe you remember something else? Maybe you remember something that you've read recently? Haven't you read anything?" the teacher said, trying to encourage me.

"As you see, I'm a volunteer at the Zwerinitz Hospital and I have no time to read. However, I did read something lately . . ."

"What is it?"

"'The Conqueror of Death.'"

"'The Conqueror of Death?'" the director repeated, pointing his beard at the ceiling. "I know the whole Russian and world literature and I never heard of this book."

"It's not a book—it's seventy or eighty little booklets that are sold by installment every week at the newspaper stands."

Tanya stamped her foot. "Enough! Enough of this nonsense." And, running to the apron of the stage where a number of scripts lay stacked, she snatched up a page and brought it to me. "We don't have time to listen to eighty books. Read one page of the inspector general's part and that will be enough."

Her action was like a fresh needle jabbed into the director's hypersensitive skin; still, he forced himself to go along for practical reasons.

He stretched out against the back of his seat, crossed his legs, and slapped his knee three times as a signal for me to begin. But a second didn't pass before he slapped his knee a fourth time and exclaimed, "Goddam it, I've torn my garter!" He pulled up his trouser over his pale, womanly leg. "This is very unlucky in the theater. Not because I'm superstitious, mind you, but because it's a well-established fact that when a windowpane or a mirror breaks—or a garter tears—the play is sure to be a flop."

"That's all we needed," Tanya said and turned to the others with her hands helplessly extended as if appealing to them to get involved and do something at last.

For Gerasim Isakovitch this was the final straw, and he jumped up in a rage. "Your cynicism smacks of impudence and this I won't allow."

The man with the cataract again tried to explain that Tanya hadn't meant anything derogatory by her remark, but the infuriated director waved his hand in disdain to indicate that he didn't need an attorney in the face of such an open insult, because even if superstition *was* a sign of obscurantism, any professional theater person would confirm that whistling during rehearsal or bringing an umbrella backstage wasn't tolerated even by such progressive authorities as Stanislavsky and Gaydeburov.

Tanya cringed like a whipped dog.

"Excuse me, I didn't understand what you meant. I thought you wanted to cancel the performance just on account of a torn garter."

"If the performance is canceled it will be because of you, not because of my garter," he said, and he flung the torn elastic into a corner.

From this, everyone understood that Dalski had finally come to terms with the notion of personally playing the inspector general. But just at that moment, someone knocked quietly on the door.

Two little girls came into the hall. Holding hands and speaking as one in trembling voices, they announced that their father wouldn't be coming to rehearsal because their mother didn't want him to wander through the streets any more and risk his life for some foolishness and therefore she wouldn't let him out of the house. Therefore, Father was sending back the part.

"Tell your father he's a swine," Gerasim Isakovitch roared at the terrified children. "What does your father think—that he's the only father in town?"

The children broke into tears. Tanya took the mayor's part from them and, stroking their hair, pushed them out the door. Then she came up to the director and, with a gay smile as if she had just experienced the greatest thrill of her life, she said, "Gerasim Isakovitch, you're right. We'll teach *him* a lesson. *You* will play the mayor and he'll burst from envy." And with that, she thrust the mayor's part into his hand.

"Yes, yes," Gerasim Isakovitch agreed, brandishing the part in the air as if it were a sword, "I'll show him so he'll have something to remember! Yes, yes, *I'll* play the mayor and *he*"—pointing to me—"will play the inspector general!"

"Help me put the table on the stage," a happy Tanya said to the man with the cataract.

"No, no, we'll rehearse right here in the hall. We mustn't lose any more time. Take your places . . . you sit on the right, you on the left . . . I'll come in from the middle."

Everyone took his script, and Tanya, holding the prompter's book, quickly began to read aloud. "Everyone is sitting in the reception room. The mayor enters."

Dalski took off his jacket and soon, under the pretext that he felt a draft, put it back on again. As he read his part, he excused himself a few times, saying that his vision had been troubling him lately and that he needed glasses. Several times he questioned Tanya about her prompting, as if he were losing his hearing, too. And finally he turned to the man with the cataract and said, "What time is it?"

"Eight o'clock."

"Oh, too late for rehearsal already. On account of that irresponsible dilettante we lost a whole evening, but tomorrow, precisely at seven, we'll begin some real, intensive work. I ask everyone to learn their parts by tomorrow and to be exactly on time." And he went off to get his hat and coat.

Tanya brought me the rest of my part and rebuked me for wrinkling between my restless fingers the first page she had given me to read. "Don't lose any time. Run straight home and try as hard as you can to memorize at the least the first act by tomorrow."

With renewed energy, she began to mix the paint with which to correct the poster that would now read: "The celebrated theatrical personality Dalski in the role of the mayor."

I jumped down from the stage, nearly knocked over the man with the cataract, and raced down the stairs and into the street.

I was forced to stop a few times to let long columns of retreating soldiers pass by. I started to shove the fluttering pages of my part into my pocket and noticed that I had dropped some of them on the run. When I found them again, they were completely shredded by thousands of boots that had trodden over them.

XXVIII

～✵～

THE FOLLOWING EVENING, Gerasim Isakovitch entered and promptly announced that he wouldn't be playing the part of the mayor after all, that he was only a director, and that he had never nursed any acting ambitions. The mayor was traditionally played by a heavyset man with a bulbous nose and a fat, smooth-shaven, piglike face. His lean cheeks and especially his beard definitely excluded him, and he wouldn't shave his beard under the circumstances, since to do so in such times meant to risk one's life. The only solution to the dilemma was to postpone the performance until someone else could be found for the role.

Tanya wrung her hands. "No, no, we can't postpone it. I've already sold the tickets, hired the hall, sewed the costumes, and painted the poster . . ."

"I won't shave off the beard . . ."

"Then take the part of the inspector general. The inspector general can have a beard."

"Tanya, your asinine proposals have annoyed me enough already," he said, bowing his head and looking up from under his brows like an aroused bull, "If I play the inspector general, who will play the mayor?"

"He! He!" she pointed to where I was sitting.

Dalski slapped his hips. "Ha, ha, ha . . . what's this—a child's game? Don't you know that in the fifth act the mayor says that he'll squash the inspector general like a bedbug in a greatcoat? How can he say this when he himself looks like a bedbug in a greatcoat?"

"It doesn't matter," Tanya argued. "He'll pad himself. I'll sew a belly for him. He can be fitted with a bulbous nose."

"That's sheer idiocy. It's mockery . . . it means deceiving an audience. If you want to do this—do it without me."

"But how can you do such a thing? After all, you talked me into all this. Where would I get the money now to repay the people?"

Tanya ran up to the wall, sobbing, seeking a hole there to bury her face.

Several members of the company tried to soothe her while others took the director aside and let him know that he had gone too far. The woman was hysterical. Who could tell what she might do?

Gerasim Isakovitch bit his lips and after a short pause drew up the tie around his restless Adam's apple, put his hand on my shoulder, and asked, "If I'll play the inspector general, are you ready to play the mayor?"

I shrugged. "What's the difference what part I play? I'm too young for the inspector and too small for the mayor."

"You can see what a terrible spot we're in, and you must help us out. So if you're prepared to take on the mayor's part I'll let you go now so you can go home and study it. And in the meantime I'll begin to rehearse my scenes as the inspector . . . Re-hear-sal!" He growled like a field marshall getting his troops ready for a last stand.

Tanya wiped her tearful eyes and ran up to me. "Give me back the inspector's part, and here is the mayor's."

She snatched the stack of pages from my hand and replaced it with another. She carried the first stack to the director, took a seat at the prompter's table, and began to read from the book. "A hotel room. The inspector enters . . ."

Dalski stopped her. "Wait a minute. When does he enter? Where does he enter? I don't see in my script that he enters. I see here on the first page that he's already in the room and eating his lunch."

"It can't be," Tanya said, leaping to her feet, "I copied the script myself."

"Then you copied it badly. You've left out nearly half an act. How can I begin by eating lunch when I haven't even entered the room? God Almighty, what do you people want of me? I can't! I can't! I'm ready to make good all the expenses . . . I'll go into hock, I'll borrow, only let me out, release me!" He flung the pages to the ceiling, grabbed his hat and coat, and fled from the hall.

Tanya ran after him. The company began to quack like a flock of migrating ducks. They cursed Gerasim Isakovitch's behavior and defended director Dalski and at the same time stuck up for Tanya and vilified the old maid. But all in all, they were delighted that the boil had finally burst and that they were rid of the entire mess. And after a whole half hour had gone by and neither Dalski nor Tanya had returned, the cast began to sidle out the door as if through a crack in a broken fence, so that when Tanya finally came back all sweaty and excited, there was no one left in the hall but me.

She looked at me with an angry, suspicious stare. "There'll be no rehearsal today. You can go home."

"I understand . . . But I gave you a package yesterday. I've gone crazy looking for it. It's a very important package."

"I don't remember where I put it. Look over there."

I climbed up on the stage and began to search among the pile of costumes.

She began to straighten the scattered chairs and gather the fallen pages of scripts that the members of the company had abandoned in their escape. She angrily threw everything into the wastebasket, then grabbed her knitted green hat and handbag and exclaimed, "Where are you? Come on! I must put out the lights, lock the hall, and give the key to the house manager."

"I must find that package."

"I don't have the time. I must go."

"Go, go. Leave the key and go. You just have to tell me what time tomorrow's rehearsal will be."

"There'll be no more rehearsals. The performance is canceled." She irritably shoved the hat down over her head. "And believe me, your former teacher won't get away with it so easily. I'll force him to return his advance and cover all the expenses. That disgusting windbag . . ." She put her finger on the light switch by the door.

"He isn't entirely at fault. You provoked him too much. I could have played the mayor."

"But there wasn't anyone to play the inspector."

"I could have played the inspector, too. I could have played both parts," I said with vexation. "I once staged a performance in which with the help of only a phonograph, I played the violin, recited a poem twenty-four pages long, and took a live chicken out of a boiled egg . . . You don't have to cancel the performance or give back the money. I myself will perform the whole thing."

"You're a baby. You know nothing about the theater. *The Inspector General* isn't a recitation, it's a performance. The audience paid a half-ruble to see a play . . . *The Inspector General* is a well-known comedy. Everyone has seen it and knows it."

"If they would pay a half-ruble for a thing that they already know and have seen, they might pay a whole ruble to see something they've never heard of, as, for instance, 'The Conqueror of Death.'"

"I don't know what you're talking about. Isn't that the eighty books you mentioned yesterday?"

"If you'll only give me a few minutes, I'll read it to you."

"How can you read eighty books in a few minutes?" An uncertain smile began to crawl out from between the folds around her lips.

"I'll begin from the first book, and when you feel that you've had enough, stop me." And, not waiting for her consent, I quickly shucked off my greatcoat and cap and began. She slowly sat down on the edge of a chair in the rear near the door. A few times she delicately interrupted me: "I don't understand . . . French . . . ? Who condemned whom to the guillotine? How did he get himself out of the clutches of the executioner?" I ignored her questions and went on with the story. She opened her knitted bag, took out a comb with some missing teeth and a little mirror that she balanced on her knee, and began to fuss with a stray lock on her forehead, mumbling, "What a tangled, stupid tale . . . Do I have to sit and listen to eighty books of nonsense?" But I went on with a mounting passion illustrating my words with movements of my body and delineating the various characters with appropriate accents.

When she was through fussing with her hair, she looked up and remarked, "It's a pretty name, Chantille Jeantaigne Delacroix."

I stopped. I thought fast. "Yes, that's the name of the doctor."

"But why did he rob the patient after he hypnotized him?"

"That was a false accusation fabricated by his own wife who had betrayed him with his best friend, who had an even prettier name—Francois Albert René Laroshe Marquis Debushon."

There was a smile on her face. "It couldn't be that only by his wife's say-so he'd be declared insane and put in an asylum."

"Perhaps you're right from a legal point of view, but at the moment you have a greater legal inconvenience. You have to return money that you've spent so recklessly. And I am here to help you."

"Excuse me, but may I ask you—how old are you, and are you really a soldier?"

"We're all old enough and soldiers in this wretched, besieged city," I said and in the same breath proceeded, "We're now at the point when Doctor Delacroix is confined in a straitjacket and tortured with drops of cold water trickling down on his shaved skull for days." And after a few extravagant vocal and physical expressions of pain, I finished with a shattering scream on the highest possible pitch, "Ah-h-h-h-h."

She jolted as if she'd been touched by an electric wire. Her purse slid off her knee, but she didn't bother to pick it up. Pink blushes colored her face while I continued to demonstrate the perennial triumph of human imbecility and cruelty. Delacroix had once again been confined behind the heavy iron bars of a prison, and once again he managed with his remarkable eloquence to persuade the guard to change clothes with him and, so disguised, slipped out through the heavily guarded gates of the prison and fled from country to country, changing his language, his face, his body . . . Now he was a hunchback, now an old toothless beggar, now a blind street singer, now a jolly drunk . . .

Tanya was now all ears and eyes lest, God forbid, she lose me in my swift talk and amid the rapid transformations to which I now gave full rein. She breathed heavily. When I noticed the emotional strain was more than she could bear, I stopped abruptly and bowed deeply. She jumped from the chair, ran uninhibitedly through the hall up to the stage, and, seizing my bowed head, kissed it.

That same evening, Tanya turned the poster to the other side and painted the following announcement:

Saturday evening the 22nd
In the magnificent Chorus Hall
Will be presented a grand musical-theatrical concert.
Making his debut in the city
Will be the mysterious doctor
Chantille Jeantaigne Delacroix.

While she painted I found my package. I tore apart the rag in which it was wrapped and took out a bag of chickpeas.

"It's very late, and I haven't eaten yet today. I'm sure you're hungry, too. I can't offer you any ice cream or marzipan in these times, but there is enough of this—this I can still get."

"What is it? Where did you get it?" she asked, leaning with a grateful smile over the chickpeas.

"It isn't mine. I was supposed to take it to a certain rabbi. But it doesn't matter. I'm sure that the rabbi and even God Himself will forgive me."

XXIX

THE CONCERT was a resounding success. A week later it had to be repeated. But this was only the beginning. In the next three weeks, Chantille Jeantaigne Delacroix put on no less than seven performances, a record in the theatrical history of the city.

Tanya was nearly exhausted as organization after organization insisted that she provide what's-his-name—that crazy Frenchman—for a concert in their behalf. The fact that the cannonade over the horizon grew clearer and closer each day and that the German armies were already just fifteen to twenty miles from the city didn't seem as important as whom Tanya would honor with the next charity concert.

To satisfy the growing demand, Tanya decided to shift our operation to the more spacious Town Hall. I saw her only in the evenings when she came home from a hard day's work and passed along to me the compliments she had been hearing all day and the news that Gerasim Isakovitch had attended every concert and, standing in the doorway, had plucked every hair from his beard in jealousy and vexation.

Intoxicated by her repeated praises, I walked home late, filled with pride that not only had I saved her but I had now become the only provider of entertainment for the whole city. As usual, I encountered long columns of retreating soldiers marching toward me.

I would sometimes come to her house early and visit with her sister, Rosa, and her mother, a small woman with clever, darting eyes in a delicately carved face. Her husband, a Hebrew teacher, had passed away after a long and hard illness, leaving her with two little girls, one of whom was mute from birth. The mother would treat her older daughter's boyish visitor with gracious, occasionally even exaggerated politeness, and offer him hot glasses of tea, sliced raw carrots, or even a whole apple.

With tactful modesty, she avoided every question that might have placed the visitor in an uncomfortable position. All that interested her and all she demanded was that I predict when the war would end. She couldn't imagine how a soldier who spent all his days among the military wouldn't know the precise date when the war would be over. But when I revealed to her one night that although I wore a uniform I was far from being a real soldier, and that I no more knew the answer to her question than anyone else in the city, a spark of suspicion and disappointment flashed in her eyes. She gripped her pointy little chin with a pale, veined hand and sighed deeply.

"If you're nothing more than a plain civilian like the rest of us, then I can speak to you as person to person. Would you like to hear Barve's Son on this same question? You know him, don't you?" said Tanya's mother.

"Of course, by all means. Who doesn't know Barve's Son?"

"'The war will last at least ten years because there are too many people in the world now, and there isn't enough room for all of them. Therefore, the war won't end until a great number of people are killed off . . . Young people are foolish. They fall in love, marry, have children. For what? Why breed more people? The earth remains small, but people increase and nations grow bigger. They rub against one another and when things rub together, this starts a fire. Well, so why add to this mess? Love, friendship is fine, but you have to be careful about children . . .' This, of course, is what I say. You understand? No children . . ." In sharp contrast to her daughter, her face didn't reveal the slightest sign of what she really had in mind. She looked at her daughter's silent and embarrassed friend with a sudden indifference, yawned and excused herself saying that she was tired, and, leaving her mute daughter to continue the conversation, went off to the bedroom.

With her usual vacuous smile Rosa sat near the kerosene lamp on the table and knitted a jacket with remarkably skillful fingers. A few times she put down the needles and began to knit with her fingers in the air. I wasn't sure whether she was speaking to me about the jacket or about something else, and in order to bring the discussion closer to my understanding, I held up ten fingers and asked, "Do you agree with your mother that the war will last ten years?"

Rosa shook her head and, making a small circle in the air, she held up ten fingers, then two more, to indicate twelve. Tanya later told me that a circle in the air and twelve fingers indicated twelve o'clock, but at the time that I heard (or to be more accurate saw) this, I took it to mean twelve more years of war, and I sat there brooding and depressed.

I wouldn't have taken the two women's predictions so seriously if my own impatience to have the war end hadn't assumed such climactic proportions. I had begun to lose interest in the hospital and tire of the horrors at the train depot. After the first concert, I had begun to neglect my duties and even skip days at the hospital. And now another ten or twelve years of this? Possibly this was a slight exaggeration, but who could be sure? Maybe the mother was right, or maybe the truth lay in the mute's tongue.

Rosa tried a few times to launch a conversation with me, but I only blinked my eyes and shrugged with embarrassment. She looked at me a moment with her congealed smile, as if deploring the fact that I was even dumber than she, but soon she wound the knitting around the ball of yarn and stuck the needles into it, and, handing me a book, made a final effort to explain something to me with her shouting fingers. And when I still stared at her like a fish out of water, she winked slyly and walked off with mute laughter.

Soon, Tanya bustled in with a happy cry: "Don't come near me, I look a wreck! I haven't had a chance to sit down all day." She threw her hat and coat down on the sofa and ran into the kitchen. From behind the wooden wall came the sound of vigorous splashing, and a few minutes later she emerged combed, washed, and wearing a fresh blouse. Her pale face seemed to shout "Important news!"

But I didn't give her a chance to speak and ran up to her. "Tanya, when do you think the war will be over?"

"In two weeks," she said gaily.

"I'm serious."

"But I'm telling you—in two weeks," she repeated with firm assurance.

"I see that you're in high spirits. What happened?"

"Let me at least catch my breath and drink a glass of tea. I haven't had a bite all day . . . After I had arranged everything, it turns out that the Town Hall isn't available. The city officials have been evacuated and the municipal buildings are under the control of the military commandant, who didn't even know that there was such a hall in the city. Finally they found a decree by which the Town Hall was closed. There are no lights, the chairs are broken—in a word, the hall can't be used until it's repaired.

"And this won't be done until after the war. And if I were to tell you that I got the hall anyway and with the promise to have everything fixed for the concert three weeks from now, doesn't this mean that the war will end at least a week before then?" she asked, folding her hands proudly in her lap. I seized the edge of the table, which began to shake as if it were being tipped during a seance. Rummaging in her handbag, she went on. "It won't do anymore to use hand-painted posters for a concert at the Town Hall. We need professional posters done by an expert. I'll take care of that. In the meantime, I ordered some small flyers." And she threw a pink piece of paper on the table: "On Saturday, the . . . the . . . In the magnificent Town Hall—"

"Oh, my God . . . !"

Tanya put her hand on my lips, warning me not to wake her mother and sister. "Tanya, forgive me," I said. "But you don't know . . . this is the same hall where Paganini the First and Second—and now me . . ."

"I must confess that at times I don't understand you. Drink your tea before it gets cold."

We sipped the tea. The autumn wind rattled the windowpanes and from behind the wall a muffled snoring duet could be heard.

I looked at her face, which seemed to plead with me not to resent her ignorance—for how could she know who Paganini the First and Second were? As far as she was concerned, she wouldn't trade me for any concertmaster in the world. If only I didn't disappoint and leave her . . . for even if she was poor and no longer young or pretty, she still could take care of me as if I were her own son and help me grow up to be a man in the fullest sense of the word who could play the inspector general despite anything Gerasim Isakovitch said . . .

I leaned across the table to get closer to that expressive face and she leaned toward me as if anxious to reveal all her innermost secrets. The mother groaned heavily in her sleep, and we looked at each other like burglars about to enter a locked door—alarmed, ashamed, whispering words of encouragement to each other and ready to plunge together and be devoured by desire.

XXX

⟨~⟩

A FEW DAYS LATER, sitting late as usual at Tanya's house, we heard a loud burst of thunder outside.

"I'd best go home," I said.

Tanya cocked her ears. "No!"

"Those are the Germans!" the mother's frightened voice sounded from the other side of the wall. I grabbed my coat and cap, and holding hands we ran outside. There was no one in the street except the wind frolicking and dancing a quadrille with several pieces of paper.

"Go back to the house, Tanya. You're liable to catch cold. I'll find out what happened and be right back."

On deserted Butcher Street two soldiers were swiftly shedding their uniforms while from a window above civilian trousers, ties, and hats rained down on them. Three men came running from Church Street in their drawers. They banged on the doors pleading for old clothes or to be allowed inside. Swifter than the wind, I raced home. My mother was pacing dazedly in her nightgown and when I came in she wrung her hands and exclaimed: "Where is your father?"

Instead of answering I quickly ran to the dresser. "Quick, give me one of Father's old suits. I'll take it to him at the hospital."

"No, no!" she cried, grabbing my sleeve. "Maybe they'll bomb the city."

"The streets are quiet. There's no one there."

She ran to the window. All she saw were frightened faces looking out from behind carefully drawn curtains in the other windows.

"It'll only take me a half hour to get to Father," I reassured her.

"Wait till the sun rises . . ."

"In a few hours the Germans will already be in the city. I saw many soldiers getting rid of their uniforms . . . Father can save himself this way . . . Give me a cloth in which to wrap the suit."

"No, no! I won't let you go." She blocked the door, but I pushed her aside and ran out into the hall. "Why don't you change your own clothes?" she asked.

"I'm no soldier," I replied from the street and, with the bundle of twisted clothes under my greatcoat, I ran to the Zwerinitz Hospital.

At the curb of Glass Street, a fire fought a death struggle against the wind over the remnants of a charred military greatcoat. At the corner of Church Street a soldier leaned against a wall, vomiting furiously. Next to him lay three empty vodka bottles. A group of soldiers stood by the Zwerinitz Bridge. They blinked at me with small lanterns and shouted, "Hurry! Hurry!" I felt that in another minute my lungs would burst and, panting like a horse in the final moments of a race, I dashed over the bridge. The soldiers pulled a string and with a deafening roar the bridge flew into the air in little pieces.

I didn't have to salute at the hospital gate. The guard was no longer there. In the center of the yard stood dozens of high wagons into which frantic soldiers loaded big bundles of various hospital items. The coachmen, in the terrible rush and excitement, angrily kicked and punched the heads and bellies of the horses tangled in the straps of their harnesses.

I raced through the long corridor to where my father had his own room. Through the open doors I saw overturned cots from which the patients had been taken, pillows, mattresses, and all. In other sections, the seriously wounded had been abandoned on sheets spread on the floor. The drawers in the office stood open and the papers lay scattered all about. It was obvious that the evacuation had been effected in a state of complete panic. Before I could manage to look inside my father's room, a passing hand clapped me on the shoulder. "Come, come, hurry! Your father must be in Minsk already. He was sent out with the first transport hours ago."

My bundle of clothes dropped to the floor. Too late! My father surely would have saved himself if I had only come a few hours earlier . . . What now? Go back home? The bridge was down, and even if I could have gotten back to the city through roundabout ways— what would become of my father? What would I tell my mother?

The answer came simultaneously with a fresh explosion in the food stores. I grabbed my bundle and ran out the back door. It was drizzling. With fiery tongues enormous smoky beasts gobbled up the chickpeas and black groats in the storehouse. I scampered like a cat up a loaded wagon, the last to leave the hospital. I scurried to the very top and clung to the ropes to keep from sliding off the wet tarpaulin. A brutal slash of long whips accompanied by a wave of ten-degree oaths soon put the horses and wagons on the muddy highway.

Elderly peasant women stood by their broken shanties, wiping their tearful eyes with the hems of their dresses. They crossed themselves and seemed to be mumbling, "May God protect you and help you catch your father." At the side of the well hung the Redeemer on a white cross. Even he seemed to bewail the little Jew's misfortune.

Soon we reached a strand of thin saplings leading to a grove of thicker trees that made the highway even narrower; the wagons pushed forward, twisting and jostling the trees, which were cracking, groaning, and screeching. They were soon joined by swarms of trees rushing in from all sides, and as evening approached we were surrounded by a dense, grumbling, growling forest. Several times we stopped to join up with other, even bigger transports that were taking the same route to Minsk. We even let small and then larger companies of artillery with their field pieces drawn by horses pass through. From behind the trees slipped out small and then larger groups of lost, weary soldiers asking each other the way to Minsk.

I sat on top of the rocking wagon, bundled up in my greatcoat. Younger trees pushing in on me with wet, fluttering hands were patting, tickling me to help me forget the trouble I was in. Good birds tried to lift my spirits by whistling, cawing and chattering. Thousands of fireflies tried to emit some light into the gloomy air. Millions of insects whizzing and buzzing were trying to lull me to sleep. Suddenly an angry tree poked me with such force that I nearly slid off the wagon. I quickly seized the ropes beneath me, but—oh, God . . . the whole mound began to topple over. Men and trees began to shout, "Stop, stop!" The coachmen whipped the horses frantically, cursing the trees. The trees, swooning and falling, overturned the wagons. Those in the rear began to tumble over the front ones. The soldiers walking ahead began to push backward and bumped into the artillery groups, and soon a jumble of horses, trees, and men ensued. One stepped on another, not knowing which way lay forward and which backward.

In this frightful confusion of man, horse, and trees, all trying to help themselves in whatever way they could, I was lying under the overturned wagon with my nose squashed into my face and my cheek pressed against a sharp, pointy protrusion at the foot of a tree. The soldiers, dazed by the uproar, bewildered by fear as they realized that they had been driven into the forest from three sides to be ground into one heap of flesh, were scrambling in different directions. Looking for an exit, throat-splitting voices were ordering, "Push, push," which rebounded in heart-breaking pleas, "Back up, back up!" The exasperated trees began spitting fire; a rain of bullets came from above and fountains of shrapnel from below. The wounded were trying to hide under the dead, crying, "Enough. Enough. Raise your hands!"

"Raise something white . . . white shirts! Who's got a white shirt?" The sun quickly turned its face away from that ugly picture, and night fell upon the scene with a primordial darkness.

As if by the magic wand of a conductor, the pandemonium froze into silence, whereupon the trembling voices of the soldiers conveyed to each other the first orders of the Germans in a muffled refrain:

"Rifles, bayonets—throw away, throw away."

"Sit down!"

"Lie down!"

"Stretch out!"

"Face down! Hands over heads. *Schnell, schnell, schnell!*" The soldiers burrowed their heads into the ground and, crossing their hearts for the last time, they mumbled, "God Almighty, those Germans, what hell do they spring from?"

In the early morning, when the rays of the sun began to spread apart the trees and open little paths for the prisoners, new orders came from the Germans:

"*Stand up. Schnell, schnell, schnell!*"

"Leave ammunition on the ground."

"Raise your hands."

"March! Out of the woods!"

"Out, out to the open fields." "*Schnell! Schnell!*" "Quick! Quick!" the trees translated with human voices. With raised hands and trembling knees, the trapped and mauled mass rushed over the piles of wreckage, fearing a sure death awaited them in the open field. Among them stumbled along a little soldier profusely bleeding from his torn cheek, his crushed nose wrapped in the lining of his father's jacket. On the ground, the severely wounded soldiers crawling on their bellies pleaded, "Brothers, take us along." But there was no time, no ears, no eyes under the lashing German order, "*Schnell, schnell, schnell.*"

Yet I stopped for one split second, letting the rushing mob pass by me. At a distance my eye caught a glimpse of a body sprawled facedown over the legs of another body. The upper back part of the body on top seemed to have a remarkable similarity to the heavyset shoulders of my father. I was ready to push myself through the racing crowd and . . . But at that very moment one of the infuriated soldiers kicked me violently in my buttocks with his boot. I slumped and would have been crushed to death had I not immediately regained my balance. Holding one hand over my head and with the other pressing the rag, ripped off my father's jacket, against the frightfully bleeding hole on my cheek, I caught on to the rhythm of the stampede. Soon commanding voices coming from left and right ordered, "Stop, stop!"

Breathing heavily in a ferment of rage and fear, the soldiers looked at each other.

"Say, brother, do you believe they'll let us live?" "It's forbidden by God to shoot a prisoner." "They say the Germans don't believe in God." "They say the Germans speak the Jewish language." "This damned push into the woods is no doubt a Jewish trick." "Those ahead of us must have already reached the open fields—had they been shot we would have heard it." "Yes. It's quiet . . ." "Be blessed, Tsar in heaven . . ."

On the second stop: "Hey, brother, did you ever see a German?" "Don't worry, you'll see them soon." "They say instead of a rifle they carry a saw." "Holy Mother, what for?"

The open fields were empty.

"Where are the Germans?" "There, there . . . there's one." "No, two, two . . ."

Two small figures stood bathed in the full splendor of the rising sun in the open field, helmets on their heads and carrying rifles with broad, sawlike bayonets. One held a match to the other's pipe with cool indifference.

The thousands of prisoners jostled to catch a glimpse of the two

strange creatures. "Only two?" they wondered with foolish, embarrassed smiles.

Soon a brace of motorcycles escorted a couple of cars into the
field, and several foppish German officers in light gray coats nipped
at the waist and wearing monocles alighted. They said something to
the two soldiers, who immediately began to bark for the prisoners
to come forward into the field, line up in rows of twenty, and follow
them. Like frightened children treading on each other's feet, the
mass of prisoners hurriedly obeyed the order. The cars and motorcycles swiftly departed; the two Germans again lit their pipes and
started calmly forward. Behind them trailed the silent horde, each
man sunk in his own ruminations. From time to time, unable to
contain his astonishment, one whispered to another, "Where are the
Germans? These two are not enough to kill us all."

"Maybe they're taking us to Berlin to kill us there," one tried to
guess.

"How far is it to Berlin?" a few asked, but no one could supply the
answer.

After a six-hour march with only one short rest, the procession
came to a place where a large barbed-wire compound had been set
up. A great number of squatting prisoners already filled the compound. They assailed the newcomers with chattering teeth: did anybody by chance have a crust of bread on them? Because in three days
they had only had three bowls of hot water mixed with some black
bark that the Germans called "coffee."

"Do they shoot prisoners?" was the first question asked by the
newcomers.

"No, no, they don't shoot, but they don't feed either."

"They don't have anything to eat themselves," one of the old-
timers explained with importance. "You never see their mouths
moving."

"How do they treat you? Do they beat you?"

"They don't bother us, they're even polite sometimes, but they
don't feed us."

"They do feed those they send to work. I saw it myself," one of
the older prisoners swore. "Every morning a commission comes and
picks out several thousand men from the compound. They probably
send them to Berlin to work. There's probably more to eat there."

"Why didn't they pick you?" the newcomers wanted to know.

"It seems they only need doctors, engineers, and technicians, not peasants."

"How about carpenters?" someone asked.

"Could be they do."

"And a shoemaker?"

"That's not sure."

"A blacksmith?"

"Maybe."

"What about a watchmaker?" a voice piped up from the back of the crowd. No answer was forthcoming. There had never been a watchmaker in the compound before.

"A watchmaker isn't a common peasant nor a simple worker, mind you, a watchmaker you might say is a kind of engineer," the watchmaker said, pushing his way to the center of the crowd. Those standing in the rear stood on tiptoe and craned their necks to catch a glimpse of such a privileged character.

The guards marching around the compound suddenly barked sternly, "To sleep!" The whole rabble dropped to the ground as one man and, burrowing into their greatcoats, snuggled up against one another.

Early the next morning, the commission made its appearance. Outside the gate of the compound a long table had been set up for a row of noncommissioned officers. The prisoners presented their documents, papers, loose change, and other trivia, and told their occupations.

"Peasant," the first prisoner mumbled with a pitiful smile.

"To the right. Next."

"Peasant."

"Right."

"Locksmith."

"Left."

"Baker."

"Right."

"Blacksmith."

"Left."

"Butcher."

"Right."

"Watchmaker . . ." A short pause.

"Back in the compound."

A sigh from the right and the left.

I came up to the table. My face was completely wrapped up to the eyes.

"Documents! I can't hear you . . . Take the rag out of your mouth."

I took off my father's coat and presented a terribly bloody face with a hole in the cheek through which the tips of the back teeth could be seen. With a grimace of horror and revulsion, the Germans repeated, more calmly now, "Have you no documents?"

A German standing by shook out my pockets from which fell a string, several chickpeas, and a folded, colored sheet of paper.

"What's this?" one of the noncoms asked, passing the paper to the other.

The latter read in fluent Russian:

> On Saturday, the twelfth,
> In the magnificent Town Hall
> Will be presented a grand evening
> Which will again feature the famous
> and extraordinary
> Chantille Jeantaigne Delacroix.

Running his eyes from the paper to me and back again, the German asked, almost pleasantly now, "What are you, an actor? How much do you weigh?" I tried to mumble something but the words stuck in my throat, which was clogged with blood. The men at the table looked at each other smilingly and pointed to the right, where a few thousand souls were already lined up by tens following a single German soldier's command.

At the train depot the mob was again broken up into several groups, each with a separate number, and after a long slow ride in freight cars over damaged rails, the group with the long number 148649 was brought in the middle of the night to the town of Shirvint.

It was still dark when they roused us with a shrill whistle, served us "coffee," and, with the same *Schnell, schnell, schnell,*" the blacksmiths were given axes and led off to a nearby woods to chop trees. The locksmiths were handed saws to saw the hauled-in logs into long boards, and the carpenters were given measurements according to which they were to cut the boards into planks that would quickly snap together in such a tricky fashion as to form walls and floors for the trenches without the use of nails.

The "actor" was handed a pail of tar with a long brush and sent behind the barracks to smear the walls of a building with a pit, over which lay three boards, above which hung a placard bearing four Russian words which happened to rhyme:

> *Nie boltat a strat.*
> No talking—just shitting.

XXXI

THE PRISONERS in the compound were right—no food. Otherwise the Germans weren't particularly brutal. An occasional slap in the face or a kick in the rump, but this was still a far cry from shooting. Only when a guard said something to a prisoner in German and he didn't understand, then called a second prisoner to explain, and the second prisoner called a third, and the third also shrugged helplessly, only then would the guard lose his patience and slam the rifle butt against the head—of the third prisoner. To be the third man became a very unlucky role in the compound.

But that was only in the beginning. As soon as I learned to speak a little German, I became the first whom the guard called to translate for the prisoners. And that's how the "little Russian" quickly became an intermediary between the guards and the prisoners.

The peasants couldn't stop wondering how such a small, skinny creature weighing less than eighty pounds could in such a short time master such a hard language as German. So that in spite of my low assignment as keeper of the latrine, the fact that I often kept them from getting an extra smack in the head was enough for them to treat me with respect. There was another, more important reason for their friendliness toward me. Some among the carpenters could carve comic wooden figures, and the locksmiths could pound out rings, brooches, and bracelets from the Russian bullets that the guards jealously collected. The trade between the prisoners and guards exchanging a handcrafted souvenir for a piece of bread or a raw meat bone was conducted through me.

We were awakened at 5:00 A.M. for "coffee," then led off to work. Around noon we were issued a slice of bread and some gruel of indeterminate color in which floated several groats, a few bones, and, occasionally, a worm or two. Coming back from work there was again soup and again their famous "coffee." Heavy black clouds hung in the sky. The ground was covered with dirty snow, and the predawn winds tore through the worn boots and greatcoats. With each passing day the faces of the prisoners grew more sallow, the watery sacks under their eyes swelled, and their gaze grew hazier. Not the least contact with the outside world was permitted. Even speaking to a passing civilian was punishable by solitary confinement. Nor could you write or receive mail. By now everybody knew we were doomed to slow starvation.

But one day three odd-looking civilians showed up in the barracks. They wore red crosses on their sleeves. They brought packages, which they distributed among the men. The prisoners couldn't believe their eyes when they found ten slices of real bread, a dozen biscuits, several lumps of sugar, a bag of tobacco, and a small bar of chocolate inside each package. Some wept with joy. They clasped their hands in pious prayer as if confronting three angels from heaven, fell to their knees, crossed themselves, and kissed the cuffs of their benefactors' trousers. Soon came an even greater surprise. The three angels issued each prisoner a postcard and told them to write several words to their parents, wives, and children. At the same time, they supplied selected words that were allowed to be used:

"I'm alive."

"I'm well."

"I work."

"I feel good."

"Don't forget me."

"We'll see each other soon."

Those who could write a little held the pens like chisels in their shaky fists and promptly began to copy the permitted words in large, crooked squiggles. They grew deeply depressed when they realized that no more than five or six of the permitted words could fit on the small postcard; in still greater distress were those who were only able to sign their names with three crosses. They looked for me to help them, but I was not in the barracks. I had accepted my package along with the others, but when it came to writing the postcards I went off and hid in the building with the rhymed placard. Why and what should I write? Should I write that I'm healthy and working? Where? In a latrine? Should I write that I'm alive and feel good? How could I dare—I who had let down my father by not bringing him his clothes in time, thus condemning him to God knows what suffering? For according to rumor the Germans were already deep inside Russia and my father, if he wasn't already dead in the woods, was certainly a prisoner by now. And what was a furrier? Not a doctor, not an engineer, not a mechanic—this meant that chances were good that the father, just like his son, was cleaning latrines somewhere . . .

Should I write my mother that I'm alive and feeling good and that we would see each other soon? How could I? How could I ever tell her where I had spent those last few days and nights, when I should have gone to the hospital? How could I even show my face to her again? Never . . . So why deceive? Why write that I'd be coming back and that she shouldn't forget me? On the contrary, let her think I had died somewhere in pursuit of my father. Let her forget me as quickly as possible, because to forget forever meant to forgive forever . . . I'd never see Tanya again, either. I had decided this even before they brought the postcards.

It happened one day that I found a piece of broken mirror and for the first time saw my squashed nose and torn cheek. I flung away the piece of glass reflecting my repulsive face—which, as my teacher in cheder had once assured me, was created in the image of God—and in great despair I fell to the ground, sobbing, begging that the earth swallow me . . . So what did a postcard mean to me now except salt rubbed in the wounds of my deformed face and pepper on my bloodied conscience? No, the disguised angels with the postcards weren't for me. Let the ignorant, boorish peasants with their hunger-swollen bellies who still hoped to go home one day write that they shouldn't be forgotten. In their ignorance, they didn't know that the war would last another ten or twelve years and the little pieces of chocolate wouldn't carry them through it.

I didn't know the world. This prison camp was my first stop on my first excursion out of my native city, but one thing was already clear to me—whether or not it was true that there wasn't enough room on this earth for all the people, as Barve's Son had suggested—there surely wasn't enough food. So I would do better to expire here in the latrine, to make room for those remaining after me . . . But the peasants found me and pleaded, "Write, little brother, write. Have pity." I tried, but I couldn't, and I collapsed at the table.

The three angels stood around pushing a little bottle up to my nose. They examined the running wound in my cheek, shook their heads, wrapped themselves in their fur wings, and flew from the cold barracks. Still, before leaving the camp, they wrote down the number of the "little Russian" with the dangerously neglected wound.

The next morning, an extraordinary event took place. Even before everyone had been awakened for work, the "little Russian" was hustled from the barracks to a car waiting outside. They didn't tell me where they were taking me. Would they take a prisoner in a car to be executed?

Before the car had stopped, I recognized the familiar smell of a hospital. Without a word, they pushed me out of the car, shoved me into a bathroom, tore off my clothes, rammed me under a cold shower, thrust me naked into an operating room, flung me onto a table, stuck a hose in my mouth, and told me to count to twenty.

During the time of my recuperation, I managed in casual remarks to the nurses and orderlies to exhibit my familiarity with hospital procedures. One day, an opportunity presented itself to tell one of the doctors how I had worked as a civilian volunteer in a military hospital, and how I had been innocently dragged along by the retreating Russian army. Thus when I was discharged from the hospital four weeks later, I was given an old pair of pants and a ragged coat and told to report to the office for civilian workers. That very same day, I was transferred to the town of Oran, which was the temporary center of the upper-eastern train network. Now I had four angels to bless. Added to the original three was the good doctor from the hospital. One thing, however, wasn't clear to me: how did an angel from heaven come to be wearing a German military uniform?

In Oran, I found two groups of workers—one that had been rounded up for forced labor, and another that had reported for work voluntarily. I was put in the first group. The work was equally hard for both, the only difference being that the forced laborers got forty pfennigs a day while the volunteers got eighty. In the second month, after I had gathered my courage, I voiced my resentment to the stationmaster over this injustice against one who already had so much experience in routing trains. The stationmaster heard my complaint amiably and sent me to the office of the head registrar to transfer me to the list of eighty-pfennig workers. When I came into the room my heart nearly burst from amazement. Behind the large desk sat Gerasim Isakovitch Dalski, minus the beard.

He looked up. "What do you want?"

I turned my face to the left and he snapped his fingers in surprise. "God in heaven! Chantille Jeantaigne Delacroix! What are you doing here?"

"I'm a railroad worker."

"A volunteer?"

"Yes."

"Good. Very good!" The ex-teacher came out from behind his desk and closed the door. "I have no words to describe how happy I am to see you. How are you? Where were you all this time?"

In order to adjust to the joyful greeting, which echoed to me as if from distant space yet at the same time seemed so intimate and near, I asked with forced cheerfulness, "Gerasim Isakovitch, did you by chance hear anything about my mother?"

He nervously began to feel around for his missing beard and, with the other hand, directed me to a chair. "Unfortunately I don't know your mother, but I asked around several times for you at Tanya's."

"Tanya . . . how is she?"

"I don't know, exactly. I did hear that she got involved with a group of revolutionaries, and it seems that they smuggled her into Russia, but when I saw her she told me that you and your father had disappeared with the Russian army. This, I felt, was very foolish of you. You should have stayed and gone into hiding, as many people did. Had your father done so he would still be alive today."

"Is he dead?"

"According to rumor he was heavily wounded on the way to Minsk and evidently died in the field."

I wanted to correct him; not in a field but more likely in the woods. But before I managed to open my mouth he proceeded. "Yes, yes, my friend, war is no game. And I'm pleased that you're taking the bitter news like a man. I remember you as a boy, but I see that in this short time you've matured. The fact that you volunteered for work is a sign that you're a responsible person who can adapt to a given situation. Here you will find idiots who don't understand that when you report voluntarily for work you get a bigger piece of bread, a fatter soup, and a whole forty pfennigs more than those who are brought by force . . .

"Tell me, why are your face and nose so smashed? What is it, a sword slash? Good! Excellent! Among the Germans, this is a decided advantage. The Germans are a remarkably warlike race, and they love it when someone carries his wounds exposed. I assure you that this will help you a lot in the future. The Germans aren't like the Russians. They're a cultured people. As for the war, there can be no doubt that the Germans will win. Just look at how neat and clean their soldiers are, and how gallant and natty are their officers. How can you compare them to the dirty, lousy Russian peasants to whose right foot you must tie a piece of straw to show them left from right? We must side with the winner.

"Besides, haven't you noticed the placards—'Long live the Poles,' 'Long live the Lithuanians'? I wouldn't be surprised one fine day to see a proclamation, 'Long live the Jews.' You can expect anything from a cultured people. But what are the Jews doing? Especially the market Jews? A plague on their heads. They're sorry for the Russians. They're longing for a pogrom. They laugh, they mock the Germans. They call them shit ass. They forget that this carries the penalty of death.

"Since there's nothing to sell, they have closed their stalls and gone underground. You wouldn't believe it—they dig tunnels under the military cordon around the city to get to the country, where the peasants sell them some potatoes, a bunch of carrots, a dead chicken, which they have hidden from German confiscation. Sometimes the Jews pretend to be dead, let themselves be carried and 'buried' at some far corner of the cemetery, and the business is carried on among the graves. And with all that, a quarter of the population has already perished from hunger, and still they hide out so as not to work for the Germans.

"And what do the girls and women do, even those who have lost their husbands in the fierce battles around the city? They open coffeehouses with signs, 'Music and Roast Goose,' but you understand there isn't even a whiff of roast goose there. This is only to attract the German soldiers. All you can get there is a pot of dirty water and music from a squeaky phonograph. The guests pay with a little square of bread or a pinch of marmalade. And since it is punishable by death for the Germans to sleep with foreign women, which is another reason to be grateful to the German hygienic culture, the whole marketplace has become one big coffeehouse.

"Good. So serve the coffee already—but no, they go and piss in the pots, and the German dum-dum drinks it. You talk to them and they scream, 'Where should we get tea or coffee when there isn't even enough piss in the city?' I ask you, does that befit a Jew? They're really a disgrace. They wait for the Russians to conquer the Germans, which is as likely as hair growing out of my palm. What was I to the Russians? A crummy little teacher, not God forbid in a university, not even in a government gymnasium, but in some poor Jewish junior high school.

"What else would a Jew be? Did you see any Jewish officers in the Russian army? Nary a one! But in the German army, Jewish officers are thick as flies, and not only lieutenants but captains, colonels . . . You see, here I am the registrar. I'm supposed to control and keep lists of laborers. Naturally, this is only temporary. After the war the region will belong to the Germans, and I have great plans. In the meantime I'm getting to know the various train networks. And everything is possible when you deal with a cultured people. I may yet attain a high post such as, let us say for instance, Minister of Train Connections in the Occupied Upper East . . .

"Yes, yes, my friend, everything is possible and not only for me but for you as well. I have a proposition all ready for you. You'll work under my personal supervision . . . You understand, you have to approach the matter from a historic-cultural standpoint. Take, for instance—"

I jumped up. "Excuse me . . ." But I remained speechless. An excruciating pain ran through the crude stitches on my face and nose. I crumpled my lips and let my moist eyes speak the words: How dare you! I came to ask you for an extra spoon of soup or a larger bite of bread, and you are presenting me with a lecture on historical culture or cultural history. How dare you mention to me German-Jewish generals and captains when a German bullet killed my father? Perhaps my father, shooting, killed a German, then maybe a Jew killed a Jew, so what good is the proclamation "Long live the Jews"? What for? To kill each other? Aren't you ashamed to insinuate that my mother, who was considered even by the pigeons of the market as the gentlest creature of the city . . . At the very moment she appeared, they would circle around her head and rest upon her shoulders, eat from her palms, and kiss her on the lips . . . Why, even the dog and the cat were following her day and night—out of sheer self-respect and dignity she spoke Russian to the dog, Polish to the cat, and Yiddish to her children.

Have you no limit to your vulgarity to imply that perhaps forced by need and hunger she may be dancing now with a German? Drunk on Jewish wine? Fie—to think that you were my teacher! Are you talking to me like that because I've lost my human face and will perhaps remain for life a figure of ridicule, like the Victor Hugo character after his face was deformed? Have you forgotten that when you were still my teacher I was forty-five years old already, and after you asked me to help you with a recitation at a charity concert for the starving children, *you* got cold feet? Just at curtain-rise you disappeared and left me alone, throwing the whole beleaguered city upon my shoulders. And now you stand scoffing and deriding the people who put themselves in coffins and play with death to support their miserable lives. Well, well . . . know that I am now saying good-bye to you for good. Never will you see my face again. I'm going to join this wretched army of the "dead," for it makes no difference who'll make the final kill—the Russians or the Germans. I'm on the side of the "dead" already, for it will be like in "The Conqueror of Death"—the dead will survive.

And I sat down.

"What's the matter? You don't feel good?" he asked me.

Carefully I opened the side of my mouth and spoke in torn phrases. "Excuse me . . . interrupting you . . . no question about your proposition . . . I thank you, but the truth . . . I'm a prisoner of war, transferred to civilian group of forced laborers . . . I accidentally found out that my . . . teacher was here. I asked the stationmaster permission for ten minutes to exchange regards . . . regards weren't happy ones, still I thank you for everything, especially for the new post . . . you offered . . . I will surely accept in a day or two . . . Meantime, I must run back. I don't want to anger the stationmaster who's been so good to me . . ."

"Excellent," Gerasim said, slapping my shoulder. "This shows discipline. Give my your work card, and I'll transfer you to the list of volunteers. It'll only be a difference of forty pfennigs, but in a time of hunger even a hog's bristle is good enough."

"First thing tomorrow I'll come to get my volunteer card, thank you again . . . now I must run . . . Excuse me."

With assumed calmness I slipped out of the office and headed for the freight depot. Once there, I quickly crawled under a pile of broken wagons where I waited for the sun to fade from Oran, then, using the two moonlit lines of the rails to guide, I headed for the city and the old marketplace.

XXXII

◦~◦

THE GERMANS ENTERED the city at the beginning of September. At first, only a small group of riders on glittering horses pranced down broad streets. They threw candy to the youngsters running behind, and kisses to the girls in the windows. That same day, around noon, a small detail of infantry marched down the same street led by several musicians piping on small, thin flutes and kicking their legs in the air in a strange wild fashion. And that was it. No more Germans showed up. The fact that such a small group of Germans should possess such satanic powers as to drive out such enormous hordes of Russians who for weeks on end had been dragging through the streets in endless regiments, brigades, and divisions made an awesome impression upon the city. At night, only one soldier stood guard by the garbage bin in the marketplace and, if not for the moon's reflection on his bayonet, even that one wouldn't have been seen and there wouldn't have been any indication that the White Russian, Ukrainian, Lithuanian, Polish, Russian, Jewish market-place was now a German marketplace.

Early the next morning, strangers in long blue capes appeared on Market Street. On the building walls they posted brief greetings to the city, which began:

Since the German occupation troops
have come to liberate
the city from the yoke of the Russian barbarians . . .

and ended with a blessing upon the entire population.

But soon, another kind of news appeared on the walls, evoking amazement. It read more or less like this:

In relation to the spread of cholera, all men, women, and children regardless of age must report to the specially set up baths where they will be bathed, deloused, and disinfected. Those who have found a bedbug or a flea at home should report immediately with their pillows, mattresses, and clothes to the above-mentioned place. Failure to obey is punishable by six months' imprisonment.

"Six months for one bedbug? Are they *verruckt?*" some of the people joked. But they found out that the thing wasn't as funny as they thought when a day or two later new information appeared on the walls:

Entering or leaving the city is strictly forbidden under the penalty of death.

"What's this, what does it mean?" And before they had time to consider further, the "blue capes" hung a new ordinance on the opposite wall:

Whoever has bread, butter, or cigars must present these items to this and that address. Whoever has copper, iron, tin, or zinc must bring it to this and that address. Failure to obey is punishable by four years' imprisonment.

And the very next day came a fresh postscript to yesterday's directive:

Samovars, candlesticks, bells, copper pans, pots, door latches, window hooks, brass buttons from trousers . . . must be promptly brought to this and that address—six years' imprisonment.

The same penalty was posted a few days later with a new announcement:

Whoever owns a horse must cut the hair from its tail and mane and present it to this and that collection center.

And a bit later the same day:

Along with the cut hair, the owner must also present the horse.

From this, it became apparent that the Germans were not at all *verruckt* but simply out to drive the city crazy.

I entered the city at night. The streets dozed in indolent slumber and whispered quietly under my careful footsteps: Where have you been, little one? Where do you come from? Might you have any food to spare, perhaps?

And the buildings with the darkened windows breathed through murky mouths: Food . . . food . . . food . . .

When I came to Market Street, the wall of a house blocked my path: Stay, stay and read what they have posted on my sunken breast for you . . .

Entering or leaving the city is strictly forbidden under the penalty of death.

Everyone ten years and older must carry his passport at all times. Failure to obey is punishable by ten years' imprisonment.

Men from sixteen to sixty must register for work in coal mines in Germany.

Evading this edict will cost those able to pay six hundred marks, and those unable to pay, six years in prison.

All inhabitants of the city between the ages of fifteen and sixty who possess all their limbs must pay a head tax of six marks, a hand tax of eight marks, and a foot tax of four marks . . . or six months' imprisonment.

Concealing former Russian soldiers or war prisoners is punishable by death.

Every family must provide one blanket per member for the freezing soldiers at the front. Failure to comply—four weeks' imprisonment. Failure to obey—two years' imprisonment . . . four years . . . six years . . . nine years . . .

All in all, I quickly figured out that for the ten minutes that I had been in the city, I had more than a hundred and thirty years of prison and several death sentences coming to me.

I drew myself up to my fullest height next to the old, familiar wall. This colossal penalty hanging over my head evoked a proud feeling of devil-may-care within me. Such a punishment befitted only a criminal of the highest rank, a master criminal next to whom all the forty thieves of the *Arabian Nights* and the sixty legendary Russian bandits were mere amateurs.

With sure footsteps I ran up the stairs of my house and knocked on the door with a firm hand.

"Who is it?"

"Me!"

A woman's figure appeared through the partly opened door.

It vaguely resembled my mother. The same face but somewhat smaller, and instead of light brown hair, two thin gray braids dangling over her shoulders.

Nor did Sarah—standing there, huddled in an old cotton jacket and holding a kerosene lamp—recognize her son immediately. He had grown somewhat taller and leaner, and although the hair was the same, the face certainly wasn't. For a moment we looked at each other like strangers—as if I had knocked on the wrong door by mistake. Then I pushed the door open and stole in sideways like a thief in the night. My mother burst out crying, but I told her that we had no time for idle sentiment: that I faced three sentences of hanging and that she had better tell me right off what she had heard of my father.

"Shush, quiet, the neighbors are liable to hear." And, lighting the way with the tiny lamp, she led me into the rear room and whispered confidentially, "Someone spread the rumor that your father was wounded with shrapnel while fleeing with the Russian army. He must be lying in some hospital right now and we'll be hearing from him any day."

"How?"

"By letter."

"You're expecting a letter from Father?"

"Yes, very soon."

She was never a liar, poor woman. What's become of her? I thought. Or, maybe she doesn't know that Father is dead? Should I come right out with the truth or should I let her keep breathing a while longer before I deal her the death blow?

"How do you know Father is alive?"

"I don't *know,* still I'm sure of it."

"How can you be sure of a thing you don't know?"

"How can you know a thing you're not sure of?"

"But the rumor is he's dead."

"Nonsense!"

She angrily shook the lamp in her hand, and her shadow grew ever bigger on the wall. "I heard the same rumor about you, and here you are alive and well, only a little scratched around the face. It can be the same with your father. He may come back with a wound or two—that's only natural. To come out of a war without a scratch would be too much to expect. You need only to have patience until the Germans get their comeuppance. All we need do is outlive the Germans just as we outlived the Russians . . . Don't take off your coat, it's colder in the house than outside. It's weeks since we've heated the oven. You can't get any wood, but I do have enough to eat." And she put a loaf of bread that was slightly larger than my fist on the table. "You get this as a weekly bread ration for five people. But you can finish it because, thank God, we have enough to eat."

I pushed the bread away. "No, I didn't come here to take the last bite of food out of your mouth. I'll get bread tomorrow."

"How? Do you have a ration card?"

"No."

"To get a ration card you need a passport."

"I'll get a passport."

"Do you want to risk your life?"

"What's life worth, anyway?"

"Nonsense. One live dog is worth more than thirty dead lions. With a passport you get a ration card and with a ration card you get a quarter of such a loaf. Let them choke with their passports and those cards."

"But if they catch me without a passport?"

"You won't go anywhere, so you don't need a passport. So far, they haven't searched the houses. And if they do, there is an attic here and a good cellar—I found a couple of old beds there, too. And as for food, I told you, you don't have to worry about it. You understand . . ." She put her mouth closer to my ear. "The city is like a prison—no coming in, no going out. The slightest attempt to disregard it is punishable by death. But what punishment can stop the hunger of children? So people have begun to match themselves against the Germans in daring and ingenuity. They try to smuggle in a little flour or a sack of potatoes from the nearby villages . . .

"I've joined such a group of smugglers . . . I'm a mourner. My job requires joining a group of twenty or thirty people following a funeral cortege and crying as loud as possible. But instead of a body, the coffin contains a sack of flour or a side of beef. The cortege forms behind the city, then after it has passed the German guards it turns toward the Jewish cemetery. There, the 'corpse' is removed and divided into small packets that the women carry out in their bosoms or under their dresses. They bring it to a certain gathering place. The Germans are still a bit more considerate of women. They don't shoot them right on the spot. If they catch us, they strip us naked and give us a few lashes across the behind. They only caught me once, but blessed be the Almighty, I got away with four or five lashes, and I pray to God they'll never catch me again."

With these words, she stood up and looked to see if the curtain over the window was tightly drawn. She rolled up her sleeves, stuck her hand deep into the chimney of the wall oven, and pulled out a big Sabbath loaf, a half triangle of dry white cheese, a few eggs, a small jar of chicken fat, and a bag of yellow sugar and laid it all on the table in front of me.

I watched the shriveled woman with the mighty shadow looming over her— she turned, and the enormous shadow vanished inside her. In her tattered jacket, holding the kerosene lamp above her head, she sidled up to me and looked me straight in the eye as if making sure that the youth with the scarred, unfamiliar face was un-mistakably her own child whom she could finally entrust with her deepest secret. "When you're finished and you go up to the attic, don't be frightened. Your father is sleeping there . . . He came a week after you left. He hid among the sacks of barley in the food storehouse. When the running Russians set fire to the storehouses, your father got his arms and legs burned. Now he is better, but he still can't get around. He didn't believe you would come. But now, he will see that I was right. One must believe, wait, and hope."

The bite of food stuck in my gullet to make room for the flow of tears that spurted from my whole body to my eyes.

"Oh, you little mother of mine, how majestically marvelous you are in your ragged jacket, and how small and insignificant is your son beside you. You're beautiful because you speak so little and love so much—your children, your husband, and your God . . . You're beautiful because you're always the same under all circumstances. You're always you with the same unbounded trust in perhaps, in maybe, in wait and see, because waiting means living and living— outliving the Russians and the Germans. But I who was never I, what do I need a passport for? Whose name shall I put on it— Paganini, Vaska Sibiriak, Chantille Jeantaigne Delacroix? No, no, I won't go up in the attic. I'll take your place on that dangerous path to the graves of the cemetery. I'll be the smuggler, and you will stay home. If they catch me, whip me, or hang me, it'll be a small loss for the city, but without you and those like you, what kind of face could the city present and what worth would the whole world have?"

And I began to gobble the food with all the hundred mouths of the Arabian and Russian bandits.

XXXIII

⟨∽⋙∽⟩

THE BAND OF smugglers consisted of twenty-two persons, none of whom knew the others. If there were some who knew each other or were close relatives, they made believe they were strangers. No names were used, only "you" and "he." The smuggled-in bundles were designated as "this corpse," "that corpse," "the other corpse," and so on . . .

The leader of the band was a cantor nicknamed Cold Itche. Two qualities singled him out as leader. First, he lived at the very edge of the city, the third house from the cemetery, where he served as the permanent cantor. His house was therefore the most suitable spot from which the band could steal out late at night, then steal back at dawn. Second, he was a cool character, as his name implied, not because he was overly daring but because he hadn't the slightest notion of the fearful risk in which he placed his wife and four children by making his home the headquarters for this dangerous business.

A quiet, unquestioning man who, after having lived twenty-five years near a cemetery, was still afraid to enter a dark room alone, he had managed to save up a nice bundle with which he had eagerly and with assurance—as if investing in a government bank—subsidized the entire venture. Amiable and honest too, he saw to it that none of the participants were cheated and that each received his rightful share. The only trouble was that after the smuggled-in goods had been distributed among the band, nothing remained for the leader, and he couldn't understand how this could happen. That a piece should be missing from a wedge of cheese or the soft inside be scooped out from a loaf of bread or that an egg be lacking a yolk, this he could understand, but in heaven's name—where was *his* share?

It was very hard to keep track of the business, since everything was reckoned without writing for security reasons and the leader's memory was poor when it came to remembering who was supposed to bring in what and who had brought in which.

"What's going on here?" he harangued the band. "It *should* come out right. Approximately twenty-two corpses are brought in each day, six days a week, which comes to some hundred-odd items divided by twenty-two, which should come out to about six corpses per person. So where is my share?"

One evening during such a session when the leader again began to reiterate his complaints, the youngest and newest member of the band, who sat in a corner reading a book and awaiting the signal to get going, mentioned with casual indifference that six times twenty-two wasn't some hundred-odd but one hundred thirty-two, which had to be divided not by twenty-two but by twenty-three, amounting to five and seventeen twenty-thirds per share.

When Itche heard this over his shoulder, he turned to the speaker and said, "If you're so good at mathematics, young man, why didn't you speak up before? It's enough that I've given my money and my house, must I also carry around such a crazy thing as seventeen twenty-thirds in my head?" He turned to the whole group. "No! Let the young man take over the bookkeeping, all I want is my share." And thus, only two weeks after joining the band, I became book-keeper for the entire enterprise.

Itche couldn't get over my remarkable memory. Not only did I remember which smuggler was supposed to bring in a slaughtered rooster, I also remembered which woman had tucked a salt herring under her breast, and could even recall which breast. Itche couldn't praise the bookkeeper enough.

Now that he was rid of the headache of keeping count and his share was controlled down to the tail of a herring, Itche should have been a bit more cheerful, but exactly the opposite prevailed. His face grew sadder from day to day, lending a strange kind of moroseness to his calculated coldness, and he seemed like a corpse from the cemetery that had attached itself to the band.

This was too obvious for the band not to notice, and when they were in the cellar waiting for the moon to set to go their separate ways, they amused themselves by trying to unravel Itche's secret. With a word here, a word there, the story soon unfolded.

Itche had a son of eight, an ugly lad with slightly crossed eyes who took after his mother, herself a kind of hag. But to make up for it he had three daughters, each one prettier than the next, particularly the eldest, who was sixteen. And it was she, Gutia, who now caused Itche such anguish.

It seemed that one day Gutia had gotten herself pregnant. But this wasn't the main problem. After all, Itche had money, and with money you can cure anything. The fact that Gutia was just sixteen and the prospective father only a month or two older didn't irk Itche as much as the fact that the boy's parents—prominent society people—were making every effort to break up the romance.

It never occurred to him that the parents' greatest concern was that their son might be caught in a smuggler's house, and if someone had pointed this out, he wouldn't have understood. What was the fear? What was the danger? But the boy's parents knew better. They read the newspapers, and they knew that a day didn't go by that a smuggler wasn't caught and, according to the German system, all those seized with him were equally condemned. Itche, who didn't begin to realize that his head was in a noose or at least on the brink of a long prison sentence, interpreted the parents' disapproval as the snobbery of aristocrats toward the daughter of a poor, simple cemetery cantor—and without a voice, yet. He justified himself in his own mind by telling himself that no one came to a cemetery to hear Caruso . . . But what was the use of talking? It was the old story of the prince and the servant girl.

If the girl had at least been homely—but such a beauty? So decent and refined and able to speak such nice Russian even though she had never gone to school? Then again, what were the boy's qualifications—two and a half years in junior high school? But the fashion was such that one aristocrat wanted his child to marry the child of another, and what was he but a common cantor? And maybe not even that, for a cantor was someone like Kvartin, Sirota, Razumny. Was it his fault his father hadn't sent him to a cantorial school?

In this dark, self-deprecatory mood it is understandable that the new bookkeeper's skill in mathematics made a tremendous impression upon the cantor. The fact that the youth with the torn face and squashed nose spoke excellent Russian was immediately apparent, but when he heard him argue with a passing German in fluent German—this stunned Cold Itche completely. And when he noticed him one time sitting in a corner and reading a thick German book, he called him to his room and began to question him about his background.

In careful fashion I explained that I had neither parents nor relatives, that I had finished the gymnasium before the war, and that I spoke and read German because I had once been in Germany.

The fact that such a well-traveled, well-educated boy should become a smuggler seemed perfectly natural to Itche, but why not hire him to tutor his children in German at a time when it was the main language of the city? All right, Gutia was a lost cause already, but the two younger daughters and particularly the boy could still be saved and made into aristocrats.

"It's not a question of money," I said with hesitation. "We have to go out to the villages late at night, do our business early in the morning, then go home, which takes a long time because I have to sneak along side streets so as not to get caught by the 'blue capes.' This does not leave time even to sleep."

"You can sleep at my place," Itche said. "I have enough room. I have an extra bed, and if you are as you say—an orphan—I can sell your 'corpse' to my customers and you can come live here with us."

"I'll take care of the 'corpse' myself, but if you let me live at your house, no matter what you pay me for the lessons it will be enough," I said.

That same day Itche introduced me to his three younger children and gave me complete authority over them. If they didn't listen or neglected to study, I could even slap them. But this never proved necessary, for they took to me from the very first lesson. It wasn't because they valued my pedagogical skills, it was more out of pity for my woeful appearance with the broken nose and torn cheek. They didn't call me "teacher," since it was no secret to them that by profession I was a smuggler, but they didn't consider it fitting to call me "smuggler" either, so they compromised with "Mister Bookkeeper."

It just so happened that I made the best impression on Gutia. After she had rid herself of her "plague" and her relationship with her seducer had been terminated, she wandered around as if in a vacuum, not knowing what to do with herself. One day, out of sheer boredom, she joined the group.

All that she knew about me was that I was a smuggler without parents, home, or name. And no one needed or dared know anything more. But her curiosity about me was sharpened one evening when in a moment of weakness I revealed my name, Yosik, which was a variation of her lover's name, Osik. She swore several times that I reminded her of her lover not only in name, but in speech and manner as well.

"It's true," she added, "you don't resemble each other physically, you're as different as a baked potato and a fresh apple. Your squashed nose and his nose . . . well, well . . . He has the nose of an angel. Still, when you speak, I could swear that either you were disguised as Osik or he was a masked Yosik."

In her longing she was pleased to have, at close quarters, if not the original then at least a poor reflection of her lover.

From day to day she grew franker and more trusting. One evening when we were left alone, she confided her story to me.

It had happened when her father had been forced to buy a ticket for a benefit concert, which was to be followed by a dance for the public. Since her parents couldn't be bothered by such nonsense, it was decided that the eldest daughter would go. Until then, she had never attended such an affair because she lived on the outskirts of town and coming home late at night was a very dangerous thing. It was therefore decided that she would sleep over that night with her Aunt Feigel, who lived in the center of town. At this concert she had met her angel. "Yes, an angel!" she said, leaning closer to me. "You think I'm naive and silly. I see that you're laughing at me."

"If you think that I'm laughing at you, it's probably because of my torn cheek. But you should know that I happen to believe in angels. I beg you—go on, go on."

When the concert in which the angel took part was over and the dance for the general public began, he, the angel, came up to her and asked her to dance. She had never danced before, so it was natural that after the first few dances she should grow dizzy. He kept her in his arms and carried her out. Where to, she didn't remember. But it wasn't to Aunt Feigel's . . .

Since it was impossible for her to meet him in the city, he used to come to her house, but here the angel's mother intervened (she wasn't called "Mother," but "Maman"—may a plague descend on her). When Maman learned of the affair between her son and the smuggler's daughter, she began to move heaven and earth to break it up. She even threatened to denounce the cantor to the "blue capes" and hinted to her son that if he didn't stop seeing the girl, she would turn him over to the Germans. Osik stopped seeing Gutia when she was already in her second month.

The fact that Osik knuckled under to his mother's threats (proving he was a coward) was something that she could understand and even forgive. Her greatest anguish and resentment stemmed from the fact that when she was in her third month she found out that her angel was again appearing at a benefit and once more declaiming the same poem or recitation or the devil knows what under the name of Chantille Jeantaigne Delacroix . . . and was probably dancing with another girl as well, and—

Before she could utter another word of her confession, I kicked over the table in a terrible rage. "How dare he! I never gave him permission to use my name. I know him, that angel of yours. He is one of those three angels who came to Abraham and made his wife pregnant . . . the angel who came to Jacob in a dream and twisted his legs. Why must I rot here in this cemetery and from the open grave hear my name blackened by some impostor?"

"What's the matter with you? What are you talking about? Who are you yelling at?" she asked, backing away from me in bewilderment. "I thought you were an intelligent person with whom I could exchange a few serious words, but I see now that you too are nothing but a petty cheat, a bamboozler, a smuggler. Get out! Get out of here!"

Her cries soon brought her mother and brother and sisters in a chorus:

"What happened? What's wrong?"

"He must come here!" I shouted. "I'll tear his face and smash his nose. He must come here this minute! I won't be scared off by any 'maman' or 'papan' . . . I'm not afraid of any aristocrats or even of the Germans because I am . . . I am Chantille Jeantaigne Delacroix."

They didn't understand a word of this sudden outburst and were sure that the bookkeeper had gone berserk. They ran off to fetch Itche.

When Itche saw that his bookkeeper had lost his senses, he calmly scratched his goatee. "What's so surprising? A boy who in a half second can figure out thirty-two times seventeen couldn't remain normal for long." In a subdued and trembling voice I tried as best I could to explain the reason for my sudden flare-up and concluded that although it might look to them as if I was mentally deranged, for me it was a matter of life and death. Since I couldn't wander freely through the city, I would write this impostor a letter demanding that he come to me. All I wanted them to do was to deliver the letter to him early next morning.

At first Gutia argued that he would ignore the letter, then agreed that he might come, but how could she face him? She might die . . . She had better not show up . . . She'd stand behind the door and eavesdrop, but she wouldn't have to . . . because he wouldn't come, and so on and on far into the night.

The next morning the little boy, accompanied by his two younger sisters, went off to the city with a brief note:

> I've just now come to the city.
> I'm staying in the third house from the cemetery.
> I would like to see you personally.
> Yours,
> Chantille Jeantaigne Delacroix

The angel, who, thanks to his special papers, was able to travel freely after curfew, showed up that very same evening.

That his appearance suggested an angel was indisputable. On a tall body was a handsomely fashioned head with a chiseled nose and black, rounded eyebrows over a pair of cheerful cheeks. He managed to give the impression of being not of this city and not of this world. The free and unconstrained manner with which he entered the house could only issue from one who had come down from heaven. He spat out a candy into a hanky and joyfully embraced me.

"Chantille Jeantaigne! It's you—I recognize you! On stage you looked somewhat different, but yes, I do recognize you. How are you? Where have you been all this time? How do you come to be in this house? I'm so happy to meet you! Oh yes—I've known you a long time. I saw you perform several times at the Chorus Hall. Oh, what an impression you made on me." And rather than describe his reaction verbally, he depicted it in pantomime, mimicking the characteristic movements of my performance.

"I wanted so badly to meet you in person but soon afterward I heard that you had perished somewhere with the retreating Russian army. Is it true you were a soldier? A real soldier? Ha, ha, ha, I can imagine you as a soldier—ha-ha-ha." And he mimicked the retreating Russian soldiers and the grotesque pomposity of the advancing German troops. "But now I see that you're alive . . . That's good. Bravo, I'm so glad you're alive! Maman was very happy too when I told her I had received a letter from you. She asked me to bring you home. She wants to meet you."

"I don't know your Mamannn," I snorted through my broken nose.

"She's tall, heavy . . ." He puffed up his neck, thrust out his breast, and raised his rump to present the approximate image of his mother.

"No, I don't know her."

"But she knows who you are, and she knows your father, too. She says that he was extremely handsome. They used to be . . . friends— ha, ha, ha. So you see, we aren't such complete strangers after all. But tell me, what are you doing here—in this house?"

"I live here. I work here."

"In the cemetery?"

"Yes, I'm a tutor. I'm teaching the dead German."

"A German teacher, ha, ha." And he whirled in lightning zigzags through the room. "That's really a surprise. I was under the impression that you knew French—*je vous pris, mes enfants, il famous Chantille Jeantaigne Delacroix*. Remember? Ha, ha, ha. I didn't know that you knew German too. I could recommend a few pupils to you. I myself could use a good German tutor—Papa comes from Germany and speaks fluent German . . . *Ich habe, du habest, er habet*," he recited, mimicking his father. "I'm not too good at languages. When the war broke out I had only three and a half years at junior high school . . . And you have become a teacher, of all things? If I introduced you to my papa I'm sure he would hire you on the spot and you'd get paid well, too. If you're up to it, I'll take you to my house right now."

"I thank you, but I can't take on any new students. My time is all taken up as it is. Besides, I'm here without proper papers."

"That can be easily arranged. Papa has big connections with some very important Germans. He has already helped quite a few people get exemption cards. He could do it for you, too. Come, let's go. You don't need a passport. I often go around without it. Don't be afraid. If we're arrested we'll be released immediately. Papa will take care of it. Get your coat and let's go."

"What for?"

"I have a lot to discuss with you."

"So talk."

"It's not comfortable for me here in this house. If not for you, I wouldn't have come here at all."

"Why not?"

"If you're living here, you've certainly heard something about me."

"No one has ever mentioned your name."

"Not even Gutia?"

"I tutor the younger children, I hardly know Gutia."

"Gutia is a wonderful girl. We were very good friends, but her parents are common boors, especially her father. He plays the role of a cantor, goes around all day vocalizing—tra-la-la-la, tra-la-la-la—but you know what he is really? A smuggler. I beg you, don't tell anybody on account of Gutia, she's really a very fine girl. I wouldn't want her to find me here."

"She isn't home. No one is."

"That's good. Still, you would do me a favor if you'd come with me now, if not to my house, at least outside for a stroll. I have lots to tell you."

"I don't know what you have to tell me, but I have something to tell you, and I can say it right here. I heard that you're doing my recitation 'The Conqueror of Death.'"

"Yes," the angel admitted, "and not only I, but our whole group. Do you know a certain Talakovsky? He's very tall and has a basso voice." He raised himself up on tiptoe and began to speak in a deep-from-the-belly voice. "Do you know Mishka Kazanovitch, a fat fellow with short legs? He lisps, 'Tantille Tcantaigne Delatrua,' ha, ha, ha . . . Everyone imitates you. You infected us all with that Frenchman's madness. We're a whole group that dreams about the theater. I'll introduce you to them."

"I thank you very much, but times are bad and I have to earn a living. Maybe some other time. I called you just to let you know that Chantille Jeantaigne Delacroix still lives, and that one crazy Frenchman is enough for this city."

I went to the window and turned my back to the visitor.

Osik took a fresh candy from his pocket and spoke in a somewhat restrained tone. "I only performed your recitation a few times. Naturally, I wouldn't have dared do this if you were still around, but people spread the rumor that you were no longer living. Well, I thought, if that was the case, it couldn't hurt you anymore. I never failed to mention that I was reading the piece according to your interpretation. Naturally, I lacked many of your nuances. In certain places I couldn't for the life of me remember what you had done. For example, the place where the doctor is taken to the insane asylum—"

"He isn't taken but flung there," I said, my back still to him.

"Yes, yes, they fling him in and the guard says—"

"Not the guard, but the doctor says—"

"Yes, yes, that's what I mean. I mixed this spot up a little, but now that we've gotten together, you'll have to help me with a few directions."

I faced him. "Do you mean to say that you intend to use my recitation again?"

"No, not publicly, only for my brother. My older brother, Alex, is an actor and he's getting ready to go to America. He may go first, and I will follow him because Maman says that one actor son is enough. That silly old duck goes 'Quack, quack!' But it won't help her. I'm going to America! I told my brother that I'm dead set on becoming an actor. I even performed 'The Conqueror of Death' for him. He was critical because in a few places it wasn't coherent and was boring. But now that you're here it would be good if you would give me a few lessons in German, for which my papa would pay you handsomely. If you agree, I'll come by tomorrow. I'll bring my papers. Until Papa gets an exemption card for you, you can use mine. Maman will be overjoyed to see you, and my brother will be delighted too. So, it's all set for tomorrow, right?"

I heard the whole monologue, standing in a corner by the window like a mute wax figure.

"I understand that you want to think it over," Osik said after a short pause, "so I'll go now although there are still many, many things I'd like to discuss with you. But we'll leave it for tomorrow. Well, good night."

"Good night," I said and was the first to extend a hand.

"You know something," the angel said, pressing my skinny fingers within his downy palms, "I like you. Although I must tell you that I was completely wrong about you. I imagined that you would be altogether different. You're so quiet, or maybe it's my fault that I didn't give you a chance to open your mouth. I kept talking . . . I was in a hurry . . . You see, I'm on tenterhooks here. I'm afraid someone may come in. I'll tell you all about it at my house tomorrow . . . Oh, yes, I nearly forgot. Do me a favor and give Gutia this bar of chocolate for me. It comes from the German canteen. Very good, too. Give it to her so that her mother doesn't find out or else she'll kick up a fuss. Rah! Rah! Rah! That cockeyed churn-rod with the crooked legs . . ." He turned his eyes upward and, bowing his legs, waddled from side to side like an orangutan, then joyously flew out of the room.

As soon as the door slammed behind the angel, a second door opened and Gutia came in with red eyes. "No, no, he's an ugly liar! You mustn't believe a single word he says. He won't bring you any exemption card. He won't come back tomorrow, that shameless clown. He was afraid to see me, and he'll never see you again either . . ." And she began to choke on her tears.

I placed my hand tenderly on her shoulder. "Gutia, I was wrong about him, and you're just as wrong. I cursed all the angels, but apparently there are all kinds of angels. There is only one God, but there are many angels—good ones and bad ones."

"Stop making fun of me! You still can't forgive me for letting slip the word 'angel.'"

"Believe me when I tell you that I've already been visited by a number of angels who did me a lot of good, and I'm sure that this angel won't harm me either. He will come, he will take me to his mother—as you undoubtedly heard behind the door, she was once in love with my father. She'll understand. She may even be eager to see you, and I'll be the one to bring you to her house."

"No, no, I beg you, no more fancy talk," she pleaded, wringing her hands nervously. "You can drive a person crazy with your words."

"Believe me, it'll be the way I say. In the meantime, however, he asked me—" and I held up the chocolate to her. She grabbed it and flung it wildly in my face.

"You're even more repulsive than he is! I always sensed you two had something in common. All you can do is make merry by ridiculing people. Behind the door I heard everything. As brutal as it was for him to sneer at my parents, it's just a mild joke in comparison with your vileness in trying to delude me with candy so I wouldn't remember that he's escaping to America!"

"That's not true."

"I'm not deaf."

"He won't go to America," I said with assurance. "If anyone goes to America, it will be me!"

"You? I heard him say that his brother was taking him to America."

"If his brother will take anyone, it will be me. I don't know his brother yet, but one thing I feel already—if Osik is *your* angel, his brother, Alex, will be *my* angel."

"I don't understand. I clearly heard him say that Alex would take Osik to America."

"He won't take Osik and he won't take Yosik—he'll take Chantille Jeantaigne Delacroix!"

She dabbed away a stray tear and mumbled in a soggy voice: "No, no, if I told this to someone he'd say that I'm crazy, that I made it all up, that I'm imagining a story out of *The Thousand and One Nights*." She dropped into a nearby chair. I came up close to her. Placing my hand on her head, I leaned forward and whispered: "Gutia, get ready for the thousand-and-second night."

She threw off my hand with a gesture that combined impatience and aversion and, biting her fingernails, began to run around the room. I couldn't get her to stop and had to call in the mother to calm her hysterical daughter.

XXXIV

~~~

I TURNED OUT to be right. Osik came the next day bringing four documents: his passport, an exemption card freeing the bearer from forced labor, a permit to be outside after curfew, and his papa's special card to obtain liquor at the military canteen. With four such guarantees I could go to Osik's house without fear. Still, when I rang the doorbell and the door opened and a big black poodle came bounding out, barking savagely, I scurried to the rear and rushed down the stairs.

A commanding voice from inside ordered the dog to shut up and the guest not to be afraid. And thus, somewhat frightened and a bit ashamed, I went into the house.

"Excuse us, our dog is a real nuisance," the slim, elegant man who had opened the door said to me. He appeared to be twenty-eight or thirty, with long black hair over a heavily powdered face shaped like an upside-down pear. The thin oriental nose was arched between womanly brows. His most prominent feature was his pale, delicate hands with long, manicured fingers. He wore a velvet smoking jacket and broad-striped trousers. Under his soft white collar with the long points was a carefully knotted wide, black tie.

"This is my brother, Alex."

"Very pleased to meet you."

"Maman, be so good as to take the dog out of here!" Alex called.

In a moment, Maman made her appearance. "Lately, the dog has been unbearable, but you needn't be afraid. Dodie, put the dog's muzzle on him," she ordered a man in a flowered silk bathrobe behind her. He had a pointed mustache and a part in the center of his flatly brushed silver hair.

Dodie slapped the poodle aside and, under the protection of the whole household, I was ushered into the living room.

I was left there to be interviewed by Papa and a half hour later I was engaged as a German tutor for Osik at a salary of five marks per week.

The first lesson began in an unpleasantly strained atmosphere in which the teacher tried to show more than he knew and the pupil turned out to know even less than the teacher had anticipated. With an expression of utter weariness, the pupil soon pushed the German grammar aside and asked, "When Doctor Chantille is thrown into the asylum, who speaks first—the doctor or the guard?"

"The narrator. He describes the asylum and all the lunatics in it."

"Ah! And I had it completely the other way 'round . . . Tell me what his exact words are when he is led to the scaffold."

"We'll have time to talk about that later," I said, pushing the book back in front of him. "I understand that your brother is going to America in two months. If you should go along with him, then the time in which I promised your parents to teach you German is very limited. Therefore I believe that we must now concentrate more on the grammar than on other things."

A few minutes later, the pupil pointed to the wall clock indicating that the hour was almost over, slammed the book shut, and walked me to the door.

At the threshold he asked as if in passing, "How is Gutia?" He wondered why she hadn't been there the two times he had come to the cantor's house. Could this mean that she had purposely avoided him, or had she really gone away someplace?

I replied that I wasn't so close to her that I would know her comings and goings. The pupil wasn't satisfied with my answer. Didn't she ever speak about him? Didn't she ever mention his name?

"I don't know, I don't see her, I don't even know her." And I ran down the stairs and out.

When I came home that evening, I knocked quietly on Gutia's door, and we left the house together. Holding my hand, she led me across a rotted log that served as a bridge over a small, rushing stream, then turned to the rear of the cemetery where her favorite bench stood by the fence. We sat down, and I promptly began to give her my impressions and experiences in the house of her beloved.

With the same unbridled remarks and grotesque portraiture with which my pupil had derided the cantor's family, I now caricatured all the aristocrats, black poodle included.

She choked with spasms of laughter, then, wiping away tears of joy, said, "Well, and what about America? What did you hear about America?"

"Gutia, I believe in luck. Luck brought me to your house. In your house I met one brother who brought me to another brother, and that other brother will take me to America. And I have a premonition that you'll be coming along with us."

As usual, when deeply distressed, she began to bite her fingernails, and whispered, "Now I know why you carried on so the other night. Now I know who the man is with the long French name."

I seized hold of the fence pickets, feeling that her words would inflate me like a balloon that would soon rise up from earth and soar among the clouds.

"God, if it only were true!" she whispered. She leaned toward me, touched my stitched-up cheek with her moist lips, and swiftly ran home.

Beyond the fence the monuments dozed like white doves in a field with heads tucked into their wings. The delicate willows washed their bowed heads in the stream. I sat on the bench and let my thoughts accompany Gutia all the way to her bedroom.

The lessons continued for three weeks. At the end of each week Maman handed me the fee in an envelope with warm thanks for my efforts and patience with the undisciplined pupil, at the same time deploring her lack of influence on her two sons, the elder of whom had become an actor against her will and the younger of whom would probably enter the same "low profession" despite all her efforts to prevent it.

I would nod sympathetically and assure her that her son exhibited remarkable abilities and that his urge to learn was mounting from day to day.

In fact, however, the lessons grew ever shorter and less productive. Instead of concentrating on grammar, my pupil kept questioning me with ever greater curiosity about Gutia, but I would tell him only that she was seldom at home, that she was busy, and that I rarely saw her.

"Where does she go?"

"I don't know."

"To whom does she go?"

"I don't know."

It didn't make sense to him that someone living right in the house wouldn't know where she went or what she did.

For my part I constantly tried to turn the conversation to the subject of America and to ask him about his brother. How much longer would he be staying in the city?

It irked Osik more each day that the teacher asked more than he answered, and he paid me back in kind. The moment I touched "Alex and America" he promptly stuffed up my mouth with "Gutia and the cemetery."

By the fourth week, the misunderstanding between teacher and pupil came to a climax.

The maman and papa were very nice to me, probably because they had known my father so well. Besides, strange as it may seem, they were pleased with my efforts with their son. They even invited me to lunch.

The only one to show no interest in me was Alexander. His room was closest to the front door, and he was the first to hear the doorbell and let me in. "Good morning, teacher. How is the teacher? Your pupil is waiting for you."

"Oh, yes, good, thank you." And that was it.

Sitting at the table during lunch, Alexander began to argue with his mother. She had reproved him for drinking too much and she took the whiskey bottle away from the table. Alex swore that he hadn't touched a drop, and Maman turned to me to bear witness that when we sat down, the bottle had been almost full. I shrugged my shoulders.

The wrangling between Maman and her son went on until Alex finally asserted that he had had two or three glasses at most, and that she had to give him at least one more drink. When she remained obdurate, he angrily threw down his knife and fork and left the room. I had lost the opportunity to have a conversation with him, yet I felt the ice had been broken. The fact that I had been a silent witness to the intimate quarrel somehow made me part of the family, and this would lead to another invitation at which time I would not come with empty hands. I would bring a bottle of whiskey, which I would obtain from the smugglers. Ah, hurrah for the smugglers! True, this would cost me a whole two weeks' pay, but the bottle would keep Alex glued to the table.

At the end of this same week, when I rang the doorbell Alex opened the door and greeted me with the usual impersonal, "Good morning, teacher. How is the teacher?" and promptly vanished to his room.

I found my pupil pacing nervously. He closed the door firmly and turned to me. "Maman and Papa went away on a visit and left me the money to pay you. But from now on, I would like you to give me the lessons at your house."

"I have no house."

"I mean in Gutia's house."

"Gutia's house isn't my house, and you can't come there."

"Ah, now I understand the whole thing!" He grew red as a beet and, snatching back the five marks that he had already given me, seized me by the lapels and pushed me into the doorway where he hissed in a jealous rage, "If you try to take away my girl I'll split your skull!"

"I have nothing to do with Gutia. I live in a separate room, and I only see her brother and younger sisters. I don't even know Gutia," I said, throwing off his hand with indignation.

"I'm not such a fool as you might think. I won't give you the money. You're no longer my teacher. I'm going to America next month anyway, and if you want your money, write me a letter and I'll bring it to your house." He slammed the door, and ran out of the house.

The thought that I was here for the last time left me in great distress. What now? If I had had the bottle of whiskey that I had prepared to bring the next time I was invited to lunch, I would have gone to Alexander's room and once and for all revealed myself to him. I would have torn off the mask of the pathetic little teacher and cried out, "Here I am! Chantille Jeantaigne Delacroix! Here he stands in the flesh before you. Come, take me and let's go to America!" But without a bottle, who could tell how Alexander would react? Who could tell if he would even let me into his room?

For a moment I stood there debating: Yes, no, no, yes . . . Why not . . . ? Sure, certainly!

I smoothed down my lapels, patted my hair, and knocked on Alex's door.

"Who is it?"

I didn't answer but walked right in.

He stood in his red slippers, peering into a round mirror and plucking his arched eyebrows. In a tone that was neither friendly nor unfriendly, he mumbled, "Oh, it's you."

"Excuse me for disturbing you. My pupil had to go somewhere, left me alone, and if you don't have any objections—"

"What time is it? I should have already been somewhere too, but until I get dressed—have a seat . . . Would you like a brandy?" And not waiting for an answer he took a bottle out of a wardrobe and poured two big glasses.

"I hear that you're getting ready to go to America," I began.

"Mhu . . ." Alexander gulped down the drink and dabbed his lips with a handkerchief. He poured himself a second drink and winked at me not to delay him.

"I also heard that you're famous, a great actor."

"Mhu . . . that's what they say," and he downed the second glass.

To keep him company I took a sip from the glass and promptly began to lick my scalded tongue. "I'm not much of a drinker. That is, before the war I used to like to drink, but since you can't get whiskey anymore I grew unaccustomed to it and now it's hard to get used to again . . ."

In the meantime, Alexander had taken out a leather mono-grammed cigarette case and he offered me a cigarette.

"Thank you, I don't smoke. That is, I did smoke, but I gave it up. It's too hard to get good cigarettes these days . . . I haven't had a cigarette since I was thrown out of the gymnasium," I said, twirling the cigarette between my fingers and trying to get the conversation going.

Alexander showed no interest in why I had been thrown out of the gymnasium. After he had carried a burning match to my trembling cigarette, he lit his own, crossed his legs, and watched the emerging smoke rings.

"Actually, I have—or, to put it more accurately, I had—the impression that you can't leave the German occupation zone, but I understand your papa is an important person among the Germans . . ." Alexander suddenly reminded himself of something, and went to the window. I stood up too.

"Sit, sit," he said. "I only wanted to see if it's raining and if I'll need my rubbers. You can't get a droshky these days. I'll have to walk there . . . The devil take the war, it's given me enough trouble already and the end's not in sight yet."

He sat down again, poured himself a third drink, stretched out his legs, and began to pinch the crease of his striped trousers between his fingers.

"I was told that you've been invited to be the leading man of a troupe in America," I said.

"Finish your drink. Unfortunately I don't have too much time . . ."

"I also heard that you're thinking of taking your brother along," I persisted.

He stood up and began to search the room for an ashtray. I took a quick gulp from my glass and went into a long coughing fit, then mumbled in a pitiful tone, "Forgive me. I haven't had a drink since I was wounded. That is, since I received this wound." And I pointed to my ravaged cheek.

"Brandy can't hurt a wound. The fact is that when I get an occasional toothache I usually kill it with liquor," Alexander stated with the air of an expert.

"You're absolutely right," I said, and wiping tears from my eyes I poured a second drink for myself.

He brought the ashtray to the table, threw down a fourth drink, then gazed down at the wide tie under his chin.

"Oh, the devil take me. Spattered my best tie."

He deliberately moistened a pinky with his tongue, went up to the mirror, and tried to rub out the stain. Suddenly he spotted an obstinate hair on his eyebrow and tried to pluck it out with his long, polished fingernails.

"You probably don't know that I have a strong urge to go to America too," I said to the face in the mirror. "How could you know? You don't even know me. On the other hand, I don't know what I could do in America."

Alexander moved the cigarette holder to one side of his mouth and spoke from the other into the mirror. "Why? I mean, I think you could manage in America. Maman tells me she's very pleased with you. You're a good teacher."

He finished with the eyebrow and turned back to the bottle, from which he poured himself a fifth drink. "Why don't you drink?"

"I'm a little dizzy. The thing is that I'm actually not a teacher."
To support my contention, I bravely poured the brandy down my
throat.

"Your bro-zer, I mean brother, told me that you're taking him
along."

"Where to?" he asked.

"To Amerv-ica—I mean, America. He says that there are many
theaters there. A lot of charity concerts are given and they need
acto-vs . . ." I said, licking my burning gums.

"Don't listen to my brother. He's a punk, a little snotnose putting
on airs. He thinks that imitating Maman makes him an actor and he
can go overwhelm America."

"Did you hear your brother recite a certain piece called 'The Conqueror of Deaff-th?'"

"The conqueror of what?"

"Of dea-th-h-h."

"Oh, you mean that silly story with the French doctor?" Alexander said, throwing off his red slippers and putting on his shoes.

"Maybe it's because you heard this recitation from your brother
that you formed a false opinion of it."

"It's disgusting."

"Would you object if I recited it for you now?"

"Are you trying to tell me that my brother has already turned your
head too? It's the old joke with the Jew and the priest. Instead of
you making him a person, he has made you an actor."

"I'm no actor, but if you're going to America—"

"I don't understand. Do you mean to say that you want to go
with this idiotic story to America?"

"I'll recite it for you."

"What for? I'm sorry, I have no more time now . . . maybe some
other time—finish your drink and at another opportunity I'll be
happy to hear you recite that piece of trash."

With great effort I tore my rump out of the chair, swayed to one
side as if one leg had suddenly grown shorter, and cried out in an
unnatural voice, "The Conqueror of Death!"

"Not now, not now . . . Please."

"The Conqueror of Death," I announced with desperate obstinacy.
At that moment, the poodle began to bark.

"Well, that must be your pupil already . . . Excuse me, I'll go open the door." Alexander came back. "It's Maman. Finish your drink . . . I don't want her to see us here drinking." And he began to clear the table.

I drained the remainder of my drink and, holding on to the back of the chair, I again began the recitation. But after only a dozen words, I stopped and my eyes began to wander from corner to corner. I knew that I was drunk, or else why would I see two Alexanders with two glasses in hand? At that moment I couldn't decide which of the two was the real Alexander and toward which I should direct my recitation.

"Excuse me . . . would you allow me to begin from the beginning? I'll recite it quickly—it won't take long."

"Well, all right, begin at the beginning because I didn't understand what you were talking about anyway."

In order to concentrate better, I looked away from the two Alexanders and spoke to the wall where like the legendary Persian king I saw the inscription branded into the wall. "Hurry! Make it brief! Alexander has his shoes on already! Maman will soon throw you out! The dog will tear you to pieces!"

In my mad rush I quickly seized the French doctor and promptly locked him into jail, freed him with a few more words, took him to the gallows, chopped off his head, and in the same breath began to plead, "No, no, it's not this way . . . I skipped over a lot. I didn't tell you how he once became a midget. I mean, he was captured and locked up in a toilet for ten years under the suspicion of being a lampedusser . . . Let's start at the beginning . . ." And I suddenly staggered into a corner and began to vomit.

"Oh, that's disgusting," Alexander said, holding me up in a disapproving manner. "You get drunk from a few glasses of brandy and you want to be an actor in America? Take the rag and wipe the floor. If Maman came in now and found you like this . . . What a scandal, I got the teacher drunk. Better go home now . . . come, I'll lead you out so no one will notice."

"The Conqueror of Death!" I burped drunkenly.

"I wouldn't advise you go to America with this," Alexander said, pushing me toward the door. "But if you do ever go there, look me up and we'll have a proper drink together."

"I beg you, don't tell your brother. Don't tell anyone in America," I pleaded from the other side of the door.

On the way to the cemetery, a smuggler and a teacher stumbled along on wobbly legs. They held each other up while, at the same time, fearfully abusing each other. "May the epilepsy seize you! May you burn! Why didn't you let me recite?"

"I saw that you were drunk, and I wanted to help you."

"Well, as far as America goes, that's finished. You've blown your chances. But how will you show yourself now among the 'corpses' in the cemetery, and especially before Gutia?"

"Never mind about Gutia!"

"Why didn't you let Osik get together with Gutia? Does this mean that you aren't so indifferent to Gutia and really want her for yourself?"

"Maybe I do and maybe I don't."

"That's a vile, filthy business."

"I meant no harm."

"But you behaved like a louse."

"I'm not responsible," the teacher blubbered. "Each time I came to Gutia and passed along to her my conversations with Osik she jumped for joy, threw herself at me, and kissed me."

"Because you promised her with your fancy words and all that folderol that she would go to America! You wanted to take away the sweetheart of a friend who took you into his house, provided you with documents, and even paid you a good living, besides."

"I didn't want to take her away. I wanted to take her along."

"To where?"

"To America."

"What America? Which America? There is no such place as America."

"There is, there is! My father was there. Barve's Son swore that all the market people will be there someday. My mother rocked me to sleep with a song about a letter to America. I wanted to get away from the war, the cemetery, the smugglers . . ."

"Don't you know there's a war in America too? There's a cemetery there too . . . Here at least even hardly knowing German you can still be a teacher. So why did you deceive Gutia?"

"I never kissed her, she kissed me."

"But you knew that she wasn't thinking of you. She was kissing Osik's name on your lips. You wanted to seduce her with the music of your prattle, to chain her soul."

"Maybe that's how it really was. Maybe I really am a louse."

"When Gutia finds out, she'll come to hate you, and for each kiss you swindled out of her she'll send a curse down on your head."

"But enough—enough punishment for one innocent little kiss. Let me alone in my misery and pain of being a louse and knowing it."

"You horrible drunk!"

"You vicious smuggler!"

"The Conqueror of Death—aha, ha, ha!"

"The Dead Conqueror—heh, heh, heh, heh . . ."

"Aha-ha, ha, ha . . ."

They both leaned against the wall and continued to vomit.

Gutia waited at the door with her usual impatience for my report on how far along she was on her way to America. But I didn't show up that night. I went off with the two drunks—the teacher and the smuggler—behind the cemetery and, along with them, stretched out on the bench by the fence and went to sleep.

The next day I sent a note to Osik demanding that he bring me the five marks.

Osik brought the money, and this time he met Gutia. A few days later, he had a serious talk with the cantor. He declared his love for Gutia and explained that he would soon be going with his brother to America, where he would become independent and within a year and a half would be able to send for Gutia to join and marry him.

Cold Itche grew so excited that he developed a high fever and had to spend a whole week in bed. When his fever was brought down with plasters and cupping and he came back to normal, he announced to the band that a great good fortune had befallen him and that he was contributing his weekly share toward a banquet for the whole crew at his house. What this fortune was he couldn't reveal, but God willing, they would know it in a year hence.

A real celebration followed, a good, old-fashioned prewar party complete with chopped liver, gefilte fish, wine and whiskey. Deep in his cups, the cantor launched into song and finished up with his triumphal piece, the prayer for the dead with different variations—as if it were the most beautiful ballad.

There was no need to be coy with the smugglers who already knew what the "fortune" consisted of. But where were the girl and the boy? It was obvious that they had been specifically told to stay away when this scruffy crew got together. The smugglers felt offended. Did this mean that the cantor was ashamed of them? If not for the bitter times would they be coming here at all? Unless they were brought in a wooden box? If not for the damned war, would they so patiently endure the cantor's hoarse crooning unless they were already lying stretched out on the floor covered by a black cloth?

With this feeling of humiliation, they choked on every bite. All of them had once been respectable heads of households. God had punished them and broken their pride, yet it never diminished their faith that He always prepares the cure before the disease, the punishment before the abuse. The time would come when Itche would invite them to the wedding, but they would refuse unless they were dragged in chains . . .

The thought of chains wasn't so far off, for a few days later when they were figuring out accounts with the bookkeeper, the cellar door burst open and five "blue capes" came in. The whole band was led out into the courtyard where Cold Itche and his wife and children, the engaged couple among them, were already surrounded by five other "blue capes." And that same evening, the whole gang including Osik, Yosik, and Gutia were put behind bars in the big prison at Number 10 Antokol.

XXXV

DURING THE TIME I was with the smugglers I grew accustomed
to sleeping standing in a corner like a horse, or sitting on a fence like
a hen, so that when it came to sleeping in a bed like a human being,
I would toss from side to side and not be able to shake loose the
previous day. But as soon as the iron gates of the prison swung shut
behind me, I stretched out on the stone floor, snuggled my head
into the damp straw, and fell promptly into a delicious sleep.

After long months of constant fear and apprehension, the whole
band felt the sense of assurance and protection afforded by the iron
gates and stone walls, and they too fell quickly asleep.

To our surprise, it turned out that the Germans were a lot nicer
inside the prison than they were on the outside. True, the first few
days the food was as expected—atrocious—but one morning when
the prisoners lined up with their bowls in hand before the vat of the
famous "coffee," each one received a handful of biscuits and a small
cone of marmalade in addition to the usual portion of muddy water.
Some of the prisoners were afraid to taste it, fearing that the unexpected delicacy contained poison, while others explained the treat as
the usual final meal given the condemned before hanging.

Yet this didn't occur only once but repeatedly, and with each suc-
cessive day a few more biscuits and bigger portions of marmalade
were issued.

"What can this be?" the prisoners wondered. "Prisoners aren't fed
marmalade, especially by the Germans. Something strange is going
on here."

And they were right, for during the time we were in prison un-
usual things were happening in the city. It started one cold, rainy
morning when several people on Market Street saw huge columns
of Germans coming from the direction in which the Russians had
once retreated. This time the Germans didn't fire, didn't kick their
feet in the air, didn't throw kisses to the wasted female faces in the

windows or candy to the skinny children with legs bound in rags running behind. They marched grimly with heads bowed and not to the front but in the opposite direction, not to Minsk but to Berlin.

The bewildered market people promptly ran into the surrounding courtyards to tell their neighbors about it. What could this mean? Could it be that they were heading home? Could it be that the war was over? Was this the long anticipated day when peace would come to the world? No, no, it couldn't be. Because in the fever of their two-year yearning, they had fashioned a clear picture of that blessed day. Whether a Monday or a Thursday, the glorious day would be heralded at dawn by the sound of rams' horns and trumpets. The day would emerge with a sunny splendor from behind the mountains and would linger in the city for a whole week as in the good old biblical times when Joshua commanded the sun to stand still and the moon not to move from the spot.

On that glorious day, the prettiest virgins in the city would dance through the streets in white robes with garlands on their heads. Great tables would be set up the length and breadth of the marketplace and huge bottles of brandy would be placed on the white tablecloths. At the same time, the Russians, Germans, Frenchmen, Turks, and all the other nationalities would gather behind the city, throw off their powder-stained coats, and heave them into one great bonfire along with their rifles, swords, and cannon, then go dancing through the city into the marketplace and sit down at the freshly set tables.

The market people would serve them—not, God forbid, because there wouldn't be a place at the table for them but because they were famous the world over as the best bakers, cooks, and butchers. And although the celebration would be international, the dishes would be exclusively Jewish: chopped liver, gefilte fish, soup meat with dumplings, prune stew, kugel, noodle pudding, raisin strudel, carrot stew, stewed meat, lung knishes, and stuffed derma. And they would eat, eat, eat . . .

But the day came without trumpets or covered tables. The sky was grimy with clouds, and a gloomy rain was falling. There was no sun, no moon, only a gray, damp emptiness that was neither day nor night.

The Germans went home, and loaded wagons went with them.

The onlookers on Market Street recognized their stolen possessions inside the wagons: this one his bed and blanket, that one his candlesticks and samovar. The proud conquerors and brutal ruler slunk out like common thieves, leaving the tortured, pillaged city to the mercy of whoever wanted it.

So, go, go—may you break your legs and lose your crutches and come to Berlin sliding on your asses. Your tongues should grow bigger than your mouths. Corns should grow on your nose and piles on your lips . . .

With these unspoken wishes, the market people saluted the departing Germans. No sooner had the last German wagon left the city than the market people began talking louder and louder like the deaf speaking to the deaf. Talk—incredible, unbelievable talk that the war had ended and that it was starting anew . . . that the Germans had lost and that the Russians had also lost and those who had helped them hadn't won, either. That in their deep disappointment the infuriated Germans had torn out Kaiser Wilhelm's upturned mustache and that the Russians had done even more: they had torn out their tsar's mangy beard and, along with it, his head as well. That Germany had collapsed and that Russia had crumbled to bits and that these bits had been divided among many . . . One group of "revolutionaries" had seized the tsar's palace, another that called itself by the funny name of "Bolsheviks" had commandeered the tsar's silken beds, downy pillows, silver utensils, and diamond rings . . .

Those who told this sounded like so many lunatics; those who heard it nearly went out of their minds. Because who had a brain powerful enough to grasp all this?

In the meantime, the last Germans marched out of the city, chaos prevailed, and plans to take over the city were launched in a hundred places. Who wouldn't be eager to seize an abandoned city? But how do you tuck a whole city into your pocket? Those who were more slick and cunning promptly began to organize into bands to seize power. A different band formed on every street—Poles on one street, Lithuanians on another.

The more respectable citizens dashed to take over the Town Hall. The Poles brought old documents signed by King Kazimierz the Great claiming the city as their own. The Ukrainians demanded two-thirds of it and the White Russians settled for a mere half. At first they wrangled politely, but soon they began to abuse each other, and finally it came to blows and to smashing chairs over skulls.

Under the Germans the city had been like a silent cemetery, but now the corpses left their graves and entered into a violent conflict over who would own the cemetery.

"The city belongs to us!" various voices shouted in various languages on various streets. In order to know who was for what and what was for whom, the Poles tied white kerchiefs around their sleeves and the Lithuanians tied green kerchiefs around their necks. The Poles begged the assembled mob to join with them and to shout "hurrah" in Polish, the Lithuanians to shout it in Lithuanian. The confused people ran shouting from street to street, changing the language to suit the street.

Suddenly a rumor spread about a new group, a very small one— eight people in all—who had assembled at the "House of the Transit Workers" on Broad Street.

"Who are they?" "What do they want?" "What do they wear, kerchiefs or neckerchiefs?" "Red armbands." "What do they say?" "That the city belongs to no one." "How can that be? Who's the boss?" "There's no such thing as a boss, therefore the city does not belong to anybody." "That's a perverse joke." "Ravings of some madmen!" And the mob came running to see the madmen. Everyone knew of the dirty trick the Germans had perpetrated on the city before leaving—they had thrown open all prisons and asylum gates and released all the criminals and lunatics. But the things they now heard from the speakers with the red armbands they wouldn't have expected from even the wildest crackpots.

"Whereas there's no such things as a Polish city, Jewish city, or Tatar city, we therefore proclaim in the name of the red-bands' government that the city belongs to no one, but that each street belongs individually to those who live on it."

Even more astounding were the remarks of the second, third, and fourth speakers, who presented themselves as the chosen government of all the streets. They drew a box of weapons from under a table and ordered the crowd to throw down the white and green kerchiefs, put on red bands, and take the guns and go with them to guard the streets that belonged to no one.

The white kerchiefs met the approaching red armbands with

mocking laughter but, when the red armbands came closer with drawn guns and ordered them to withdraw, the mood turned grim.

"Brothers, throw down your weapons," the white kerchiefs begged. "Don't let yourselves be deceived. You belong with us. Throw down the red armbands and put on white kerchiefs."

In the meantime a group of the green neckerchiefs gathered from the neighboring streets and began to harangue the Poles with the white armbands. "Traitors, you'll pay dearly." A Lithuanian army was already forming in Kovno and in a few days would seize the city and deal harshly with all turncoats.

"Our Polish army is already formed and will be in the city by tomorrow," the white kerchiefs shouted.

"That's a filthy lie!" some shouted in Lithuanian, and soon a terrible brawl erupted. The red armbands began to shoot into both groups, and the streets soon filled with the moans of the wounded.

By evening, the fighting and shooting stopped. The red armbands had routed the white kerchiefs and green neckerchiefs, who took cover in basements and attics, and it came about as the speakers had proclaimed it—a city that belonged to no one.

Early the next morning, several starving women tried to go to the garbage bin in the marketplace to see if the Germans had left behind a crust of bread or a chewed-up bone, but they didn't manage to cross the street; they came rushing back to warn their sleeping neighbors to put on white kerchiefs because a whole troop of Polish cavalry was gathered in the marketplace.

At first, no one would believe it. Where would Polish soldiers be coming from? Since when was Poland a country and when did it begin to have an army? But yes, it was true. A small troop of cavalry was assembled in the marketplace, with a huge flag on which a white eagle fluttered.

They looked imposing. The officers wore shiny boots, silver-threaded epaulets, and square-topped caps with silver embroidery on the visors.

The government of the red armbands took positions in the windows of their three-story building holding rifles and hand grenades, while the crowds gathered between them and the Polish cavalry to observe the confrontation.

The Polish commander rode close to the building and demanded that they throw down their armbands and disperse to their houses.

To this came a shout from the building: "Whoever dares make a move will be shot on the spot!"

"Shut up, you lousy Jew," the officer cried, then turned to the crowd. "I know that there are some Poles among you who have let themselves be deluded by the paid agent from Russia whose name is Meyer Schmulevitch. Therefore I appeal to my brothers to reject this traitor and to come over to the side where all decent Poles belong."

The bewildered crowd stood silent.

"Brother Poles," the officer continued with fervor, "for generations Poland lay dead, but now it has risen. Look at your resurrected brothers," he said, extending his hand in a classical gesture toward the rider with the fluttering flag. "Which of you good Poles would dare place himself against these noble Polish knights in whose veins flows the blood of Kazimierz the Great? Which of you good Poles would allow this white eagle to be sullied by some Meyer Schmulevitch? For hundreds of years we lay under the yoke of the Meyer Schmulevitches. They drained our blood and murdered our children for Passover. Brother Poles," he declaimed with feeling, "reject these Jewish vermin—the Schmulevitches. Come over and place yourselves under the white eagle that the Schmulevitches have kept in chains so long . . ."

One of the men in the crowd bent down. It wasn't clear whether or not he had lost his armband or kerchief and had merely stopped to retrieve it, but at that moment a bullet hit him in the back and he fell into the gutter. The crowds in befuddled cross-purposes applauded—"Hurrah!"—and at the same time screamed, "He was not Schmulevitch!"

The sudden rumpus made the cavalry horses rear into the ranks of the mob that was trying to escape into the side streets, pursued by the saber-wielding riders. A while later, the Polish officers once more regrouped around the building and issued an ultimatum. "All we want is the Jew, Schmulevitch. The rest of you can go free," the officer shouted. The answer came in the form of eight hand grenades. A few of the riders were thrown to the ground—the rest hugged the side of the building in confusion. By this time a small detachment of Polish infantry had entered the city, and came racing down to help the demoralized cavalry. They fell to the ground and began to spray the building with rifle fire.

The open windows swallowed the bullets like big, hungry mouths ingesting chickpeas and spat back radishes in the form of grenades. This exchange, as the market people later described it, went on with short interruptions until evening, when a company of Polish artillery took over the siege of the building and with a couple of field pieces began to answer the radishes with whole fiery watermelons.

In the meantime, the cavalrymen regrouped in the old marketplace.

Several times that day the rumor spread that "Schmulevitch's Fortress" had fallen and that the whole government of red armbands had been arrested. But each time it turned out that the battle wasn't over yet, and the rumors grew wilder until a man wearing a white kerchief swore that he had just come from Broad Street and had seen with his own eyes how the "Jewish government" had surrendered and come out of the building with hands in the air. The only one to escape was Meyer Schmulevitch.

This information roused the cavalrymen to a new pitch and fired a wild urge to root out the escaped Schmulevitch. They smashed down doors, broke into houses, and dragged screaming women and men out by their hair. In one yard they actually found a Schmulevitch, but before he could explain that his name was Yonkel not Meyer Schmulevitch, his skull had already been split.

The most remarkable thing about it all was that in every courtyard there was a Schmulevitch, and not one but several. In fact, all the surrounding streets were full of Schmulevitches, for it turned out that nearly everyone in that section of town was named Schmulevitch! In the desperate zeal to settle with that fantastic Jew, even several Christians who were wearing white kerchiefs were also labeled as Schmulevitches and lost their heads.

The bloody farce lasted for a whole three days. And although during this time it was firmly established that the battle on Broad Street was still in full force and that Schmulevitch not only hadn't escaped but was in fact the only one still stubbornly resisting, the cavalrymen kept searching, beating, plundering, and murdering the unlucky residents of the streets around the marketplace who regardless of age or sex suddenly all became Meyer Schmulevitches.

The ultimatum first issued to the government of the red armbands had been extended from five minutes to five hours, but nearly five days had gone by and, although the building lay in ruins, the fragments still showed signs of life and continued to spit fire.

Eventually, everything grew still. The ultimatum was accepted and all eight Schmulevitches of the red-bands' government gave themselves up—dead.

This happened on the fifth day after sunup, and only one or two hours later the cavalrymen packed the loot plundered from the Jewish and non-Jewish Schmulevitches and hastily rode west out of the city. They were followed pell-mell by the infantry and artillery, since there had suddenly been heard a distant but distinct sound of band music from the east.

The Schmulevitches lay hidden under rags in the dark corners of their cellars and with trembling hearts listened to the military air that grew stronger and closer by the minute. The melody seemed somehow familiar; still, no one had the nerve to go outside and see who was playing. Gradually their curiosity overcame their fear, and they began to crawl out of the cellars and up to the rooftops, where they shoved aside the shingles and carefully stuck out their heads.

In the middle of the marketplace several men sat astride some skinny, mud-spattered nags. At first glance it was hard to tell if they were soldiers or civilians—some wore dirty, torn greatcoats, others peasant sheepskins and mangy fur caps. Only one wore a split leather jacket with a battered, military cap on his head. With them was a five-piece band: two drums, two tubas, and a large shrill trumpet.

"Who are they? Where do they come from?"

"They're Russians. I heard them speak Russian," reported one who dared to peep out into the empty street.

"They must be those—what do they call them?—those who turned Russia upside down."

"You mean the Mensche-vicks?"

"Not Mensche-vicks, but Bolshe-vicks."

"So who are the Communists?"

"Those who wore the red band here."

"The Poles call themselves Legionnaires."

"Don't mix borscht with cabbage soup. Names mean little to me. What I'd like to know is what part of the city do they claim," a grave voice demanded.

"Shush, be still. See what's happening down there!"

The man in the leather jacket raised himself, stood up with his feet on top of the saddle, and cried out through a cardboard funnel,

"Comrades, citizens, come out, join us at the market. In the name of the Revolution we declare the city free. And we congratulate you on your hard-won victory. Death to the bourgeoisie! Long live the proletariat!"

The orchestra repeated the march. The balancing on the back of the horse by the man in the jacket to the rhythm of the music—and especially the cardboard megaphone, a device never seen or heard of before—brought lively approval. Soon windows, doors, gates opened carefully. And before the orchestra finished, the market streets were already flooded with people asking each other, "Say, can you spare me a red ribbon or something?" The crowd pushed forward, while those in front, unable to shake off their distrust and confusion, pressed to the rear.

Some tried to question. "Don't be afraid—ask them why their faces are full of dirt." "Do they ever wash?" "They don't come from a wedding party. There's a battle outside the city." The man in the jacket jumped off the horse and landed on the toes of an elderly woman. He apologized and to ease her pain he put her on his horse.

"Don't be afraid," the swarming crowd insisted. "Ask them who they are and what they want."

"Water, water" came an answer reverberating from mouth to mouth.

"Bring water, they're thirsty."

"Bring bread. They're hungry, too." "Who's got some bread?" "A piece, a crust, a crumb, anything."

The aroused mass never saw the old Jewish woman on a horse, but her plea for bread had an instantaneous effect. Whatever they were, Mensche-vicks, Bolshe-vicks, or revolutionaries, it was certain that they wore torn boots, tattered rags instead of greatcoats, and were hungry and thirsty—and who in the world were greater experts on poverty and hunger than these tormented, exhausted people now surrounding the visitors? So in spite of the strange French or Turkish pronouncement of death for the burge-jois and life for probletarat, there was an immediate mutual sympathy.

Soon from all sides men rushed with pails of water and women with crusts of bread in their aprons. The bedraggled guests fell to their knees and shoved their heads into the pails. But the man in the leather jacket first brought his pail to his horse, which again evoked cries of appreciation. One man even went as far as to kiss the horse.

All these trustworthy gestures lent courage to the mass. They encircled the grimy visitors and touched them with their hands. "Will you be staying here? Are you going on?"

The strangers smiled amicably but didn't answer. The crowd, however, grew more insistent, especially one little fellow with a heavy accent: "What about us, about us?"

Suddenly a group with red stars on their caps appeared, as if they had just sprung from the ground or fallen from the sky. They made their way to the center and began pushing the crowd back. "Don't bother them, can't you see they're tired," one ordered. When the man with the accent persisted, they kicked him in the buttocks and told him to ask the commissar.

The man obstinately followed their advice and approached the man in the leather jacket. "Forgive us, mister commissar."

"Not mister, but comrade, comrade commissar," the commissar corrected him.

"Could you, comrade, advise us to which of the two classifications you mentioned belong the local Jews?"

The commissar smiled graciously. "There is no local and no Jews. There's people. And the people are either proletarian or bourgeois." The red stars strongly applauded and, raising the commissar with a new outburst of the orchestra, they threw him into the air, shouting, "Long live the proletariat, down with the bourgeoisie." The mood turned gay, and forgetting all their questions the crowd joined in the song: "Down with burdz-oi." Then, improvising, they added their own refrain: "Revolution-contribution, hoo-hah, hurrah, hurrah!"

When this ended, the commissar remounted the horse and again put the funnel to his mouth: "Thank you for your warm reception. We're only an advance unit, which has been granted the honor of greeting you, but your victorious army will enter the city right behind us in order to pay proper respect to those who fell in the struggle for your liberation. Along with the army will come a large number of speakers who will answer all your questions. We thank you once again for the good water that you gave us."

For a while the crowd stood there, touched, and quietly watched the sympathetic visitors riding out of the city, but then a strange thing happened.

The man with the accent, who had been kicked aside, now pushed his way into the very center of the crowd and again began to demand the answer to his question.

"Yes, let him talk," a few voices insisted, but before he could open his mouth he was surrounded by a group of red armbands who shielded him, like a screen. The band struck up again, the crowd began to sing, and when the music stopped, the red armbands spread apart—and the loudmouth was no longer in the marketplace. Whether he had gone up to heaven or been swallowed by the earth, no one could say.

Now the red armbands joined the red stars and ordered people to clean up the marketplace and get it ready for the parade. Soon every street was abustle with preparations. Banners made from old clothes, sheets, and shirts were brought to Market Street. On them were the same strange, incomprehensible slogans: "Death to the bourgeoisie! Long live the proletariat!"

In the meantime, eight simple, red-painted wooden boxes were placed in the middle of Broad Street. Announcements written with chalk or charcoal appeared on the walls at every street corner. They proclaimed that every man, woman, and child from the age of eight to eighty was to be on the street during the parade. In larger letters it was explicitly proclaimed that failure to do so would be punishable by death before a firing squad. Other announcements urged every citizen who owned a drum, trumpet, or violin to join the army band in playing "Down with burdz-oi." Failure to comply with this order would also be punishable by execution.

Early morning the next day the streets were jammed with every living creature from eight to eighty who could walk, crawl, or creep. The eight red boxes containing the bodies of the fallen "Schmule-vitches" were set out on a high, hastily constructed red platform, and just behind it stood the first rows of the oncoming army, which stretched through the twisted streets like an endless snake with a tail piercing the sky at the horizon.

The speakers stood poised on the platforms on Depot Street, on Broad Street, on the Boulevard of St. George, and in the old marketplace. The platforms were large and intricately decorated and were occupied by speakers who looked remarkably alike—each with a short, pointed beard, pince-nez, and a pipe in the mouth. They spoke for hours without a break. As soon as one ended another began without losing a second, while the first went to relieve a third on some other platform in another street.

They opened with a fiery greeting to the liberated city and its eight heroic martyrs. But they reached the pitch of emotion when they screamed their sympathy for the poor, the whipped, the starving, the deceived, the exploited, the humbled, the persecuted—and with frothing lips cursed the bourgeoisie and blessed the proletariat. These now familiar but still mysterious words seemed to shoot electric sparks from their grinding teeth and set fire to the crowds that gathered around them. The blazing words singed the weary, hungry hearts and beaten heads, burned the ears, and stifled the breaths— words unheard of, proclamations of comfort, freedom, peace, and redemption that far exceeded anything ever promised by a prophet, a messiah, or even a god. The speakers tore open the guts of the stupefied people, twisted them into a fiery rope, and used this rope to drag them out of the blue nightmare of the brutal world and lift them beyond to the brightest heights of the old biblical dream of the Final Day of Days.

Presently, trumpets blared and dozens of cannons fired a simultaneous salvo that shattered the windowpanes. All the bands, all the improvised drums and cymbals, erupted together and were soon joined by the crowd roaring, "Down with, down with burdz-oi," which was soon transformed into the totally unrehearsed and improvised refrain:

> Revolution,
> Contribution,
> Hoo hah, hurrah!
> Operation,
> Transportation,
> Hoo-hah, hurrah!

From all the singing, drumming, and fifing the narrow, crooked streets around the marketplace seemed to stretch as if making room for the parade. First in line were the eight red boxes borne along on the bayonets of dozens of rifles. These were followed by men in leather jackets, torn peasant sheepskins, and tattered shirts hung with revolvers and ammunition belts. With angry eyes, they marched along, pressed closely together, holding each other's arms. Behind them marched soldiers wearing greatcoats with holes eaten by lice and worms, some with loose sleeves, others on crutches, some with heavy knotted sticks on their shoulders in place of rifles.

"March! March!" the speakers roared. "March to the moon without fear of dying halfway there!"

"Revolution—contribution!" the mob cried.

"March, march! For the millions of murdered, millions of violated women and starving children."

"Operation—transportation! Hoo-hah, hoo-hah!" the mob screamed.

When the parade neared the center of town where the stone statue of the famous General Muraviev stood, thousands of hands hurled themselves at him, tore the sword from his grip, and threw him off the pedestal into the gutter, where he was trampled into dust. Then the parade came to the second and biggest monument in town— that of Empress Catherine the Great. An agile hunchback in torn pants scampered up her and to the accompaniment of raucous cries and the pounding of drums began to ride her neck as if on horseback. Then a rope was looped around her mighty breasts and she was sent crashing to the pavement. The eight boxes were placed on the pedestal, and above them a banner was stretched between two high posts: "Death to the bourgeoisie . . . Long live the proletariat!"

Everyone doffed his hat and bowed his head. The peasants fell to their knees and crossed themselves. In that split moment of silence a shrieking voice of crazed despair was heard. A woman with two little children holding on to her dress was pushing through the crowd: "Help, help, did anybody see my husband the big mouth. He disappeared, he vanished. Good people, help a poor woman with two hungry kids." But this was drowned in the last outburst of the cannons blasting in the air, accompanied by the music bands and the crowds screaming: "Down with, down with burdz-oi!"

The ground shook; the walls trembled. The sky looked down with millions of blinking eyes: What goes on in the old marketplace! The angels in their long, silver nightgowns were roused from their downy pillows and with wrinkled wings rubbed their sleepy eyes. Through the silver curtain in the porthole of the moon gazed out a bewildered and half-frightened face.

*　　*　　*

Deafened and intoxicated, the people trudged home on weary feet, drained yet sated with so much music and so many speeches—too much excitement for a human heart no bigger than a fist to absorb. They fell into their beds and mumbled drunkenly:

> Revolution,
> Contribution,
> Operation—transportation.
> Hoo-hah—hurrah . . . !

XXXVI

⟨ঌ⁂ৎ⟩

JUST A FEW weeks after the big parade, small groups of market people stood at the corners of Market Street and with fear frozen upon their faces read the proclamations about the forthcoming operation. The proclamations were printed on dark paper in a wavy type that was almost impossible to decipher, much less to understand. But taking a few words from here and there and gluing them together in condensed form, the people explained it all to each other in their own fashion:

"This city is like all the cities in the world—sick, depraved, full of miserable poverty, degradation, subjugation, and backwardness. Whether some people wanted it or not, such a city had to be cut to pieces and the pieces rearranged so that up became down, and down up. The buildings and streets of the city had to be reshuffled like a deck of cards so that where a church or synagogue stood, now a bathhouse would stand, and where the bathhouse used to stand, there'd be a barracks. The Boulevard of St. George would be transported to Glass Street, and Butcher Street to Broad Street.

"The people too would be mixed, shuffled, and dealt like cards into new categories: poor, poorer, and poorest; into workers and peasants; into enemies, greater enemies, and greatest enemies; and the fourth and last category—the unnecessary, the useless, and the dangerous. But since in the process of reshuffling and redealing it was hard to know who had been who and what had become what, everyone had to be on guard and watch one another. Haim watch Berl, and Moshe watch Shmerl. Because Shmerl was liable to be the son of a totally unnecessary father, and the father could just happen to be the brother of one of the most dangerous."

And this wasn't all. Actually by the very nature of man, all of the categories were depraved to begin with. Therefore it behooved everyone to watch everyone else so that the first was afraid of the second, the second of the first, the son of the father, the father of the brother, and so on until the city was revolutionized and its inhabitants were transformed into a new breed of mankind.

In a word, a bourgeois was a cancer and only after the cancer had been cut out would the wars end and eternal peace and freedom prevail. But so long as there was a bourgeoisie, there would be no peace, and without peace there would be no bread, no cheese, no herring, nothing at all. Therefore, until operation-transformation was performed, the city's mankind would have to make do with potatoes and some radishes, which would be distributed at a rate of five potatoes for a person in the first category, four for the second, three for the third, and only two for the dangerous and unnecessary people.

Even in the best of times, the market people had seldom overeaten, and in the words of Notte the kerosene dealer, the Germans had taught them how to make "a tasty meal out of high fever with bitter troubles and salty tears."

The new ration of potatoes never made it to their stomachs but stuck upon their trembling hearts, because the market people knew that by heritage they belonged in the last, the "unnecessary" category. Simple men though they were, they understood that according to the proclamations, all men except those who wrote the proclamations were declared to be parasites—and therefore "bourgeois." No wonder then that the huge placard hanging over the city and proclaiming "Death to the Bourgeoisie" looked down on them with a thousand piercing eyes of suspicion, and the market people suddenly and abruptly stopped laughing, for life had become a grim affair.

In all their former misfortunes they had always had one great source of comfort—their famous sense of humor. They would laugh at their own wounds and be amused by their own troubles. They left all the whys and wherefores of their hard lives and the puzzling contradictions and inexplicable lunacies of the world to God, and for themselves they reserved laughter. With laughter they erased their humiliations and revenged themselves against their enemies. With laughter they transformed the tragic into the comical and the comical into the ludicrous and thus pulled themselves out of miserable reality.

Their laughter was the antidote to their misfortunes, a temporary deliverance, a pause in the constant struggle for survival. With their remarkable sense of the ridiculous they forced every situation to its extreme—turned everything and everyone grotesquely upside down and reduced it all to comical absurdity. Thus they had managed to emerge from tsarist rule and German occupation like ducks out of troubled waters, shaking their feathers dry and quacking at the silliness of it all.

But now they had ceased laughing, for fear is the only climate in which all humor atrophies. They could laugh in pain and in hunger, but never in fear. They stood now in long, grim rows before the strictly controlled food distribution centers. At times a burst of gunfire was heard somewhere, but no one dared turn around, for the city was no longer a community of good and bad, saints and sinners, Jews and gentiles, but a strange, faceless family without mothers, fathers, brothers, sisters, aunts, or uncles.

Who could know who stood in front or in back—a first-grade revolutionary or a fourth-grade parasite? It was better, therefore, to keep one's eyes down. One look could mean arrest—one word, death. Yet without speaking, seeing, or hearing, they knew all that was happening around them. They knew that their lives now lay in the hands of strange new people called commissars, whose own lives lay in the hands of other commissars, who in turn were controlled by a nameless group referred to by a gesture of the thumb as "those of them," "he of them," or "she of them."

No one ever saw "them." They didn't appear at meetings and were not seen in the streets. Still, it was common knowledge that it was "they" who kept the city in a tight grip of terror. It was also known that most of them were young. Some of them either were natives of the city or had lived there for some time. They knew every person, every corner, every attic and cellar—you couldn't hide from them, and the most deadly of them was a woman.

The language of the polyglot city was reduced to a few phrases. "I don't know," "I didn't see," "I didn't hear," and often a desperate "I'm innocent!" or "It's a lie!"—but by that time it was already too late.

Yet everyone knew that it had been "she of them" who had shot a policeman who removed a ring from the finger of a woman who fainted in the potato line. And it was the same mysterious "she" who shot a drunken soldier who in the middle of the street had torn the shoes off a bourgeois and given him his torn boots in return.

Those who had had the luck to be born paupers and remain

paupers were now placed in the first and second categories, those who had even more luck got an extra potato, and those who had no luck at all had to be content to be allowed to live without any potatoes at all.

Included in the last category were Osik and his papa and maman, Alexander having fled when the Germans were leaving the city. The same unlucky category also included Cold Itche since cantors and crooning over a helpless corpse had been declared an "antisocial function." Gutia had managed to inveigle herself into a position as nurse in a hospital and thus entered the third category. But the greatest fortune of all happened to fall my way—I was assigned to a very special group entitled to a whole eight potatoes.

According to my social status I shouldn't have received more than two potatoes, since I had emerged from the reshuffling neither a teacher nor a smuggler but the son of a former American millionaire. The fact that the millionaire had been impoverished long before the Revolution because of chronic asthma and that he had been severely burned in the war didn't make a bit of difference. Once a bourgeois, always a bourgeois. And yet—eight potatoes! Not because I had exerted any efforts or even sought to improve my pedigree. It was as if the potatoes had been seeking me out.

Just like my mother, I had accepted the new circumstances with a things-are-all-for-the-best attitude and consoled myself with the fact that others had it even worse. In one of the potato lines, I recognized Osik's mother. All that remained of the once handsome and elegant matron with the big ostrich feather in her hat were her black almond eyes. Her cheeks were sunken, her back stooped; she wore ragged clothes, a kerchief over her head, and men's shoes. She motioned to me to wait for her on the corner of the street.

When she came up, she took a silk handkerchief from her bosom and opened it to reveal a gold dental bridge. She turned around to make sure no one was in the street, then quickly slipped it into her mouth. In a quiet, broken voice she revealed that normally Osik went for the potatoes, but he had caught a cold and had been in bed for more than a week with a high fever. Their eight-room apartment had been requisitioned, and they had been moved to a two-room cellar on a street renamed October. About Alexander, she had no news at all. A month ago a couple of "those of them" had come to the cellar and searched every nook, drawer, and pocket and then arrested her husband. All her efforts to find out why he had been arrested and where he had been taken had been in vain . . . She wiped away her tears, took out and wrapped the bridge in the same handkerchief, and left.

At least I could take comfort in the fact that I still lived on the street where I had been born, and that my father, even though very sick, was free, and that my mother, even though grown older and grayer, still had all her teeth in her mouth.

I heard almost nothing about any of my old acquaintances. They did not come to see me, nor was I able to find them. They either had vanished without a trace or had moved to streets that had themselves been transposed. The marketplace had become a kindergarten. Butcher Street was now Lenin Street. The thieves' dens that once dotted it had been obliterated. The aristocratic Boulevard of St. George had been transformed too, for the people who had lived there and from whom the burglars had used to steal had now themselves been declared criminals and were allotted five potatoes for a family of four.

Once I went to the outskirts of town to look for Gutia, but where the cantor's house had been stood a barracks surrounded by barbed wire and guarded by soldiers. I passed the cemetery and saw from afar that not only life but even death was being operated on, transformed to hoo-hah, hurrah . . . I recalled the weeping, the chanting, and prayers when the dead said farewell to the living, but now an old broken-down hearse stood there with several corpses waiting to be thrown together into a mass grave without a word said or chanted over them.

By now, like all the market people, I was aware of living in a sick city. But like the dog who knows his own remedy, I tried to cure my wounds with my own tongue. My obstinate will to survive wasn't diminished; I still believed that not even an earthquake could snap the chain of my destiny. I flew like the French doctor over the rooftops and came again to the old city, no longer to conquer death but to conquer life—for life was a thousand times more bewildering, fantastic, frightening, and incomprehensible than death.

And thus preoccupied on the way from the cemetery, I saw a man with a briefcase under his arm coming toward me. I stopped and greeted him by doffing my hat. Although his face was hidden behind the raised collar of his coat and wrapped inside a heavy shawl, he looked remarkably like Gerasim Isakovitch Dalski. He ignored me and walked by. Only after he had taken some twenty more steps did he turn and call my name. Yes, it was my former teacher.

"Gerasim Isakovitch, I greeted you, but you didn't answer."

"My eyes aren't in the best condition," he grumbled, raising out of the shawl a sour, unfriendly face in which the right cheek twitched in a nervous spasm. "I guessed it was you. What are you doing in this neighborhood? Do you work around here?"

"No, I'm taking a walk."

"A fine time to be walking."

"I wanted to visit a friend."

"Boy or girl?"

"I doubt that you know her. Her name is Gutia. How are you?"

"What makes you think I don't know Gutia. She's the daughter of a famous lumber merchant."

"No, she's the daughter of a former cantor. She lived over there . . . across from the cemetery."

"Where does she live now?"

"I don't know. I thought that maybe—"

"A boy like you would be better off working than bothering his head about girls."

"Maybe so," I said with a shamefaced smile. "But it's not so easy to get work these days if you don't have a specific profession."

"Why the hell don't you learn some constructive work?"

"I see that you're angry with me, and maybe you're right. You must forgive me that I once deceived you."

"What do you mean?" The nervous twitch drew the mouth nearly up to the right eye.

"Do you remember at the Oran depot when I promised to come and take the job you offered me . . . of a watchman, a controller, or was it a minister?" I said, trying to ease the tense mood with a jesting tone. "But you knew, after all, what the situation was. You knew—"

"I knew nothing!" he cried, the right, unparalyzed side of his mouth spinning wildly. "You didn't give even one minute's thought to the danger in which you placed me. I was accused of helping you escape and, actually, I did help you!"

"My status wasn't prisoner of war," I pointed out.

"With your behavior, you nearly brought me to the gallows. I should slap your face right now!" And he turned to go.

"Wait a while, let me explain what happened."

"If you want to explain, come up to my house. The street isn't the place for such things. You know where I live?"

"No."

"Now you will know." Rolling his eyes he burst out in whinnying laughter. "What's your status now, I mean with the potatoes?"

"I'm in the third category."

"Ah! That's it!" He buried his head in his collar and started off again. Puzzled, I followed along hesitantly. When we came up to the second floor, Gerasim took a key out of his briefcase and opened the door. The small room was in disorder, and the walls were covered with clippings from newspapers and a few pictures of Marx and Engels torn from a book.

"You'll excuse the mess. As you see, I've remained a bachelor," he said, pulling the blanket over the unmade bed. Then he took a pot of potatoes off the stove in the corner, put it on the table, pushed some dirty underwear off the chair, picked several books up off the floor, and threw them on the bed. "Sit down, I'll just light the stove. It'll warm up the room a bit, and I'll treat you to some potatoes."

While still on the street I had been somewhat disturbed by my former teacher's nervousness and unnatural laughter. Observing his jerky, sharp movements now, the twitching of the mouth and the popping of the eyes, I realized that he was mentally disturbed and I regretted having come with him. Still, I rubbed my hands in feigned gratitude and licked my lips as if preparing for a feast of marzipan. "I certainly did not expect to meet you in the street," I said.

"There you are—as you seek so shall you find," and he locked the door with the key.

His words and his locking the door warned me that I had fallen into a trap, and I impulsively jumped up. But he already had the key in his pocket.

"I said, what you searched for—you found."

"What do you mean, searched for? And why did you lock the door? I demand you let me out of here at once!"

"Young man, you're under arrest! And you undoubtedly know what it means when someone is arrested these days."

"Why should you arrest me? I didn't do anything!" And I began to pound my fists against the door. He pulled me away with brutal strength, and I fell back on the bed.

"You still think me the naive fool who would let you deceive me a second time? You still have the gall to try to convince me that you were looking for girls in the cemetery? Instead of becoming a useful, constructive citizen you've launched yourself on the path of vileness and depravity."

"Gerasim Isakovitch, you're not thinking clearly. Maybe you have someone else in mind, or maybe I'm the one who is mistaken—who are you?"

"Ah, that's the question!" the teacher declaimed like a Shakespearean. "You recall, we once dreamed of becoming actors. We tried comedy, but life fixed it that we would have to perform a gruesome drama. Don't worry, I'm the same Gerasim Isakovitch you've been searching for." And, resting the briefcase on his knee, he took out a piece of paper and put it on the table.

I didn't look at it. For I realized that the teacher was one of "those of them" and that I really was arrested.

At the same time, Gerasim took a shaving brush and a razor wrapped in a towel out of the briefcase. "This is my inheritance from my German boss. When he gave these to me he said, 'This can be used for two things, to remove the hair from your face or to remove the face from the shoulders.' But don't be afraid. I'm holding the instrument for my own face and my own throat. I only have to turn you over to those who sent you to find me. Isn't this an interesting subject for one of your recitations? Unfortunately, we're not on stage now but in real, cursed life. I locked the door because you always were a wild creature and I couldn't tame you, but now it's a different story. Now you'll listen to me or by tomorrow you'll be lying in the cemetery next to your imaginary girls . . ." And he looked into the corner as if a third person were standing there.

I came up and gently took his arm. "I don't understand why you speak to me with such anger. What do you have against me? You always liked me and we had some interesting conversations, remember?"

"That's not important," he said, shaking my hand loose. "You will tell me the truth now . . . What were you doing in this neighborhood?"

"I was looking for Gutia, the daughter of Cold Itche the cantor."

"What do you have to do with cantors?"

"I told you that I knew his daughter, Gutia."

"That's a lie. You were looking for me."

"But why? I didn't even know that you were in the city."

"Stop it, you filthy punk!" He suddenly hurled himself at me and pinched my nose between his fingers, which were like tongs. "You're an informer! I knew that someone had informed on me, and I couldn't guess who it might be. But now I know, and you will tell me why you did this to me! I was your teacher, I helped you prepare for your concerts, I helped you when you were a forced laborer under the Germans, but you deceived me, and now in such dangerous times you've betrayed me as well."

"Gerasim Isakovitch!" I shrieked. "You're not well . . . You're making a mistake. Why are you hurting me? Look, you've made me bleed!"

"You told them that I was a spy for the Germans."

"Me?"

"Yes, you! Who else? When I worked for the Germans I was a forced laborer just like you, and the only one I met from our city at that time was you. That means it can only be you and no one else!"

"I swear on my sick father's and mother's life that I never did such a thing! I don't even begin to know what you're talking about."

I was wiping the blood dripping from my nose with my sleeve. The running blood somehow exerted a calming effect on the aroused ex-teacher, and he glanced up at the ceiling the same way he had looked in the corner before.

For a minute or two we were both silent, then he shut off the stove, spooned the potatoes from the pot onto two plates, and, turning back to me, mumbled, "Eat . . . You searched for potatoes and you found them . . . A curse on it. God created the world so that man should eat bread with the sweat of his brow, but a world in which you eat potatoes with blood from the nose the devil himself couldn't conjure up . . . but that's how it is—you informed on me now, knowing that I'm a teacher at the Marx and Engels School and that I have such connections that I can destroy you so that no one will even know where your bones are. But maybe it would be a lot smarter for us both to lay our cards on the table and come out with the truth, and if you did me wrong, you might possibly fix things . . ."

"I did nothing to you, I spoke to no one about you. What do you have against me? Let me out, let me out of here!"

"From here, you can only be carried to the cemetery . . . Sit down and eat your potatoes, you dirty snake!" And he dragged me over to the table. "When Utkin called me in and asked with a sly smile if I had ever been a 'minister' of train connections for the Germans, I should have known immediately that the word 'minister' could have come from your mouth only."

"I don't know anybody by the name of Utkin."

"You'll know him after you enroll at the Marx and Engels School."

"You confuse me. I never heard of such a school. Why are you torturing me? What do you want of me?" I cried, my voice rising higher in the hope that someone might hear me outside.

"Eat your potatoes!" Gerasim said, and slammed me in the chest so hard that I fell back in the chair. "Yelling won't do you any good. I warn you—this is a question of your life or my death. You will now fill out an application as candidate for the Marx School. You will indicate me as the one who recommends you, and if you're accepted, no one can ever bother you again."

"No one bothers me now, and I bother no one. What do you need me in your school for? I gave up my studies a long time ago, and you of all people should know what a poor student I am."

"It's probably my fate to be your teacher again." He threw me a dirty towel. "Wipe the blood off your jaw. When I once tried to help you under the Germans, you ran away. But there'll be no more running. Either you'll understand the New Order, or I'll have to force it upon you. Life is no longer a game." And, after picking up a few books from a corner, he threw them on the table. "Here is an abridged version of Marx's *Das Kapital*, this is Lenin's book, and this is the Communist Manifesto. You'll look these over. In your application, you'll put down that long before the Revolution I studied these things with you. Here is a pen and ink. And a sheet of paper. Write!"

"I don't know what to write, but if you want me to write—I mean if you demand that I write . . ." My eyes wandered across the table and I stretched out my hand, but Gerasim was quicker and slammed my hand, snatched the razor off the table, and tucked it away in his breast pocket. When I stood up, he flung me at the wall in a fearful rage, so that I bounced off like a ball and again fell back on the bed. He hurled himself at me and, beating me in the face with his fists, shrieked, "You're an informer, an informer!"

I slid off the bed and, running on all fours from corner to corner like a mouse in a trap, I bellowed in a hoarse voice, "I'll write! I'll write!" and, apparently reaching for the pen, I scampered under the table. He pulled me out by a leg, grabbed me by the hair, and began to pound my head against the edge of the table with such force that the plates and the lamp fell and the potatoes spilled all over the floor.

Gerasim glanced at the potatoes with a childish expression of concern. "Ah, what a shame! And I wanted to repay you with a good meal for the favor you did the 'Minister of Transportation.'" His body trembling, his mouth twisted like an epileptic's, he again erupted in the same insane laughter with which he had greeted me in the street.

Then he stood up, lifted me by the lapels off the floor, deposited me in a chair, spread out the same piece of paper, and commanded, "Write. I'll dictate."

With a heart frozen with fear and a brain gone soft from all the pounding, I wrote with a cold, bloody hand and in total resignation: "I, the undersigned, would like to enroll at the school. I have a fifth-class gymnasium education. Although my mother and father come from a bourgeois background and belong to the useless and dangerous category, still, under the influence of my teacher, Gerasim Isakovitch Dalski, I have always been interested in social questions and have a good understanding of the works of Marx and Engels. During the war, Comrade Dalski and I were in the forced-labor battalion under the Germans. Together, we helped many of the laborers to escape. This could be confirmed by Comrade Dalski, who has known me since my childhood. Since the forced laborers in Oran were assigned to build the new train networks, and since war prisoners were used for this task as well, the two of us were the first to inform them about the great events taking place in Russia."

After I had signed my name, Gerasim handed me the key and, completely drained, seated himself moodily on the edge of the bed. Rubbing my bruised jaw, I wandered through the room searching for my hat.

"I want you to know," the teacher said with a chalk-white face and a dull gaze in his misted-over eyes, "that the pupils of the school are entitled to eight potatoes, a weekly ration of bread, and even eight chunks of hard sugar. But until you get this, take these potatoes. They can be washed and warmed up again." And, gathering the potatoes from the floor, he wrapped them in a newspaper and stuffed them under my paralyzed arm.

Going down the stairs, I heard Gerasim break out once more into the same horrible laughter. The laughter followed me all the way home and didn't leave me when I went to bed. In a corner of the room I saw a broad, open mouth with a large, extended, violet tongue floating up to the ceiling and down to the floor. I closed my eyes and sat up in bed in a cold sweat. For an instant I felt happy to drift off into the warm abyss of sleep but, to my horror, there were hundreds of mouths on all sides, all twisted in maniacal laughter.

A few times I came to the conclusion that it was all neither a dream nor reality but a vision in my confused brain, which was on the verge of deterioration. I tried to multiply seventeen by twenty, I reminded myself of the names of things and people, and it all came to me clearly, exactly, precisely, and normally. Only a few things were foggy in my mind: Whether I had actually accused my parents of being useless elements, whether the teacher was actually one of "those of them" who had lost his mind somewhere along the way, whether I had signed a traitorous agreement with a madman against "those of them," whether I had been arrested and beaten so brutally while totally innocent, and whether I really deserved to be shot now as a vicious traitor.

For three or four days I hung suspended between hallucinations by day and nightmares by night until in the middle of one night I fell at my mother's feet and confessed the whole story.

But even before I had finished my confession, my mother, who never spoke louder than a dove, began to scream like a whole troop of baboons in a primitive forest when they smell the scent of danger. "It's a lie! This never happened! You didn't meet anyone and didn't write anything! You imagined it all. You're crazy. This is a lie!"

Her screaming drove my sick father and my small sisters out of bed and all of them together, trembling in their nightclothes and not knowing or understanding what was going on, screamed to one another: "It's a lie! A lie!" Confused and deeply upset by the frightening chorus, I joined with them and shouted along with them, "It's a lie, a lie!" Then we all grew silent together.

We expected one of the neighbors to respond, but it was obvious that those who had heard the yelling had only burrowed deeper into their beds.

Helpless and resigned to the indisputable facts of an ugly nightmare and the unavoidable consequences that would surely be forthcoming, we dispersed to our beds to await what tomorrow would bring.

The next night, there was a knock on the door. From such unexpected knocks, peoples' hearts had been known to burst. And when I opened the door, a thin woman with gray hair, wearing a leather jacket and a belt from which dangled a heavy revolver, stood on the threshold.

"Tell your family to go back to bed, shut the door, and draw the curtains. No one has to know I'm here," she said in a stern voice. And only after her order had been carried out did she ask in a friendlier tone, "How are you, Yosik?"

"T-a-n-y-a!" all my limbs sang out in chorus.

"I'm not long in the city. I had it in mind several times to visit you . . . Early today among the other applications I also received your application to Comrade Utkin to enroll at the new school. This came to my attention because the teacher Dalski, who entered the application, cut his throat last night with a razor. That's why I came to you, to find out your connection with this 'Minister of Transportation.' Did you make out the application in your own hand? If you did—why did you do it? Did you really want to enroll at the school or did you want to worm your way into a better category of potatoes?"

All that I had to offer were the three standard words that had been drummed into me during the three fearful days and sleepless nights: "It's a lie. A lie. A lie!" That was all. But the moment I looked at Tanya's faintly lit face—the same unforgettable face to which I had once recited the troubled life of Chantille Jeantaigne Delacroix—I reacted like a circus horse who is roused from slumber and led into the sparkling arena, where, feeling the sand beneath his hooves and the spotlights from above, he begins to dance to the rhythm of an invisible orchestra.

She sat there and didn't blink an eye. She cupped her chin in one hand and leaned the other on the side of her revolver.

I paused from time to time to glance at her face and determine what kind of impression I was making upon her. I knew that between what I said and the way I said it, an abyss existed—and that within this abyss lay the truth of my little life. If she were listening only, she was liable to condemn me, but if while listening to my words she also saw how I said them—how I had once been her beloved crazy French doctor—she would surely come to my rescue, untie my straitjacket, let me escape down knotted bed sheets through the window . . . She might even throw away the leather jacket, the revolver, and take off with me to conquer the dying and the death that now hung over the city.

But her face, which had once spoken with a hundred wonderful tongues, was now an earnest mute mask.

I persisted with my persuasive way. But my lips grew dry, my voice hoarse, I drained myself. Then in silence, we faced each other. After a bit, she said, "Yosik, I dare not, and I will not see you anymore." And she closed her eyes and tightened her lips.

But presently, a tear slid down her cheek. This distilled drop of feeling now spoke to me:

"Listen, Yosik," the teardrop said, "had I come with the idea of accepting your application to enroll at the school, where you would be enlightened and made conscious of the times in which you live and finally taught to speak a proper, respectable language—had I had this in mind before, after three hours of looking at and listening to you, I realize that it would be easier for me to remake ten worlds than to change you.

"Just now, when you danced through the whole tragic carnival of wars and revolutions with its bands and banners, its marches, its songs, its killings and murders—its hunger and deaths . . . I recognized in your eyes the eyes of the midget in the little sideshow at the horse market. You were and you've remained the ridiculous lampedusser who looks at world-shaking events as merely a new installment of 'The Conqueror of Death,' with yourself in the starring role of Chantille Jeantaigne Delacroix . . . Shall I say that you belong to the very last category of the useless, unnecessary elements? Shall I condemn you right here and now and take away your potato ration card with the notation that after the Revolution when the whole city is restored and everyone has bread and sugar again, you, Delacroix, still mustn't get even one potato because you belong neither to the city nor to the world, nor to those who made the Revolution, nor to those against whom the Revolution was made?

"I know my duty. But how can I condemn a person who has condemned himself, a person who chose the fate of being hanged seventy times and guillotined eighty times, a person who derives his pleasure from this?" She stood up. "Remember, Yosik," she said. "I never saw you. I was never here. You never heard of that school. You never made that application. It's all a lie. A lie. You understand?" She took a paper from her bosom and tore it into shreds, then took the glass off the kerosene lamp and burned each shred separately.

At the door she turned around, looked at me again, and whispered, "No, no, never. A pity." Then she adjusted her gun belt and left.

A few days later, I got an official notice to report to point B. There, they took away my ration card for two potatoes and replaced it with one for eight potatoes.

XXXVII

FOUR MONTHS LATER, a bomb destroyed the pedestal on which Catherine the Great had once stood and which had later held the coffins of the eight "red-bands." At the same time, a second bomb tore down the red flag along with a great chunk of the Town Hall.

No one knew how this had happened, who had done it, whether it was sabotage or treason. In the next three days, bombs destroyed a good third of the city's buildings and a good fourth of its population. At the end of the third day, a Polish flag with a white eagle flew from the still-smoldering Town Hall. A new parade was announced—this time for Poles only. There were no more greens, whites, or Reds. All and everybody became Poles overnight, except for the Jews. The Jews took it in their stride. They had served, in their lives, under many flags. So once more, the Jews cowered in their old places in the attics and cellars and remembered, lamented, mourned their dead relatives and neighbors.

Again music played. Officers rode by on prancing horses in front of long columns of cavalry, infantry, artillery. At the rear of this procession, eight decomposing corpses, removed from their coffins and tied to the tails of cavalry horses, bumped rottenly along the pavement.

The "government of the Schmulevitches" vanished into thin air. Whether they had managed to escape or had fallen in the bitter battles during the three terrible days, no one knew. What *was* known was that in the still-standing wing of the Town Hall there existed a list telling who was in which category of potatoes.

Those who had received even one extra potato were now considered dangerous revolutionaries. Those who had received two extra were declared full-fledged Bolsheviks, and if you were a Jew besides, the verdict was predetermined—death by firing squad. Those who had had the earlier good fortune and now the bad fortune to receive two additional potatoes had to hide in ditches or trenches in the nearby woods. (At the first opportunity this category ran in small groups deeper inland, where their status under the Reds was unknown. To one of these groups, consisting of seven or eight people, I attached myself.)

When we assembled in the early morning I recognized three faces in the crowd—a doctor for whom I had once done a favor in the Zwerinitz Hospital, a printer who had a bookstore on Broad Street, and, to my greatest surprise, Velvele Fox, the well-known pickpocket from the old marketplace.

What their sins had been that death now faced them was something I didn't know. I myself was convinced that with eight potatoes on my conscience, I was the biggest, most conspicuous criminal of them all.

Velvele took over as leader right from the start. His first order was "that we not goof around, not fritter away the time but make tracks immediately."

No one doubted that he was best equipped to get to the ruins of King Jagiello's palace on the mountaintop; the group intended to spend the day there and, with the coming of night, to steal over to the other side of the mountain, pass unnoticed past the peasant huts, then lose itself in the distant mountains.

In earlier times, the climb up the mountain was by a twisted, well-worn trail. On hot summer Saturdays or holidays, couples used to stroll here and, in the shade of the ruins of King Jagiello's palace, drink soda water, crack sunflower seeds, and make love. But during the war years, the path had been fenced off and strewn with piles of junk and filthy garbage—we, therefore, had to approach it by a side road that was overgrown with wild, prickly shrubs, then cross a swiftly running stream, and only then climb the nearly straight, rocky wall of the mountain.

It was a gray morning with cold, damp winds, and the rocks on the mountain were too slippery to grasp. The refugees began to discard their bundles, but this didn't help much. Even Velvele, who was far in front, began to slide backward.

Several birds soared gracefully overhead. We followed them with sad, envious eyes.

Velvele was the first to reach the top of the mountain. He used twined branches to help the others up.

Shivering from cold and fatigue, everyone crawled inside the ruins of the royal castle and huddled in the corners. "Don't go in there," Velvele said, indicating a dark cave in the background. "There are rats there as big as cats. They can rip out your throats."

I licked the blood off my bruised fingers, stuffed my shirt back into my pants, and stretched out on a stone bench that was built into a small niche with a rounded window.

"Hey, you scruffy punk, have some respect for an older dip," Velvele said, grabbing my foot and dragging me from the stone slab. "In this house of worship, the east wall belongs to me. A thousand years ago the Lithuanian king used to lie on this bench . . . What was his name? Kolibolus ben Yontef XVIII . . . He used to watch through this window how his stout lads drove the Russki punks back to Moscow and the Polack slobs to the sea in Galicia."

"There is no sea in Galicia," the bookseller said.

"There was, there was. I heard it myself from Barve's Son. He was a big brain. He even said that there was a sea right here on this mountain and that my great-grandfather and his great-great-grandfather were pike in that sea swallowing each other and that is why we still enjoy herring and gefilte fish."

The doctor laughed. Velvele glared at him. "I hate a quack. Specifically, a laughing quack. If you want to listen like a mensch, I'll keep talking. Otherwise, keep your trap shut or I'll punch you out and make your blood into borscht."

Everyone turned toward Velvele, who stretched out on the bench with his head in his hands and, looking up at the round ceiling, spoke with every intention of being heard: "Here on this bench the Lithuanian prince, Kaletuches XIV, screwed the beautiful Polish princess, Jadwiga the Broad. And I should have a thousand for every time I myself screwed here . . . A thousand years from now some other dip will probably lie here on this same bench screwing some other virgin princess. Will he know that there ever was such a sinner as Velvele Fox? Here was my palace . . . here you could bury a brooch, a signet ring, a piece of heavy silver, a gold coin . . .

"In the den on Butcher Street a cop was liable to stick his nose in and start waving a sword, but if you were lucky enough to jump out the window and come up to this ruin, you were in clover. The cops wouldn't dare chase you up the mountain. This was a sanctuary as it's written in the holy Torah because even the cops respected the Torah. 'Come down!' the cops used to yell up to us, then blow their whistles and wave their swords. 'If you want me, come and get me.' Ah, this was when a man was a man, a rabbi was a rabbi, a pickpocket was a pickpocket. Now the whole world is a thieves' den—everyone with his hand in everyone else's pocket. There's no room in this world for an honest pickpocket.

"Under the Krauts, may the milk sour in their wives' tits, I sat a whole year in prison for one skinny chicken. The Kraut is by nature a dirty rat who bamboozles the world with a cannon in hand. True, the Kraut bully threw the world into a stew, but as soon as the cannon was taken out of his hand, the hard guy became a punk and wet his pants . . . War is a punk's game. But to get some sucker to look at the moon and cop a watch from his vest pocket, now that's an art and a pleasure! To hide in some filthy hole and shoot someone hiding in some other dirty hole—that's a bloody bore.

"Under the Reds, may they rot, it just so happened that I lived what you call an honest life. I convinced them that Leibele Trotsky was my mother's cousin and I got signed up for sixteen potatoes a day . . . They gave me two rods to go shoot those—what did they call them, bourgeoisie? But go shoot hungry people? I can understand an occasional belt in the chops or a black eye—that can't be helped. I had to eat, didn't I?

"My mother—may she now, as I see her, enjoy a bright paradise—used to say, 'My child, choose either an honest trade or a filthy profession.' That's what she said. I listened to her and never smoked on the Sabbath. My hand never went into anyone's pocket on the Sabbath. But now it's become a world without a Sabbath . . . A new Torah—why steal? Just kill and take. So what would the thief do?

"So all of them, even the pickpockets, become traitors and finks. My own buddies ratted on me. What could the poor slobs do when, outside of shooting and squealing, my Uncle Leibele Trotsky forbade anything else? I'm tired . . . Didn't eat or sleep for two days . . . But with those Polack cruds, may their guts get mixed up and may they be operated on with rusty knives, with them I'll get even yet! My best pickpockets in the marketplace were Polacks. I used to fence lots of loot at Jan the shoemaker's. He used to make a nice piece of change too.

"I even screwed his old lady, but one thing had nothing to do with the other. I used to give her presents . . . one time, a silk dress . . .

kept her four bastards in pants I used to cop from Lazer the old-clothes dealer . . . But the day before this last commotion started, I came to her to hide me. She shoved me under the bed. Her three younger bastards were playing on the bed. The oldest bastard—Matzek—came in with a big gun and gave the mother two pairs of pants and a big can of kerosene and said that he had just shot Notte the kerosene dealer and Lazer the old-clothes dealer . . . When they left the room I wanted to take the can of kerosene, spill it over the bed, and burn the three little bastards to death. But, after all, I have a Jewish heart. And then who knows, maybe one of the bastards is of my own creation . . .

"But I'll be back. Now I've learned to shoot . . . I buried two guns . . . and marked the place. I'll be back even if it takes a hundred thousand years . . . But in a hundred thousand years—who knows? If, like Barve's Son says, it took the pike in the sea ten thousand years to become a stinky herring, what will become of the Polack bastards in a hundred thousand years?"

What he said after that was no longer distinguishable, for it grew muffled by a quiet then a louder snoring.

The wind whistled through the holes in the ruin as if playing on a huge clarinet. From somewhere in the east, distant drums could be heard accompanied by echoing gunfire. From time to time, troops of mice danced a quadrille from corner to corner.

When it grew dark in the round window in the niche, we started to sneak out of the ruin. I wanted to wake our leader but the others stopped me and dragged me away. In the time I had been sitting with my eyes and ears glued to him, they had communicated in some strange fashion and agreed to leave him behind.

This irked me. After all, he had brought us here and helped us get up the mountain—so why betray him? Had the world actually become a world of traitors as he said? Had his vulgar language and his scabby tongue offended them? Who did they expect to hear in this stinking rat hole—Barve's Son? In the world that had evolved, maybe Velvele Fox was the most fitting successor to that gentle, scholarly dreamer. But looking at it from the other side, I understood that the band of driven, depleted, demeaned people wanted to retain at least the appearance of dignity in the face of danger, even in the event of sure death. And if I tried to sabotage their effort, I myself would be nothing more than a fink.

Through a hole in a large black cloud poked the cold eye of the moon. Alarmed, everyone scurried away from the ruin toward the other side of the mountain.

I looked for the last time at the sleeping city, which lay draped in a foggy, dirty sheet. Several green roofs lacking houses floated in the air along with a Polish flag without a pole and a white cross without a church. At the foot of the mountain was the river, a water snake harnessed to a bridge.

Epilogue

⁂

THESE EXPERIENCES CAME to my mind when I was on the *Southern Cross,* coming back from one of my frequent tours to Buenos Aires.

As usual, the ship docked in the port of Santos, Brazil, for twelve hours in order to take on several tens of thousands of sacks of coffee.

A big colored poster with my picture on it was hanging in the port with the announcement that on my way back to North America I would make one appearance in the local municipal theater. And so it was that when I stopped at Santos, a jolly group was waiting for me and welcomed me with flowers and touching greetings and escorted me to the theater.

It was a hot day and an even hotter night.

The moment the curtain had fallen for the last time I went to my dressing room, stripped off my soaked clothes, wrapped myself in my flowered dressing gown, lit a cigarette, and sat down in front of the mirror to take off the runny makeup.

A few minutes later a man burst into the room. He neither knocked nor asked permission to enter. He ran toward me and began to kiss me on my neck and on my head and to shout in a tearful voice, "Yosik! Yosik, how are you? You don't remember me? My name is Boris—Berchik the fool—the orphan from the old marketplace!"

I wasn't sure whether I couldn't recognize him because I didn't remember him or I didn't remember him because I couldn't recognize him. In his face and in his whole appearance there wasn't a single trace to connect with the name "Berchik" in my memory.

Before me stood a man with sparse, unkempt hair, a pointed pot belly under his sunken chest, narrow shoulders, a wrinkled collar, a tie askew, deep wrinkles in his forehead, and a drab mustache on a weary face that resembled the old Berchik as much as the blazing sun of Santos resembled the frosty snow of the old marketplace.

From my reticence, Boris gathered that I doubted his identity, and he began to pound his breast:

"That's me, me . . . I've waited nearly thirty years for this meeting. How is it possible you shouldn't recognize me? We were partners in a bakery . . . next to Notte the kerosene dealer's store, just across from Shlome the ritual-fringe maker's stall . . . Remember? You still owe me eight buttons! The bakery was a failure. We were about to go bankrupt. So I lent you four buttons to pay off the debts, then after I had become a musician you came again, and I taught you to play 'Perpetuo Mobile.' For that, let us say I've got another four buttons coming. So together, that makes it eight." He erupted in joyful laughter that brought a stream of tears to his eyes. "When did you leave our town? I asked everyone I met about you. I followed your successes, I saved every picture, every newspaper where your name was mentioned." And he took out of his breast pocket a pile of old, crumpled clippings and spread them out before me like a usurer waving a bundle of promissory notes under a cornered debtor's nose.

I didn't know how to react. Unable to decide, I seized upon a question: "Is it always so hot in your country?"

"I'm not long in this country. I live in Porto Alegre. I traveled a whole night. Your ship is leaving at dawn, how could I miss you? Do you recognize me? Remember the Golem from the old synagogue? Remember how you wanted to steal my violin, but I held on to its neck, ha, ha, ha! Oh, good brother, it didn't help me a bit. I am, as you see, no second Paganini. I appeared in a few concerts and got glowing reviews. It looked as if I had things licked . . . Suddenly I felt a heaviness in the middle finger of my left hand. What this was, I don't know till this day. Some doctors said that I had sprained it, but whatever the reason, I soon had to give up Paganini's 'Perpetuo Mobile' and substitute numbers that wouldn't make such a strain on my middle finger. It didn't help much.

"I was left with no other course but to join a symphony orchestra. On a certain day a famous conductor came from Italy and, get this, at the first rehearsal, out of a hundred and five musicians, he heard one violin screeching. He quickly stopped the rehearsal and told me to stand up and gave me a good dressing-down in front of the entire orchestra. In desperate fear I sat down to play again and, when the conductor saw I wasn't paying much attention to his warning, he ordered me to take my violin and leave.

"As distasteful as this experience was for me, it still wasn't as bitter as the fact that I soon had to amputate the finger before its affliction spread to the other four, God forbid. But that was that. It wasn't even conceivable that I should ever play the violin.

"When the Second World War broke out I managed to flee to Russia . . . I enjoyed you so much tonight. I was so proud. After all, an old partner . . . in my sand-cookie bakery at the garbage bin of the old marketplace. What about the eight buttons you owe me?"

There was a knock at the door.

"Wait, wait, he's dressing," Boris answered for me. "You have a good three hours yet until your boat leaves," he assured me. "I know you're tired. I won't trouble you, but one thing you'll have to tell me. You must reveal the secret that held me enthralled for all these years. What was it that time when you wanted to snatch my violin from me? Who began to shake the walls? Who jumped down from the roof? Was it really a Golem?"

"I have to pack my things," I mumbled.

"I'll help you."

"No, I'll do it myself. You tell me—what did I want to ask you?—oh, yes, how did you come to this country?"

"Running to Southern Russia with the escaping Jewish hordes, I met a woman. Her husband died on the way, from dysentery, and I helped her drag her two babies along. I promised her that, God willing, if we got out of Russia we would get married. I kept my word. But we still had to keep running, until we reached Brazil.

"After only a month and a half in this country she went to buy a dress and a passing car smashed into her, breaking her spine. She was in a hospital for months, and although she came out of it alive, she was left a cripple, a shattered creature with two children.

"Now, I had been going around, like everyone else who came here, with a pack on my back, peddling, but after her tragedy I couldn't do it anymore since there was no one to mind the children. Who would help me here? You'll laugh when I tell you—my good old violin, the one you wanted to steal from me. It suddenly occurred to me that since I was busy during the day with the children, I'd have to find some work at night. And God soon provided such a job.

"In Porto Alegre there is a kind of nightclub called the Gypsy Cave. Not a first-class spot, God forbid. You drink coffee, dance a little. It has a six-man band. The pay isn't much because the Gypsy knows that I can't give him more music than my four fingers can provide, so he doesn't demand more and leaves me alone. I'm second fiddle, anyway. All I have to do is yom-tom, tim-tom, tim-tom-ti, and, again, tim-tom, tom-tom, tom-ti. And so, my friend, I sit in the corner and scrape away. Yom-tom-tim-tom, yom-tom-tim-tom. I don't care what's being played—a tango, a rumba—I do yom-tom, tim-tom-ti, since with these few chords I can accompany every dance, even every melody.

"Look here, I'm talking and you're silent. Tell me, tell me something about yourself, it seems to me that all my life I've only been waiting for you. You wouldn't believe that months ago I had a premonition that I would meet you soon. Listen to this. I sit there in that gypsy dump and, half asleep, draw my bow up and down. Only from time to time I glance at the gypsy leader just to know where he is at . . . Suddenly I look—he isn't there and in his place is someone else. And you know who? I should not live to see my children married if I'm lying.

"Well, what can I tell you? I didn't know if I was dreaming or if I had gone mad, but suddenly I began to play 'Perpetuo Mobile' with all my passion, and I must tell you, my dear friend, that even when I still had all my fingers I never played it so well as that night when you led the miserable orchestra in that gypsy dump. It was only a shame that no one heard it, because in the noise of those dancing you can only hear the drum . . . and now I see you in flesh and blood. So, tell me, tell me about yourself—come, we'll have a coffee together. My treat, my treat . . ."

"No, no, how can I? I'll miss my boat."

I opened the door and let in the committee in charge of the evening who had come to say good-bye to me.

"Let me, I'll carry your valise." Boris blocked my path. We left the theater. I hailed a taxi and Boris forced his way onto the seat next to me.

"We have a good hour yet," Boris said as the taxi began to drive toward the ship.

"Talk . . . tell me, was it really true? How did you do it? Did you actually put the name of God into a piece of clay and it began to speak?"

Under the pretext that I had to check my baggage in my cabin, and promising that I'd be right back, I dashed up the gangplank.

It was only when the screws of the ship began to turn that I carefully stole out on deck. He still stood there with his neck thrust out, waiting for me to return.

The ship began to sway. The port with my playbill and smiling portrait upon the wall, along with Berchik, began to fade and sank into the sea. The tip of the rising sun began to show on the opposite horizon.

I went back to the cabin, shaved, changed my clothes, and went out on deck to stretch out in a chair waiting for the call for breakfast.

I hadn't lain there for more than ten minutes when a strange, sudden remorse woke me up. Why had I treated that man so indifferently? Now that the strange face had vanished from my sight I recognized and saw him exactly as he had wanted me to see him—behind the garbage bin in the old marketplace.

What kind of unforgivable swinishness was it for me to deny the debt, to so openly ignore a man—no matter how foolish, childish, or grotesque—who had once lent me eight buttons!

Was it the wrinkled, sweaty hat or the stained jacket that had affronted the aesthete within me? I was ready to knock myself out of the chair. I tried to justify and pacify myself: that my attitude was possibly a fleeting reaction to an unexpected visit, that it would pass the moment I put some breakfast into my stomach. But the obvious avoidance of the obvious irked me even further: No, No! It wasn't true. He wasn't the person who had given me the buttons, and I wasn't the person who had taken them.

Then again, where should I find buttons? I tried to comfort myself. Span the ocean and half a globe, run to the old marketplace and find the boy I was and demand buttons from him who had once borrowed from someone who was now also someone else? And where was the marketplace? The bloody Holocaust had swept not only the people and the market but even the ground on which it stood off the face of the earth. Not even a trace, a sign had remained. It was as if it had never existed, even in a dream.

That's true, I agreed, but what would have harmed me if, standing there in the dressing room, I had torn some buttons off my jacket and jokingly handed them to him—here, good brother, the payment on my debt . . . Who knows what a comforting compensation this would have been for a man who has been waiting for it a whole life? Maybe with these eight buttons I would have repaid him for the years that he had been waiting for me to tell him how I placed the name of God inside a stone so that it would speak. Oh, come back, come back you marvelous Berchik!

But if in my stupidity I had made a mistake, maybe I could still correct it. Should I write him a letter, a long letter with a thousand apologies, and disclose to him the secret of the Golem?

Although I hadn't yet fully agreed, I already had a pencil in my hand, and I began to scribble on a piece of paper.

I wrote until late that night and on all the subsequent days on board ship, lying on a chair, leaning on the rails, stretched on the floor, and continued the letter on my desk in New York.

To send this mountain of paper to Berchik in Porto Alegre was out of the question. He would surely take it as a mockery and an even worse insult than he had suffered in the dressing room. I decided to pick out only the pages that pertained to his questions, and so that he might even have a good laugh, I would put in a separate little envelope eight buttons. But . . . wait. What was his address? I knew Berchik . . . Porto Alegre . . . nightclub . . . the owner is a Gypsy.

As I had expected, after a month or so the package was returned with a postmark: no such address. I thought of the head of the committee that had arranged my appearance in Santos. I remembered his full name and, using the municipal theater to deliver the message to him, I asked him whether there were any men among his friends or any people he knew with the name of Berchik. Of course I added a description of his appearance. The head of the committee was prompt to answer that he knew only two people who might be considered, but their names were not Berchik, but simply Berl. One of them was in Santos, a teacher in a children's school, and the other one was actually in Porto Alegre but he was a tailor; both of them had all ten fingers on their hands.

I was fuming with vexation. To write such a long letter and not to have someone to send it to was really too much. I wrote a heart-rending letter to my dear friend, the well-known producer in Rio de

Janeiro, Mr. L., asking that he do everything possible to find in Porto Alegre a musician with only nine fingers. I described in minute detail his approximate height, the sound of his voice, the worn-out face with the depleted hair on his head.

My producer was not lazy. He went to Porto Alegre. He found the place. The owner was not a Gypsy, the name of the place was "Chitano" (in Portuguese a Gypsy), but now the Chitano was no longer on a back street but in the very center of the city, and it had changed its name to "Montparnasse." He also met two of the musicians who once played at the Chitano, and they remembered the violinist with four fingers on his hand, but his name was not Berchik but Pedrito. His wife had died and left him with two small children. He married the cleaning woman. She was from one of the half-wild Indian tribes and when the Chitano closed she took Pedrito and the two children deep into the rainy Amazon jungles to her parents. I bound the stack of scribbled papers with a string and stuck it away in the basement in one of my trunks. A year later I couldn't remember where I had put it, and in a few years I forgot it altogether.

How I found the dusty heap of paper and how I assembled the more than a thousand multi-sized unnumbered pages, covered with letters some as large as a finger and others too small for even a magnifying glass—how from all this I later fashioned this book—is perhaps an interesting chapter in itself. But this already has no bearing on the odd, lengthy letter with which I wanted to repay the eight buttons to my partner Berchik from the old marketplace.